❧ **THE QUEST FOR**
  SIR ARTHUR CONAN DOYLE

The Quest for Sir Arthur Conan Doyle

❦ *Thirteen Biographers in Search of a Life*

Edited by
Jon L. Lellenberg

With a Foreword by
Dame Jean Conan Doyle

◣ SOUTHERN ILLINOIS UNIVERSITY PRESS
Carbondale and Edwardsville

Copyright © 1987 by the Board of Trustees,
  Southern Illinois University
All rights reserved
Printed in the United States of America
Edited by Teresa White
Designed by Cindy Small
Production supervised by Natalia Nadraga

Library of Congress Cataloging-in-Publication Data

The Quest for Sir Arthur Conan Doyle.

  Includes index.
  1. Doyle, Arthur Conan, Sir, 1859–1930—
Biography.   2. Authors, English—19th century—
Biography—History and criticism.   I. Lellenberg,
Jon L.
PR4623.Q47   1987   823'.8   [B]   87-9529
ISBN 0-8093-1384-7

Frontispiece: Sir Arthur Conan Doyle in 1904. Already world-famous as an
author, his *Return of Sherlock Holmes* stories were now making him the world's
most highly paid writer as well. Photo courtesy of Richard Lancelyn Green, all
rights reserved.

In Memory of
John Nieminski
1929–1986

Friend, fellow editor, and Baker Street Irregular

CONTENTS

ILLUSTRATIONS

FOREWORD

Dame Jean Conan Doyle

This book is about books about my father, Arthur Conan Doyle. It is remarkable that so many books should have been written already about him since his death in 1930.

Although always aware that our father was by profession an author, it seemed quite as important to my brothers and myself that he was such a good all-round sportsman, and that he fought for justice for others and for any cause about which he felt strongly. He seemed to us to be the very personification of the chivalry of the stories of King Arthur's Round Table. We had a very healthy respect for him, knowing him to be tolerant of high-spirited mischief but capable of anger if we broke his code of honorable behavior. Perhaps too much has been made by some biographers of the incident when he clouted my brother Adrian for referring to a woman as "ugly" and told Adrian that "no woman is ugly"—but to disparage anyone's looks, male or female, would have been considered poor taste in our family. Character, yes, physical defects, no.

An asset of having an author for a father is that he works at home. You see more of him and he is able to play an active part in your life. In our nursery days he used his imagination to invent splendid games for my brothers, cousins, and myself. I realize now how much time our large genial father must have given up to inventing these games, but I am sure he enjoyed them as much as we did. He always retained the boyish streak that inspired him to write the verse that is a prelude to *The Lost World*:

I have wrought my simple plan
If I give an hour of joy
To the boy who's half a man,
Or the man who's half a boy.

It made him a perfect companion for his children. Even in the last years of his life, my brothers said he seemed like an elder brother to them, someone with whom they could discuss all their problems.

I wish I had been older than seventeen when my father died. There would have been so much to talk about—such as woman suffrage, one of the many public issues mentioned in this volume. I only heard him discuss this in the context of the possible effect within a marriage and his criticism of some of the actions of suffragettes. However, he had an open mind, admitting past misjudgments, such as telling the then Sir Robert Baden-Powell that his new Scout movement would prove too idealistic to last. He remembered this when he took me, age seven, to join the village Brownie pack, a first step leading to years in the Girl Guide movement. He certainly did not underestimate women's intelligence. He encouraged my older half sister Mary to become a journalist and often discussed possible careers for me.

Of course my father's belief in Spiritualism had a considerable effect on us as children, but that is too big a subject to embark upon here. I have found accusations of "gullibility" from those who never knew him hard to accept. He impressed upon us so often the need to guard against fraud—never to accept as genuine, messages from the departed that were not backed up by positive proof of the identity of the communicator, preferably with cross-corroboration. I have not been to a seance for many years, but those "messages from him" that well-meaning people have sent me in recent years have sadly failed to fulfill my father's criteria. It was not always so.

I saw a lot of my father during his last years. As my older brothers were following their own pursuits, when I was home for the holidays we spent most evenings together. He was such a peaceful person to be with and so sensitive toward the feelings of others; at the same time, he was such fun, not only because of his sense of humor but also because of his alert mind, always interested in new things and interesting us in them. He approved of the modern generation, getting enjoyment from hearing of my brothers' activities, and being driven at 100 mph in their racing car (a significant speed in the late 1920s). He was amused and interested also by their love for "hot jazz."

One penalty of being an offspring of a famous person is the emotion one is bound to feel when reading some biographies written by people who never knew their subject personally. One does not expect to share all the opinions of the writer, but one hopes that they will get the facts right. Alas, one so often hopes in vain. Hesketh Pearson's *Conan Doyle, His Life and Art* was the first that I read. I thought it a poor biography when it came out, as the author failed to capture the personality of his subject. It was so obvious that he had never known him and couldn't imagine what he was like. In response to it, my brother Adrian wrote his own little biographical sketch of our father. His motivation in writing *The True Conan Doyle* was splendid—filial affection and loyalty, and a wish to correct certain remarks of Pearson's which he knew to be wrong. Adrian's main objection (and mine) to Pearson's book was to his claim that our father had been "the man in the street." To say that my father's tastes and reactions were often those of the average man would be correct, but those who knew him realized that he was very out of the ordinary. The average man tends to follow the herd, the last thing my father would have done. Being "out on a limb" never worried him. "The man in the street" was an inappropriate description and gave the reader a false picture.

Friends, curious about my father, ask me which biography they should read. If their knowledge of him is scant, his autobiography *Memories and Adventures* being out of print, I recommend John Dickson Carr's *Life of Sir Arthur Conan Doyle*, although that, too, can be hard to come by today. It is not an in-depth study of his life, and there are factual errors in it, but of all the books, it conveys most clearly the personality, the nature, of the man. It is the most accurate portrait in words. If friends have already read one of the shorter biographies, I advise them to read Pierre Nordon's *Conan Doyle* for the sake of reading the extracts from my father's correspondence with his mother. No risk of the author's guesswork there. I also suggest they read Owen Dudley Edwards' *The Quest for Sherlock Holmes*. It is not a full biography, confined as it is to his early life, and it contains rather too many suppositions, but it is full of new, well-researched information—new even to me. And I suggest also that they read Compton Mackenzie's splendid book of essays, *Certain Aspects of Moral Courage* (Doubleday, 1962), which pays tribute to my father's possession of that quality and to his quest for justice for others. He knew his man.

There are only two books I advise friends against spending their time reading: Charles Higham's *The Adventures of Conan Doyle* and Ronald Pearsall's *Conan Doyle: A Biographical Solution*. It is a pity about the first, because much of it is of interest, but its factual errors are so numerous, and at times so fanciful, that justifiably or not one is bound to query the validity of any statements Higham makes, unless verified by chapter and verse. Unfortunately the wording of the author's acknowledgments may have led readers to think that my half sister Mary and I gave him significant assistance. In fact he asked me about nine trivial questions concerning the family, one of which I referred to Mary. That was the extent of our help. As we both disagreed with much in Higham's book, our ire at being "gratefully acknowledged" may be understood.

For all its faults, Higham's is undoubtedly a more interesting read than Pearsall's small volume, which is also marred by errors, less numerous than Higham's, but in line with Pearsall's feline approach. Observing the misinformation, I felt here was a writer whose own personality was so unlike that of my father's that he would find it impossible to understand the man he was writing about. One of the most important things in my father's life was his great love of my mother, and hers for him. There is no doubt that that influenced him and his work greatly. Yet there is little about this in the biographies, and Pearsall even had the gall to say that my father wished my mother had played a more active part in his 1922 American lecture tour on Spiritualism, instead of "looking on the trip as an excuse for sightseeing." What absolute nonsense! My mother was renowned for the dedicated support she gave my father on his tours. He was so proud of the help she gave concerning the bereaved, that he expressed the opinion that she could have lectured on the subject in his place. The remark would only have been a compliment, not a serious suggestion.

I won't comment here on other biographies, as the essays in this book will tell readers all they need to know. Sufficient to say that it must be difficult for a writer who has never known his subject to present a completely accurate portrait. The author's own personality so often colors the picture. Also (though I must except Pierre Nordon's book as I have not read it in the original French), all the biographies contain some factual errors: too many inaccuracies that could have been avoided and too many fantasies of the authors' imaginations—often trivial errors, perhaps, but I hate to think of them being perpetuated by later writers along with the genuine information contained in previous studies.

When would-be biographers approach me, I urge them to wait until our family papers are available to researchers. Then they will have new material to work with. Without this, the less responsible biographer may in the search for some new approach to his subject fantasize about it. Scandals sell books. Admiration, however justified, sets up a howl of "hagiography" from the critics. Until the conclusion of a family lawsuit, however, the papers are unavailable. Of course any serious biographer will need to see them. They were seen by Pierre Nordon and before him by Hesketh Pearson and John Dickson Carr, though the latter two may not have researched them very thoroughly, as their books were written fairly speedily, and the papers were in somewhat of a muddle at the time.

In conclusion, I must say how interested I was by the essays in this book. Of course I don't agree with all the opinions expressed, but it was fascinating, I found, to read the writers' personal reactions to what they had read about my father. Perhaps the essays in this book, by indicating the strengths and weaknesses of what has gone before, will stimulate scholars in new and interesting directions. I look forward to the day when a definitive biography will be written about the man whom it was my great fortune to have for a father—a biography as entertaining as John Dickson Carr's, but as serious as Pierre Nordon's and as groundbreaking in neglected areas as Owen Dudley Edwards'. When that time comes, I hope the biographer will not allow any personal opinion to color the coverage of my father's belief in Spiritualism, but will research that subject as objectively and deeply as other aspects of my father's life and as his literary works. That would be welcome indeed.

PREFACE

This book is a study of how the life of a famous man—a celebrated popular author and a controversial public figure—has been treated biographically by himself and by others. Sir Arthur Conan Doyle was, of course, the creator one hundred years ago of Sherlock Holmes, perhaps the most universally recognized fictional character of English literature. Had Conan Doyle done nothing else in his life but write the Sherlock Holmes stories, his name would still be famous today; but he was also a physician, a sportsman, the author of a wide variety of other fiction, a military historian and correspondent, a propagandist for a wide variety of causes, a social reformer, an unsuccessful political candidate, a champion of victims of injustice, and, finally, a Spiritualist missionary. Many of these activities have colored and complicated the public's conflicting views of Arthur Conan Doyle over the years, until the proletariat and professoriat alike hardly know how to conceive of the man, assess his place in literature, or account for the extraordinary creative accomplishment that is Sherlock Holmes.

This book is not a biography of Arthur Conan Doyle, although readers will learn much about his life from the essays in it, especially the first several chapters that provide an overview of his life and career and an examination of his autobiographical writings, both fictional and nonfictional. Each essay may be read on its own, I hope, as a description and assessment of the particular biographical or autobiographical work that it covers. But in the sweep of all the book's essays, I have tried to ensure that the reader can discern patterns of biographical treatment—and mistreatment—of Conan Doyle's life, played out both in the creation of half-truths and misleading images of the man and in the peeling away of appealing myths to expose very different, but no less interesting, realities about Arthur Conan Doyle. If I have not succeeded, the fault is mine and not my contributors'.

I am grateful to my contributors for their efforts, in particular to Edward Lauterbach who gave me a needed nudge at the right time. I also want to thank Dame Jean Conan Doyle (Lady Bromet), Sir Arthur's surviving child, for her cooperation and assistance and her kindness in writing a Foreword to this book, which contains some views and judgments of her father that she does not share. The late John Nieminski, my

Baker Street Miscellanea co-editor until his untimely death in December 1986, read the book in manuscript and made many helpful comments. And last but certainly not least, my wife Mary never stinted encouragement nor begrudged the time that this project required.

Sir Arthur Conan Doyle was a man of letters and a man of action, a Romantic unable to come to terms with his own age, and a mystic oriented toward the unknown. In Sherlock Holmes he surpassed himself and created a literary treasure that has given pleasure to countless millions of people. If this book helps correct some widespread misperceptions of the man and encourages a more scholarly assessment of his life and work than they have tended to receive, it will do all that I hope for it.

❧ THE QUEST FOR
SIR ARTHUR CONAN DOYLE

Introduction ∘ THE QUEST FOR SIR ARTHUR CONAN DOYLE

Jon L. Lellenberg

The place is London, the greatest city in the world, and Queen Victoria is on the throne. The time is the 1880s, and Great Britain is building the greatest empire in the history of the world. It is an enlightened age: the pace of scientific discovery and invention is quickening, laying the foundations for a new era that promises to be the ultimate in modernity, convenience and security. Even so, human troubles and social problems persist. In England's highly stratified class structure lie seeds of discontent and conflict; 1887 will see unprecedented labor riots in the heart of London, quelled ruthlessly by the Guards. The following year will see a different sort of problem: through the late summer and autumn of 1888, Jack the Ripper will stalk the slums of London's Whitechapel district by night, murdering and mutilating horribly a series of London's innumerable prostitutes, then disappearing into—some suspect—more fashionable precincts, to live the respectable half of a psychologically deranged double life.

The police will never apprehend him. Crime does indeed exist in the huge metropolis of London, seat of empire, and elsewhere in England; in fact, vice and crime flourish as the underside of proper Victorian society. The police, once despised by English society, are now respected, but not yet highly efficient, guardians of public safety and social order. They could use help. So could many people whom the police are unable to help, or who fear to go to the police at all. There are many detectives in London, but they are a mediocre lot at best, lacking the knowledge and skills they need to solve mysteries and track down criminals.

To Baker Street in early 1881 comes a young man named Sherlock Holmes. His origins are unclear, his education eccentric and incomplete, and he is alone and as yet friendless. But his intellect proves to be of a brilliance and acuity that comes along perhaps once in a century, and he has trained himself with single-minded dedication to be more even than the world's first consulting detective. He is Reason tuned to its ultimate expression in a human personality, he brings light where otherwise darkness would prevail, he is a bane to evil abroad in the land, a refuge for the beset and helpless. . . .

He is only a character in fiction, of course, but people will soon respond to his name and what it symbolizes as if he lived. And even a century after emerging into the world's consciousness, his adventures will still be read with astonishing avidity, despite tremendous changes in the times and people's tastes. Sherlock Holmes will prove to be one of the most remarkable phenomena of the creative impulse.

In this case, the impulse belongs to a young and obscure doctor named A. Conan Doyle.

i

If Sir Arthur Conan Doyle had never done anything else but write the Sherlock Holmes stories, he would still be famous today.

If he had *not* written Sherlock Holmes, he might be forgotten today, despite all his other writings and accomplishments.

And those two propositions would have distressed Sir Arthur Conan Doyle, who came to resent his most famous literary creation as a distraction from "more important" work, and who wished to be remembered primarily for other things—his painstakingly researched historical fiction, his contributions to social and legal reform, his chronicling of his country at war, and finally his work on behalf of Spiritualism, which occupied most of his time and energy for the last ten years of his life.

But Sir Arthur Conan Doyle *did* create Sherlock Holmes, and after one hundred years, a certain if unclear place for them both in the pantheon of English letters seems secure. It was in *Beeton's Christmas Annual* for 1887 that Conan Doyle, then a young doctor in general practice in the Southsea suburb of Portsmouth, England, published *A Study in Scarlet*, a mystery novel featuring Mr. Sherlock Holmes of 221B Baker Street, London. In the concept of Holmes, Conan Doyle owed a good deal to Edgar Allan Poe, something the literary character denied but his creator affirmed on many occasions. He was only twenty-eight years old at the time.

Arthur Conan Doyle had been born in Edinburgh, Scotland, on May 22, 1859, second of a large number of children born to Charles Altamont and Mary Foley Doyle. From his granduncle and godfather Michael Conan, a distinguished journalist, he (and his older sister Annette) received the compound surname of Conan Doyle. His family was of an artistic bent, with a number of prominent artists and illustrators to its credit, and his father had some talent along those lines, though he earned a rather meager living for his large family as a civil servant in Scotland's Board of Works—until his declining ability to cope with alcoholism lost him both his livelihood and his family situation. What young Arthur's father may have lacked in character, however, his mother more than made up. A gentle but determined personality, Mary Doyle instilled in her son Arthur a strong sense of personal honor, a lifelong fascination with a romantically conceived past, and an admirable if anachronistic sense of chivalry that he applied in daily life.

Arthur Conan Doyle's upbringing (the world learned only many years after his death) was not a happy one. It was not just his family's growing poverty. At home he grew up watching his family deteriorate, his mother striving to hold things together while his thoroughly irresponsible father became less and less capable of doing his duty by his family. The painful experience gave Arthur Conan Doyle a lifelong respect for women, but it also gave his mother and her strongly held views considerable influence over him for the remainder of her life, the consequences of which are now debated by biographers. Conditions at home deteriorated to the point that Arthur was sent away to school for his own good. His schooling was the strict, sometimes brutal, Jesuit environment of Hodder and Stonyhurst schools in Lancashire, England, with his horizons broadened a bit by a final year at a third Jesuit school in Feldkirch, Austria. He seems never to have regretted this schooling, but its insistence on faith in Roman Catholic dogma weakened his allegiance to the religion in which he had been raised, leading finally, during his university days, to conscientious adoption of an agnosticism that was, he knew, very much at odds with his family. At Edinburgh University he studied medicine, under several noteworthy physicians who would influence his subsequent career as a writer—in particular Dr. Joseph Bell, a prominent surgeon with an uncanny gift for observation and deduction in diagnosis that left his students breathless.

We know less than we would like about Arthur Conan Doyle during this period: his life at home again with a failing father, who would finally be permanently institutionalized in a number of asylums until his death in 1893; his earliest ambitious attempts at writing around this time; and the deep influence of a somewhat older medico, Dr. Bryan Charles Waller, who came to live with the hard-pressed Doyles as a boarder and was soon paying the rent and taxes on the house himself—a "very strange, brilliant and eccentric man" whose importance in Arthur Conan Doyle's life has been acknowledged by the latter's family,[1] and who gave Mary

1. Letter from Adrian Conan Doyle, January 20, 1966, to William S. Baring-Gould, editor of *The Annotated Sherlock Holmes* (New York: Clarkson N. Potter, 1967). The letter is in the Philip S. Hench Collection at the Univerity of Minnesota Library.

Doyle a home for many years, but whom Arthur Conan Doyle seldom if ever mentioned in later years.

Conan Doyle earned his baccalaureate of medicine from Edinburgh in 1881, having already developed a taste for personal adventure from two voyages as ship's surgeon, while still a student, on a Greenland whaler and a West African freighter. Ready to embark on his medical career, he accepted the junior place in a partnership with an extraordinary former upperclassman of his named George Turnavine Budd, in Plymouth. It lasted only a few months, but that short time proved a tumultuous experience in a practice that, in Budd's hands, crossed the limits of medical ethics and bordered on quackery. The relationship ended volcanically. Conan Doyle took up practice on his own in Southsea, and stayed there for the next eight years. As a doctor, he did not particularly prosper during this period. But he did receive his M.D. from Edinburgh, with a dissertation on the syphilis-related condition of *tabes dorsalis*; he met and married his first wife, Louisa "Touie" Hawkins;[2] and he began to be published, and noticed a little as a writer.

A Study in Scarlet was published in 1887. It was his third attempt at a novel, but the first to appear. It was no particular success, and neither was a second Sherlock Holmes novel, *The Sign of the Four*, in 1890. While Conan Doyle's stories and even his novels were getting published now, it was not yet a living nor might ever be, and so he decided to specialize in ophthalmology and to practice in London, where he moved at the beginning of 1891. But halfway through that year, as he waited in his consulting room for the patients who never came,[3] so the story goes, he wrote and sent his first two Sherlock Holmes short stories to the brand-new *Strand Magazine*. They were an electrifying overnight success. Sherlock Holmes rapidly became a sensation throughout the world, and in time perhaps the best-known character in fiction—the subject of countless books, plays, movies, radio and television, and more, Holmes without end. Sherlock Holmes is a cultural icon today.

As for Arthur Conan Doyle, the success of Sherlock Holmes permitted him to give up his none too busy medical career, and devote himself to writing. Besides Sherlock Holmes—soon regarded by his creator as a nuisance and an impediment to a serious literary reputation—Conan Doyle wrote tales of the Napoleonic Wars, historical novels of the Middle Ages, and novels set in other periods of English and French history; novels of contemporary English life, stories of adventure, romance, the supernatural, and much more. He revolutionized the detective story

2. The name is mistakenly given as Louise by most biographers.
3. A blessing on them, as Christopher Morley, founder of the Baker Street Irregulars, remarked in his classic foreword to *The Complete Sherlock Holmes* (Garden City: Doubleday, 1930).

and pioneered science fiction with stories about the boisterous iconoclast Professor Challenger.

He became active in public affairs, too. He did volunteer medical work in South Africa during the Boer War and returned home to stand unsuccessfully twice for Parliament as a Liberal Unionist. He was knighted in 1902 for his defense of Britain's conduct of the Boer War, and he led social reform movements in divorce law and criminal justice. In the latter area, his work on behalf of two men—one a half-caste Parsee solicitor, George Edalji, convicted of cattle maiming, the other a petty criminal, Oscar Slater, convicted of murder—received nationwide publicity and contributed to the establishment of Great Britain's first Court of Criminal Appeal. Less popular but equally conscientious was Conan Doyle's unsuccessful defense of the Irish patriot Roger Casement, accused of aiding Germany in World War I, tried, and executed for treason in 1916.

Conan Doyle's personal life was a physically vigorous but emotionally strained one during these years. His first wife, with whom he had two children (Mary and Kingsley), contracted consumption (tuberculosis) in the early 1890s and finally died of it in 1906 after years of failing health. The following year, Conan Doyle married Jean Leckie, with whom he had been in love for ten years: all that time keeping their relationship discreet—and platonic—for the sake of his invalid wife and his own sense of personal integrity. They would have three children (Denis, Adrian, and Jean). Younger by seventeen years, Conan Doyle's beloved wife survived him by ten.

During World War I, Sir Arthur Conan Doyle came close to giving up fiction altogether, devoting himself largely to a military history of the British campaign on the Western Front, which he had visited under dangerous conditions. In 1916 he became convinced of the truth of Spiritualism, a phenomenon he had studied, at first skeptically, since the 1880s. He devoted the last decade of his life to a worldwide crusade on behalf of the Spiritualist message, unfortunately at the expense of his reputation as a serious man of affairs. He died at home in Sussex on July 7, 1930, at the age of seventy-one. It had been an unusually active, vigorous, and diverse life. He felt he had much besides Sherlock Holmes to his lasting credit. But (and despite his periodic attempts to kill off his own most popular character), Sir Arthur Conan Doyle remains universally known as the creator of Sherlock Holmes.

ii

All things about Conan Doyle—rather to his dismay—harken back to Sherlock Holmes. During March and April 1886, while he wrote *A*

Study in Scarlet, the young Southsea doctor had hoped that this mystery would advance his fledgling career as a writer. After several discouraging rejections, the novel was finally accepted by a London publisher, Ward, Lock and Company, but it insisted on holding the story over until the next year—the market was already flooded with cheap fiction, the young writer was told—and on owning the entire copyright, for a none too lavish twenty-five pounds. It was neither a flattering nor a generous offer. But the young doctor agreed, reluctantly, in order to see his novel published.

By 1927, having long ago become one of the best-known writers in the world, Sir Arthur Conan Doyle had published four novels and fifty-six short stories about Sherlock Holmes over a period of forty years. Holmes had gotten off to a somewhat halting start in his first two novels, but in 1891 came his astounding success in *The Strand Magazine*. After two series of immensely popular short stories, *The Adventures* and *The Memoirs of Sherlock Holmes*, Conan Doyle decided in 1893 to kill off the child of his imagination and concentrate on other work. But an especially good story idea persuaded him to bring Holmes back posthumously eight years later in *The Hound of the Baskervilles*; and in 1903 Conan Doyle succumbed to the most lucrative offer ever made to a writer up to that time, giving Holmes a renewed lease on life in a new series of stories called *The Return of Sherlock Holmes*. The last Sherlock Holmes novel, *The Valley of Fear*, appeared in 1914, and a fourth short-story collection, *His Last Bow*, in 1917. Following World War I, Conan Doyle was loath to waste time on fiction, but to defray the considerable expenses of his Spiritualist crusade he wrote one final series of Sherlock Holmes stories, collected in 1927 as *The Case-Book of Sherlock Holmes*.

It did not take people long to begin treating Sherlock Holmes as reality, discussing his adventures as if historical fact. It began in 1902 with England's *Cambridge Review* and America's *Bookman* analyzing *The Hound of the Baskervilles* as if it were fact, not fiction. The "Higher Criticism" of the Sherlockian canon was given a formal structure ten years later in an Oxford University undergraduate paper, "Studies in the Literature of Sherlock Holmes" by Ronald A. Knox, later one of England's leading Roman Catholic prelates. Knox's purpose was satirical, lampooning the biblical scholarship of the day by applying the same exegetical approach to the Sherlock Holmes stories, but in doing so he established the approach that he and a growing number of Sherlock Holmes enthusiasts would employ to create, in time, a huge corpus of "Writings about the Writings."

Soon after Conan Doyle's death, the first book-length studies of the Sherlockian canon appeared. In England, *Sherlock Holmes and Dr. Watson* by H. W. Bell (Constable, 1932) chronologically ordered all sixty tales on the basis of their internal evidence; in America *The Private Life of Sherlock Holmes* by Vincent Starrett (Macmillan, 1933) gave the great detective his first biography, and the Baker Street Irregulars (founded the next year by Christopher Morley) a rallying point for their future development. In 1946 the *Baker Street Journal*, followed in 1951 by England's *Sherlock Holmes Journal*, provided regular periodical opportunities for Sherlockian scholarship, and a quantum leap was the result: "never has so much been written by so many for so few," Morley quipped. In 1967 the publication of *The Annotated Sherlock Holmes* made the by now well-developed Higher Criticism known to the public at large, and further growth was ensured.

Perhaps in paying tribute to Sherlock Holmes, Sherlockiana helped obscure Conan Doyle's real and very remarkable accomplishment. In order to make Holmes seem real, little room was made for Conan Doyle in this game, who when mentioned at all was usually relegated blandly to the minor role of Dr. Watson's literary agent. Sir Arthur Conan Doyle would probably be speechless at the vast industry of Sherlockian scholarship; and some observers have branded it as tedious and irrelevant. But for many years the latter paid precious little more attention to Conan Doyle than the Sherlockian scholarship did.[4]

Of course, Conan Doyle had made himself a difficult person to reconcile with Sherlock Holmes. From Holmes' superrationalism to an affirmation of faith in Spiritualism was a great distance. What kind of man was it who, conceiving the one, dedicated himself to the other? People looked in vain to Conan Doyle's writings for a satisfactory answer, even though some of his work took an autobiographical direction since his earliest days as a writer. His first novel, *The Narrative of John Smith*, written when barely twenty-two, had been strong-toned social and political comment of an autobiographical sort; but the manuscript was lost in the post. One of Conan Doyle's biographers, Hesketh Pearson, quotes him saying years later that "my shock at its disappearance would be as nothing to my horror if it were suddenly to appear again—in print."[5] What did appear along autobiographical lines was a later novel, *The Stark Munro Letters*, based on the brief turbulent partnership with Dr. Budd. Late in his life Conan Doyle wrote an autobiography, entitled *Memories and Adventures*—aptly, because a full and candid account of his life it was not. The first edition was published in 1924, and a second edition, revised and updated, appeared shortly before his death in 1930. And a number of other autobiographical works shed light on some of his travels, his later family life, and the Spiritualist crusade.

4. See Cait Murphy, "The Game's Still Afoot," in *Atlantic Monthly*, 259 (March 1987): 58–63, for an up-to-date look at the Sherlockian "Higher Criticism."
5. In *Conan Doyle, His Life and Art* (London: Methuen, 1943), p. 75.

But despite these, Conan Doyle has always been an enigma. His autobiographical writings did not answer the questions that critics and scholars found most intriguing about him. They have always been confounded by the fact that Sherlock Holmes was created by a man as seemingly unHolmesian as Arthur Conan Doyle—Watsonian in appearance, none too dedicated as a physician, a commercial writer, a British patriot, a spokesman for some unfashionable causes, and finally a Spiritualist missionary. Did this British author with a scientific education have a simple or complex psyche? Some "obvious" evidence seemed to indicate the former. But if simple, how could he create characters and a milieu with such universal appeal and lasting strength? If complex, with creative powers as strong as that, why have most of his writings been dismissed as mere popular fiction? And how could a scientifically educated man embrace Spiritualism wholeheartedly, and be deceived by a hoax like the "Cottingley fairy photographs"? But if shallow and gullible by nature, how could he have excelled in cases of miscarriages of justice, vindicating men convicted of crimes they had not committed? Who was Conan Doyle's model for Sherlock Holmes: Joseph Bell, his superobservant professor of medicine, as Conan Doyle claimed? Or Conan Doyle himself, as son Adrian would later argue? Why was he so reticent about his father, people wondered for years—and still a subject for curiosity today is the reportedly deep influence of his sometime mentor Bryan Charles Waller, whom he never mentioned.

What autobiography failed to provide, biography has attempted. Since Conan Doyle's death in 1930, thirteen book-length biographies have been published in England and America—quite remarkable for a writer seldom taken very seriously by academia. The first published, in 1931, was by a trusted colleague in the Spiritualist movement.[6] The second came twelve years later from a prominent English biographer, Hesketh Pearson, who undertook the project with the family's blessing and cooperation; but when they read the book, with its irreverent treatment of Sir Arthur, Conan Doyle's sons attacked it bitterly. The third,

6. The year before, a biography did appear in Sweden: *Sir Arthur Conan Doyle: liv och minnen* by Viktor Olsson (Malmo: Världslitteraturens Förlag, 1930). According to Mr. Ake Runnquist, senior literary editor at Sweden's oldest publishing house (Alfred Bonniers Förlag), the book's publisher specialized in cheap editions of classics in the public domain, translated by students from the nearby University of Lund; the author was probably a graduate student, and the biography commissioned as a useful introduction for a large Swedish audience buying Conan Doyle from the publisher. It was a superficial popular biography, based on published accounts of Conan Doyle's life and career, and as it made no mark on the development of the public perception of Sir Arthur Conan Doyle nor any new contribution to our knowledge of him, and has never been available in English, it is not discussed further in this volume.

written by one of the sons, critics scorned in its turn as sheer hagiography. The subsequent biographies have focused on Conan Doyle the man of action—or Conan Doyle the contemplative author; on Conan Doyle, the true Sherlock Holmes—or Conan Doyle, the man who hated Sherlock Holmes; on Conan Doyle, a mystic with secrets to conceal—or a Colonel Blimp too simple to conceal anything; on the young and troubled Conan Doyle—or Conan Doyle the public figure and defender of the underdog. Perceptions of Arthur Conan Doyle have varied remarkably, and research has never been easy, for he *did* obscure some details of his origins, life, and emotional experiences, his papers have not always been available for research, and they remain unavailable today pending settlement of a legal dispute.

iii

It is time now, after a century of Sherlock Holmes, to examine the principal problems in Conan Doyle biography and assess how well Conan Doyle and his biographers have dealt with them. He has had little standing in the academic sight of things, regarded there as merely a popular writer of escapist mysteries, adventures, and outdated historical fiction. Yet people return again and again to study Conan Doyle and his work, Sherlock Holmes especially. His widely read stories and novels continue to appear in one edition after another, translated into many other languages, and rendered into many media. Conan Doyle remains incontestably the creator of one of the most powerful figures in fiction. But many who look to Sherlock Holmes as the supreme literary spokesman for rationalism feel dismay and bewilderment about his creator having become a leading champion of a doctrine that seems at odds with his education and literary ideas.

Conan Doyle's life deserves a careful and thorough academic treatment, which only a few of his biographers have given to it or to his literary output and the philosophy, character, and outlook that led to it. The challenge of seeing Conan Doyle as he really was has scarcely been helped by some of his biographers concentrating on one aspect of him at the expense of others, by taking too admiring or denigrating a view of his literary and public accomplishments, or by trying to explain the essence of his personality in a catchphrase, subjecting the details of his life to Procrustean abuse until they seem to fit. There are six major problems of Conan Doyle biography that have posed serious problems for those trying to render a portrait of this man, his creative impulse, and its remarkable literary and cultural results. Five of them are conceptual hurdles, the sixth a problem of research materials.

Simplicity or complexity: was Conan Doyle simply "the man in the street"? Hesketh Pearson, the biographer much despised by Sir Arthur's sons, thought he was and made that the theme of his life of Conan Doyle. Many other observers have felt much the same. But Pearson's conclusion rested on a hasty and superficial examination of Conan Doyle's life and work; whereas a deeper examination than Conan Doyle sometimes received from his biographers seems to reveal a man whose commercial success as a writer, and advocacy of causes like the Boer War, masked a readiness to break with tradition, authority, and public opinion over issues of conscience—his family's religion, the justice of his country's courts, or Spiritualism, which cost him the respect of many. All his literary life—certainly since the Spiritualist period—Conan Doyle has been too easily dismissed as an intellectual and emotional lightweight who wrote with no particular depth of thought or feeling. But we have recently come to know more about serious difficulties in his life, in childhood and later, enough to begin to discern their reflections in his writings, which occur more often than has been generally supposed.

Unfortunately for his critical reception, Conan Doyle received little credit for any depth of emotional sensitivity or experience until quite recently. One of his more acute biographers, Pierre Nordon, discusses certain of his personality traits—deliberate masking of his personality, a constant effort to give a phlegmatic appearance of even temperament, a tendency to compensate for childhood frustrations by emphasizing personal toughness—which no doubt contributed to the general image that the world has had of Conan Doyle. No doubt he did his own artistic reputation no good by presenting to the world a demeanor that could scarcely be taken seriously as that of an *artiste*. And his son Adrian sometimes advanced such sweeping claims about his significance that serious assessment seldom followed the critical rejection of what seemed filial rodomontade.

Was Conan Doyle Holmes? The role of Bell. In part, the answer to this question depends on the answer to the preceding one. If Sir Arthur Conan Doyle was essentially a simple soul—the man in the street, as Hesketh Pearson would have it—then someone other than the creator of Sherlock Holmes must have been the character's model. Surely Sherlock Holmes could not have been created out of Conan Doyle's inner resources. Conan Doyle himself gave public credit to his former medical professor, Joe Bell, and others, like Robert Louis Stevenson, were able to recognize Bell in Sherlock Holmes. But was there nonetheless something substantial of Conan Doyle himself in Holmes? Bell himself tried to give the credit back to his former student.

Some biographers could only see Dr. Watson in Conan Doyle. His sons reacted vehemently to that notion, and Adrian did everything he could to stress the "Conan-Doyle-is-Holmes" theme to an unimpressed world—even threatening Irving Wallace with libel suits for including Dr. Bell among Wallace's "Fabulous Originals."[7] Yet there may be some truth in Adrian's contention, which need not rely entirely on a few captive biographers' claims for Sherlockian powers on Conan Doyle's part in the Edalji and Slater investigations. Conan Doyle himself dropped autobiographical clues in the Sherlock Holmes stories: when Holmes first came to London, prior to Watson, for example, Conan Doyle gave him lodgings in Montague Street (see "The Musgrave Ritual")—just as he had taken lodgings in Montague Place, right around the corner, when he first moved to London in 1891. More literary detective work is needed than Conan Doyle's writings have so far received.

Conan Doyle's psychology, and his work as the mirror of his mind. It is difficult, perhaps presumptuous, to put an author on the psychologist's couch more than fifty years after his death. Conan Doyle's biographers have tended to walk gingerly around the subject of his psychology. Nor do we know enough yet about Conan Doyle's early life to make judgments in sufficient confidence that we know where all the pitfalls lie. Not that that hasn't been attempted. The first undertaking was a full-scale one, published around the beginning of what Baker Street Irregulars remember with some distaste as the Sherlock Holmes boom of the 1970s: *Naked Is the Best Disguise*, by Samuel Rosenberg (Bobbs-Merrill, 1974). Rosenberg demonstrated that a determined effort could make Conan Doyle's work look like nothing *but* a reflection of his psychological state: delving deep into the concepts of Freudian psychology, he lay bare the Sherlock Holmes stories, and some of Conan Doyle's other prose and poetry, as a mainly conscious encrypting of the paraphernalia of an obsessed, even tormented psyche. Rosenberg saw Conan Doyle as an immensely literate man who used fiction for brilliantly allegorical exorcism of his sexual and religious demons. Scarcely a passage of the Sherlock Holmes canon did not illustrate what Rosenberg called the "Conan Doyle syndrome," a linking of mentions of the printed word with references to sexual deviance and mass murder—which Rosenberg interpreted as evidence of a very personal obsession on Conan Doyle's part with evil and punishment.

Rosenberg's view of Conan Doyle's psychology and its influence on his writings went to the extremes of Freudian diagnosis, armed with only a sketchy knowledge of the facts of Conan Doyle's life. Yet without going that far, there is something to be said for the contention that Conan

---

7. See Wallace's *The Fabulous Originals: Lives of Extraordinary People Who Inspired Memorable Characters in Fiction* (New York: Alfred A. Knopf, 1955), pp. 22–45, and *The Sunday Gentleman* (New York: Simon and Schuster, 1965), pp. 392–415, for an account of Wallace's difficulties with Adrian Conan Doyle over this essay.

Doyle *was* influenced by psychologically powerful factors in his past and present, which found their way into his writings. One comprehensible trace, recognizable now that we know about it, was his father's alcoholism. Conan Doyle's horror at the abusive effects of alcoholism turn up time and again, in his public view that dipsomania is "the foulest of all insanities,"[8] in his agitation for divorce law reform, and in fiction like the Sherlock Holmes story "The Adventure of the Abbey Grange," about a woman suffering intolerably from an alcoholic brute of a husband, whose violent death at the hands of a rival Holmes sees fit to excuse. Christopher Redmond, a contributor to this volume, points out, in a perceptive study of "the sexual elements in Arthur Conan Doyle's stories of the Great Detective,"[9] that Conan Doyle spent ten years married to a woman with whom he had come to feel at most an affection, and whose eventually fatal disease made a normal marital life impossible—while keeping his relationship with another woman, with whom he had fallen deeply in love, strictly platonic until after he was free to remarry. The sublimative possibilities in circumstances like that are boundless, but only very recently have biographers and critics begun to consider the effect that factors such as these in Conan Doyle's life had upon his literary work.

His place as a writer: literature or popular fiction? For many years, the consensus of critical and academic opinion placed Conan Doyle's literary work (both the historical fiction that he considered his best and the Sherlock Holmes stories that have had the strongest grip on the public) in the easily ignored category of popular fiction. According to this judgment, his work is without significant value or influence on the development of English literature (public devotion to Sherlock Holmes by poets and writers like G. K. Chesterton, T. S. Eliot, P. G. Wodehouse, Graham Greene and others notwithstanding). True, as eminent a critic as Edmund Wilson acknowledged Sherlock Holmes as transcending what he regarded as a disappointing genre: "My contention," Wilson said, "is that Sherlock Holmes *is* literature on a humble but not ignoble level, whereas the mystery writers most in vogue now are not."[10] But if not actually dismissive, antibourgeois critics like Wilson damned with faint praise,

8. See his February 8, 1918, letter to the *Sussex Daily News*, in *Letters to the Press* by Sir Arthur Conan Doyle, ed. John Michael Gibson and Richard Lancelyn Green (Iowa City: University of Iowa Press, 1986), p. 264.

9. *In Bed with Sherlock Holmes*, by Christopher Redmond (Toronto: Simon and Pierre, 1984), well worth reading for its study of psychosexual elements in Conan Doyle's Sherlock Holmes stories; see the editor's extensive review of the book in *Baker Street Miscellanea*, no. 42, (Summer 1985).

10. "Who Cares Who Killed Roger Ackroyd?" *Classics and Commercials* (New York: Farrar, Straus, 1950), p. 267.

and for the most part, mainstream criticism and academic curricula have had little time for Conan Doyle. They continued to regard him as a talented but essentially shallow stylist, who used the language very well on occasion to tell his tales, but whose fiction lacked depth, feeling, and expression for wells of pain and frustration and alienation in the human personality; whose work lacked significant social and political content; who created not literary characters in the true sense of the term but, rather, individual collections of memorable characteristics.

Nevertheless, Sherlock Holmes has maintained his astonishingly strong grip on the world for a century now, despite tremendous changes in the times and public tastes. Conan Doyle has begun to be taken seriously in recent years because Sherlock Holmes has proven himself to be timeless, and because of increasing recognition of the great range and contemporary impact, in both America and England, of his other work. To the surprise of many, Conan Doyle and Sherlock Holmes (as something other than a purportedly real figure) are increasingly subjects of serious study by mainsteam critics and scholars: Oxford University Press publishes a comprehensive bibliography of Conan Doyle's works; American university presses underwrite the publication of journals devoted to the lives and times of Sherlock Holmes and Conan Doyle; scholarly examinations of character and creator continue to appear in growing number; and a critical reappraisal by the academic community is well under way now. The Sherlock Holmes canon "amply repays study" concludes one American professor of English literature: "the range of life—of people, settings, ideas—that Holmes encounters or reflects upon in that time is extraordinarily wide. . . . the canon as a whole—with its observant, analytical hero who comes into professional contact with all strata of urban and rural society from kings (e.g., "A Scandal in Bohemia") to beggars (e.g., "The Man With the Twisted Lip")—offers an unrivalled and largely overlooked source for the study of late-Victorian ideas, attitudes, and culture."[11]

Largely overlooked, indeed. The irony is that Conan Doyle is now being taken most seriously by the academic community in terms of the fiction to which he himself gave little respect.

The Spiritualist crusade. This has been a most difficult aspect of Conan Doyle's life for his biographers to deal with. There is no question that after 1916, Conan Doyle gave his heart and mind to Spiritualism, and in what seemed to many an uncritical way. He always contended that he insisted on proofs of mediumistic claims, but others felt that he was satisfied with very little in the way of evidence, that he was easily de-

11. Pennsylvania State University's Christopher Clausen, "Sherlock Holmes, Order, and the Late-Victorian Mind," *Georgia Review* 38 (Spring 1984): 106.

ceived, and even others in the psychic research movement, who recognized the presence of charlatans in their midst, considered him naive. Although Conan Doyle had a scientific education, did he subject the evidence for Spiritualism to scientific examination? One character in *The Land of Mist* (1926) spoke for him in saying: "What is really not science is the laying down of the law on matters which you have not studied. It is talk of that sort which has brought me to the edge of Spiritualism, when I compare this dogmatic ignorance with the earnest search for truth conducted by the great Spiritualists." Finally his interest in the subject, active since the 1880s, won him over during the traumatic days of the Great War. The popular perception that Conan Doyle turned to Spiritualism because of his son's death in the war is wrong; Kingsley and Sir Arthur's younger brother Innes, with whom he had always been very close, died two and three years respectively after Conan Doyle's conversion to Spiritualism. But hundreds of thousands of other Britons *were* dying in the war, including several close to Conan Doyle, and this played an important part in his giving himself to what he thereafter regarded as a great Crusade: to bring mankind the truth of life after death and the affirmation thereby of a merciful God.

He had doubted the existence of God for many years. When he came to believe, it was in his wholehearted way. Yet when he did surrender to the supernatural, if one cares to think about it that way, it did not destroy his creative judgment. If he did make his beloved Professor Challenger a convert to Spiritualism, in *The Land of Mist*, it was because Challenger served as a symbol of the debate between skeptical science and spiritual faith, and because Conan Doyle identified more than a little with Challenger personally. He never committed the artistic misstep of making Sherlock Holmes, the supreme nineteenth-century materialist, a convert. "This agency stands flat-footed upon the ground, and there it must remain. The world is big enough for us. No ghosts need apply" was Holmes' dictum in a case ostensibly involving the supernatural, written at the height of Conan Doyle's Spiritualist commitment.[12] It demonstrated that whatever one thought about his conversion to Spiritualism, it had not destroyed his artistic integrity and sense of discrimination. But that Conan Doyle could believe in spirit communication with the dead and, worse than that, in fairies (the subject of two essays and a book during the 1920s) shocked and chagrined people who up to then were prepared to treat him respectfully as a writer. The Spiritualist episode probably set back his chances of gaining a serious reputation as a writer for decades. Not that he would have cared by then. By the time of his

12. "The Adventure of the Sussex Vampire," written in late 1923 and published in *The Strand Magazine* in January 1924.

death, he would gladly have traded any literary reputation he could have won for success in bringing the Spiritualist message to mankind.

Family cooperation and the archives. Conan Doyle's family would have preferred him to have both. From the earliest days following his death in 1930, until his son Adrian's death in 1970, the family strove to restrict and control what people wrote about his life and work. An early attempt by W. H. Hosking to write a biography was squelched, and Sir Arthur's widow, who shared her husband's commitment to Spiritualism, gave the task to the Reverend John Lamond, a trusted friend and Spiritualist colleague.

A decade later, Sir Arthur's sons entertained the idea of biography that, by encompassing more than Spiritualism, would advance their father's literary and public reputations and establish among the public their own perception of the father and knight they loved and admired. The Conan Doyles possessed large archives of papers, letters, and other documentary materials relating to Sir Arthur's life and work, and access to those archives has been selective. Hesketh Pearson had partial access while researching his biography; when Conan Doyle's sons turned against him, Adrian denied ever afterward that Pearson had had any access. John Dickson Carr was permitted access for his authorized version of Sir Arthur's life, and after Carr, Pierre Nordon, for his independent-minded literary biography of Conan Doyle. Since the mid-1970s, however, the archives have been unavailable to scholars, owing to litigation over the disposition of Sir Arthur's estate; and while his surviving child, Dame Jean Conan Doyle, has never cared to exercise the sort of censorship that her brother Adrian pursued, it is fair to say that she regards the archives as her *family's* papers, not something to which the outside world has an obvious, inalienable right.

Yet lack of access to the family's archives has not prevented biographies of Conan Doyle from being researched, written, and published. And while some would no doubt have been better for access to the archives, lack of access has usefully pointed some scholars in other directions, to sources that had lain unsuspected and unexploited by their predecessors. Owen Dudley Edwards' explorations in the records of nineteenth-century Edinburgh, for example, turned up noteworthy new data about Conan Doyle's early years there; and likewise, Richard Lancelyn Green's researches in even less likely places have made possible biographical discoveries to be found in *A Bibliography of A. Conan Doyle* (Clarendon Press, 1983, compiled with John Michael Gibson), and his 134-page introduction to *The Uncollected Sherlock Holmes* (Penguin Books, 1984).

iv

There is danger in taking every incident in a novel like *The Stark Munro Letters* as autobiographical fact. Nonetheless, some insight regarding Conan Doyle's life can be gleaned from his autobiographical fiction. Conscious of the dangers, Ely M. Liebow searches for personal experiences veiled in pseudonyms by Conan Doyle in *The Stark Munro Letters* and some less obvious novels and stories. Conan Doyle wrote most of his autobiographical fiction before he wrote his autobiography, and the former is examined here first for that reason.

Memories and Adventures was Conan Doyle's own selective presentation of his life. In it he laid emphasis on action and adventure at the expense of personal revelations, making it difficult to approach by those seeking the man behind the celebrated author and public figure. The life that Conan Doyle presented to the public, and its contribution to our knowledge about the man, are assessed here by England's foremost living authority on Sir Arthur Conan Doyle, Richard Lancelyn Green. Besides *Memories and Adventures*, Conan Doyle also wrote a number of other autobiographical works, reminiscences in aid of personal image and public causes, particularly the Spiritualist crusade, which are reviewed here by Andrew S. Malec.

Thirteen biographies of Sir Arthur Conan Doyle have followed, but the light they have shed on their subject has been variable at best. The following essays cover the biographies, addressing their treatment of the principal problems of Conan Doyle biography while examining the considerations that make literary biography rise or fall: the biographer's background and credentials; the biography's publishing history, where noteworthy; its intended audience; the approach taken by the biographer, and how well he deals with the biographical problems; the biographer's attitude toward his subject and his works; the biographer's areas of concentration and neglect; the sophistication of the biographer's literary criticism and handling of the relationship between the subject's life and work; the book's supplementary material, for example, its bibliography, index, illustrative material, and the like; and the biographer's sources, extent of family cooperation, and access to the family archives.

In the Reverend John Lamond, Sir Arthur's widow entrusted the task of the first biography of her late husband's life to a friend of the family and a trusted Spiritualist colleague. The Spiritualist issue would thus be in safe and respectful hands, and so it proved. However, Lamond, it seems, was conscious of his limitations as a biographer and leaned toward making his *Arthur Conan Doyle: A Memoir* essentially that—a brief, affectionate appreciation of the Spiritualist crusader.

Philip A. Shreffler, the editor of the Baker Street Irregulars' quarterly *Baker Street Journal*, explains that as biography it failed to satisfy.

A professional biography came along twelve years later in Hesketh Pearson's *Conan Doyle, His Life and Art*. Expected by a cooperative Adrian Conan Doyle to be a respectful study of Sir Arthur's life and literature, it turned out instead to be a good-natured debunking of Conan Doyle as "the man in the street." Adrian went into a rage that lasted for the rest of his life, throughout which he pursued Pearson with threats of lawsuits and attempts to suppress further printings of his book, and any other commentary about Sir Arthur Conan Doyle by Pearson in print or on the air. Nicholas Utechin, editor of the Sherlock Holmes Society of London's *Sherlock Holmes Journal*, appraises the cause of the uproar that convinced Adrian to do everything he could to shape what was written about his beloved father's life.

Determined to refute Pearson, Adrian published his own comment on his father's life two years later in *The True Conan Doyle*. Unfortunately for Adrian, his rather strident counterattack met a cool reception from the critics, who thought it absurd for him to imply that his father's life should be exempt from outside criticism. Looking back at this ill-advised episode in the history of Conan Doyle biography is James Bliss Austin, who in amassing one of the world's most illustrious collections of Sherlockiana and Doyleana came to know Adrian Conan Doyle well, and not unappreciatively.

Not long thereafter, Adrian learned that a well-known American writer of classic mystery fiction, John Dickson Carr, was planning to write a new biography of Sir Arthur Conan Doyle. At first Adrian reacted strongly, but when the dust settled, the two men emerged in a cozy relationship. Howard Lachtman casts a critical eye at Carr's "authorized" version of *The Life of Sir Arthur Conan Doyle* (1949), long considered the standard treatment: a respectful, some have thought worshipful, account along the same lines that Conan Doyle himself had set in *Memories and Adventures*.

In 1959, Adrian had published a memorial album to mark the centenary of his father's birth, which included a biographical essay by a French scholar named Pierre Nordon. Working toward his doctorate in Anglo-Saxon literature at the Sorbonne, Nordon wrote his dissertation on Conan Doyle, and this solid piece of literary criticism relating life to work was published in France in 1964. An English translation followed two years later, but in the process Nordon's *Conan Doyle* was transformed from a scholarly work into a still useful but undeniably more "popular" biography. Assessing both versions here is the bilingual Canadian scholar Donald A. Redmond, whose *Sherlock Holmes, A Study in Sources* is a pioneering analysis of Conan Doyle's creation of the Sherlock Holmes characters and milieu.

From the mid-1960s to the early 1970s, four lesser biographies of Sir Arthur Conan Doyle appeared, and their differing perceptions are apparent in their titles: *The Man Who Was Sherlock Holmes* by Michael and Mollie Hardwick (1964); *The Real Sherlock Holmes: Arthur Conan Doyle* by Mary Hoehling (1965); *The Man Who Hated Sherlock Holmes* by James Playsted Wood (1965); and *Conan Doyle, A Biography of the Creator of Sherlock Holmes* by Ivor Brown (1972). As Edward S. Lauterbach points out in his essay comparing these four minor biographies with a similar but conflicting central theme, the first of them was instigated by Adrian Conan Doyle, but by the time the last appeared, Adrian was dead, and his era of tight (if not airtight) control over Conan Doyle biography had come to an end.

In the early 1970s, a Royal Shakespeare Company revival of William Gillette's 1899 melodrama *Sherlock Holmes* triggered a great renewal of public interest in the subject. Among those taking advantage of it was a hastily researched but interesting biography, *The Adventures of Conan Doyle*, published in 1976 by a controversial American biographer, Charles Higham. Peter E. Blau joins me in evaluating the pros and cons of a biography that, though marred by avoidable error and questionable speculation, did draw attention to aspects of Conan Doyle's life and work that had been neglected in the past, and that have received more attention since.

Little as Adrian might have cared for Higham's biography, he would have disliked the next one even more. Ronald Pearsall's 1977 *Conan Doyle, A Biographical Solution* was another debunking of the subject's life and work, but a deliberately snide one this time where Pearson's at least had been good-natured. David R. Anderson gives it more attention here than it has tended to receive from others, like another Conan Doyle biographer who remarked once that Pearsall's book "wants its readers to know that its author is more worthy of admiration than its subject, and despite its enthusiasm for this enterprise, fails."[13]

The 1970s closed with *Portrait of an Artist—Conan Doyle* by Julian Symons, a reexamination of Conan Doyle's life and work by not only a master of modern mystery fiction, with an acknowledged debt to pay to Conan Doyle, but also one of the genre's most important historians and critics. Richard Lancelyn Green, who covers Sir Arthur Conan Doyle's *Memories and Adventures* earlier in this volume, returns to review this book as well.

13. Owen Dudley Edwards, *The Quest for Sherlock Holmes* (Edinburgh: Mainstream Publishing Company, 1983), p. 20. Admittedly, Edwards finds all the Arthur Conan Doyle biographies preceding his to be wanting.

Conan Doyle is not forgotten in his native Edinburgh, and next came a biography of his early life there, *The Quest for Sherlock Holmes* by Owen Dudley Edwards (1983), an Edinburgh University historian who left few local stones unturned in the attempt to shed light on the family turmoil, religious disillusionment, and portentous education of the child and youth who would become the author and public figure. Edwards' biography is assessed here by Christopher Redmond, author of the previously mentioned *In Bed with Sherlock Holmes*.

v

As we saw earlier, in discussing the development of the "Sherlockian" scholarship, people studied Sherlock Holmes long before they studied his creator. They may have done it with tongue in cheek, but they were responding to a remarkable achievement of art's power over life; and on the whole, they went about their mock-serious scholarship in a dedicated frame of mind and with a methodology that would have served them well in other areas of the humanities and social sciences. In doing so, they helped foster the sense of Sherlock Holmes' immortality that in time made his creator a subject of serious, if belated, scholarly interest as well.

Most of the contributors to this volume, including its editor, have been contributors previously to the "Higher Criticism" of Sherlock Holmes, and expect to be again. But with a difference. Unlike Sherlockians for whom Holmes' creator holds little interest, they have been much interested in Sir Arthur Conan Doyle's life and career. By 1975 that interest was strong enough to prompt the founding of a new Sherlockian quarterly journal, *Baker Street Miscellanea*, which since then has avidly pursued the notion that Sir Arthur Conan Doyle is just as real, and just as interesting, a figure as Sherlock Holmes. Most of the contributors to this volume are veterans of both lines of literary research and scholarship. They are Conan Doyle scholars and collectors, professors of English literature, editors and critics, humanities and research librarians, from England, America, and Canada, with a huge volume of published work on Conan Doyle and Sherlock Holmes already behind them. They know, often much better than the biographers whose work they consider herein, about the relationship of Conan Doyle's life to his literary work, particularly in the case of his most powerful creation, Sherlock Holmes. They have diverse views on the subject: Donald A. Redmond and Christopher Redmond, for example, are father and son, each with his own list of accomplishments in this field, and each convinced that it is he who is covering in this volume the most important biography of Conan Doyle. The essays that follow provide a rich mixture of both the biographers' and their critics' insights into the life and work of Sir Arthur Conan Doyle. We shall see at the end of them how well the subject and the important biographical problems have been treated to date, what the answers to the more challenging questions about the creator of Sherlock Holmes appear to be, what questions remain unanswered, and what research undone as we enter the second century of Sherlock Holmes.

❧ *Part I*

AUTOBIOGRAPHY

1 ° EXPERIENCE VEILED IN PSEUDONYMS

Ely M. Liebow

Conan Doyle's Autobiographical Fiction

A Joyce scholar once said of *Finnegans Wake*, to his colleagues at a huge literary convention: "Let us each take one sentence and expound upon it. That way we'll begin to understand the book."

I am not sure the autobiographical contents of Arthur Conan Doyle's fiction present a much simpler problem. Others using Conan Doyle's fiction to explore biographical questions must feel as I do: every time we turn around we find more theories, more notions, about Conan Doyle's mind, his memory, his ego, id, and intentions. Was he a simple or a complex man? If he used half the literary allusions that Samuel Rosenberg claims for him in *Naked Is the Best Disguise*—a study viewed by some with contempt, by others as a *tour de force*—then he was an unbelievable literary genius. What about his psychology and the ways in which it is reflected in his work? If he was half as frustrated as Charles Higham says in *The Adventures of Conan Doyle*—from the time he met Jean Leckie until their marriage was consummated—then he must have spent his days in literary sublimation and his nights in cold showers.

The difficult thing about autobiographical content in Conan Doyle's fiction is that he was such a book lover; he had such a retentive memory; he was such a Romantic. One must try to clear away some of the underbrush. In a perceptive modern afterword to one of Conan Doyle's early novels,[1] Jack Tracy says: "While *The Firm of Girdlestone* is in no way autobiographical, he wisely confined himself, for the most part, to his own experience." What does Tracy mean by that? That Conan Doyle did not undertake to tell his own life's story in *Girdlestone*? But while young Tom Dimsdale, the hero of the novel, is not Arthur Conan Doyle, he too played on his university football team; is fond of "putting on the gloves" with fellow students; his preliminary medical examination is a carbon

1. A. Conan Doyle, *The Firm of Girdlestone* (1890; Bloomington, Ind.: Gaslight Publications, 1980).

copy of Conan Doyle's; and he objects to the same irrelevant courses. Autobiographical, perhaps, in some minor ways; autobiography, no.

There is, in Conan Doyle's fiction, autobiographical content of various kinds. In some, it amounts to little more than traces of experiences— in *Girdlestone*, as we have seen; in the quasi-Sherlockian story "The Recollections of Captain Wilkie" (1895) and others like "The Captain of the Pole-Star" (1883) and *The Parasite* (1894). More substantial experiences of Conan Doyle's, formative in their influence on him, show up in certain other work, such as his *Round the Red Lamp* stories (1894) and two historical novels, *The White Company* (1891) and *Sir Nigel* (1906). And a few works contain overt slices of his life: *The Stark Munro Letters* (1895) relates an episode of his early professional life, for example, and both it and *The Land of Mist* (1926) reveal much about his internal religious debates at different times of his life. *Beyond the City* (1891) and *A Duet* (1899) reflect a good deal of his domestic life. Conan Doyle did draw upon his own life and experiences and attitudes to varying degrees in his fiction, in ways sometimes clear enough to be useful to those trying to improve their understanding of the man. Even so, caution is recommended. Conan Doyle himself warned against reading too much about an author into the words of his characters: to one critic's poetic suggestion that Sherlock Holmes's contempt for Edgar Allan Poe's Dupin was really the author's, Conan Doyle retorted (in part):

> Have you not learned, my esteemed commentator,
> That the created is not the creator?
> . . . .
> . . . is it not on the verge of inanity
> To put down to me my creation's crude vanity?
> He, the created, the puppet of fiction,
> Would not brook rivals nor stand contradiction.
> He, the created, would scoff and would sneer,
> Where I, the Creator, would bow and revere.
> So please grip this fact with your cerebral tentacle,
> The doll and its maker are never identical.[2]

With this important caveat in mind, let us see what sort of autobiographical insight may be found in Conan Doyle's fiction.

Following a chronology of his life rather than his published works, we are led immediately to those two novels upon which Sir Arthur long

2. "To an Undiscerning Critic," first published in *London Opinion* on December 28, 1912. The critic was Arthur Guiterman. See *The Uncollected Sherlock Holmes*, ed. Richard Lancelyn Green (London: Penguin Books, 1983), pp. 160–63.

hoped his fame might eventually rest: *The White Company* (1891) and *Sir Nigel* (1906). There is no doubt that Conan Doyle's fascination with the Middle Ages, chivalry and all their trappings, has its origin in his mother, Mary Foley, the Ma'am of all his letters. There can also be little doubt that in Dame Ermyntrude (in *Sir Nigel*, which relates the early life of the protagonist of *The White Company*), he is describing his mother as he saw her: a truly gentle but firm lady for whom any knight would lay down the gauntlet, as conversant with heraldry, the rules of jousting, the formalities of war, as any knight in the realm. But while biographers like Pierre Nordon and Charles Higham recognized his mother in Dame Ermyntrude, it is strange that no one has said very much about the curious depiction of Sir Nigel in *The White Company*. A good case could be made that the thin, wiry, gallant knight, eager to pursue one last possible dream, is, in effect, Conan Doyle's father—as sunny a tribute as his somewhat disaffected son could manage to pay to old, thin, wiry, sick Charles Doyle, still full of unrealized dreams (but institutionalized for the rest of his life).

Edinburgh looms larger in Conan Doyle's mind and fiction than many biographers have realized. Julian Symons' 1979 biography of Conan Doyle says that he "took away little from Edinburgh except his degree." But Edinburgh University's Owen Dudley Edwards, on the other hand, has remarked that Sherlock Holmes could well have attended Edinburgh, for all the traces of the city in the Sherlock Holmes stories.[3] And indeed it is amazing how *little* Conan Doyle left out about Edinburgh—if one knows where to look. In *The Adventures of Conan Doyle*, for example, Charles Higham says that the address of 3 Lauriston Gardens, where the first murder in *A Study in Scarlet* takes place, did not exist, and that Conan Doyle plucked it out of the air. But Lauriston Gardens did exist—not in London, but in Edinburgh, just off Lonsdale Terrace where Arthur Conan Doyle lived with his family while attending medical school.

In 1894 Conan Doyle published a volume of stories dealing with medical life, *Round the Red Lamp* (the visible symbol of a doctor's residence in Victorian England). The stories nearly all deal with Conan Doyle's medical school days or early practitioner's life, and there are many traces of Edinburgh. The one based most obviously on his medical education there is "His First Operation," wherein a third-year man brings a squeamish first-year student to witness an operation for the first time. On the way to the clinic, the older student greets a fellow out-patient clerk:

3. See his introduction to *The Edinburgh Stories of Arthur Conan Doyle* (Edinburgh: Polygon Books, 1981).

27

"Anything good?"

"You should have been here yesterday. We had a regular field day. A popliteal aneurism, a Colles' fracture, a spina bifida, a tropical abcess, and an elephantiasis. How's that for a single haul?"

. . . The tiers of horseshoe benches rising from the floor to the ceiling were already packed, and the novice as he entered saw vague curving lines of faces in front of him. . . .

"This is grand," the senior man whispered; "you'll have a rare view of it all."

When the neophyte asks about two men at the operating table, he is told:

"One has charge of the instruments and the other of the puffing Billy. It's Lister's antiseptic spray, you know, and Archer [a surgeon] is one of the carbolic acid men. Hayes [another surgeon] is the leader of the cleanliness-and-cold-water school, and they all hate each other like poison."

What the neophyte—read Conan Doyle—was learning is that not all the doctors at the famed medical school accepted the great Lister's antiseptic technique. Conan Doyle's mentor Joe Bell believed in Lister's theory, but Conan Doyle also knew that the celebrated Dr. James ("Dismal Jeemy") Spence led the opposition to the germ theory of Lister, Pasteur, etc.— even eminent scientific men may refuse to believe in a thing if they cannot see it, a lesson Conan Doyle no doubt remembered years later when debating other scientific men about the validity of Spiritualism.

(While Conan Doyle acknowledged Sherlock Holmes' debt to Joe Bell's analytical and diagnostic method, he said relatively little about Bell outside his autobiography and a couple of magazine articles. But in "The Recollections of Captain Wilkie," Conan Doyle did allude to his keen, grey-eyed professor with the sharp aquiline profile. "I used rather to pride myself on being able to spot a man's trade or profession by a good look at his exterior," says the story's Holmes-like protagonist: "I had the advantage of studying under a Professor at Edinburgh who was a master of the art, and used to electrify both his patients and his clinical classes by long shots . . . and never very far from the mark.")

One autobiographically interesting story—because of what it says about Conan Doyle's attitude toward women—seems on the surface not autobiographical at all. Conan Doyle was opposed to the suffrage movement. None of his medical classmates had been women. But in 1894 he published "The Doctors of Hoyland." Dr. James Ripley practices in a small town. Because of his modern methods and scientific spirit, he easily vanquishes his few rivals. For some years he reigns unchallenged, but then he learns of a Dr. Verrinder Smith newly arrived in town—educated with distinction at Edinburgh, Paris, Berlin, and Vienna, culminating in the coveted Lee Hopkins scholarship.

Anticipating a kindred mind and welcome company, Ripley calls on the newcomer and meets "a little woman, whose plain, palish face was remarkable only for a pair of shrewd, humourous eyes." He is shocked to learn that *she* is Dr. Smith. "He had never seen a woman doctor before, and his whole conservative soul rose up in revolt at the idea. He could not recall any biblical injunction that man should remain ever the doctor and the woman the nurse, and yet he felt as if a blasphemy had been committed." What makes it worse is that her scientific knowledge is obviously more up to date than his. In a fairly adroit manner, Conan Doyle has the young lady save Dr. Ripley's leg after an accident on the road; we see him not only change his mind about her but even prefer her ministrations to those of his brother, a London surgeon. Finally he proposes to her, whom he had thought of as "an unsexed woman." "What, and unite the practices?" she asks. She finally tells him she intends to take a position in Paris. And so once again there is only one doctor in Hoyland—a wiser but lonelier one.

Undoubtedly Conan Doyle had in mind Sophia Jex-Blake and the turmoil in Edinburgh over her medical ambitions. After failing to gain admission to Harvard Medical School in 1865, Jex-Blake had been allowed to enroll at Edinburgh but had to take classes alone. Told that such an arrangement was prohibitively expensive for the school, she returned with six other qualified young ladies, all of whom were reluctantly admitted. They were reviled, humiliated, spat upon, and sued. Sophia Jex-Blake took Edinburgh University on in the courts for five years, leaving bloody-but-unbowed for Paris and Bern and returning a few years later as a doctor to establish a women's hospital in Edinburgh. Conan Doyle came along at the tag end of the litigation. Women doctors were on everyone's minds. He was well aware of the role played by the young women's great champion, Joe Bell's mentor and probably Edinburgh's greatest surgeon—Dr. Patrick Heron Watson.

The final *Red Lamp* story we will take time to consider, "Behind the Times," is about a figure depicted by Conan Doyle in many of his novels and stories: the old and out-of-date, but strangely able, family doctor. In Conan Doyle's own life it was Dr. Reginald Ratcliffe Hoare, of Birmingham, with whom he did several stints of assistantship as a student. In a few stories Conan Doyle calls him "Dr. Horton," but here he is Dr. Winter. The narrator is a clever, competent new doctor, who was brought into the world by Dr. Winter. No one knows the old man's age. He is opposed to the use of chloroform, just as many of the "lightning-fast" school of surgeons of that day were leery of the stuff.[4] Dr. Winter refers to the stethoscope as "a new-fangled French toy" and "the germ theory of disease set him chuckling for a long time, and his favourite joke in the sickroom was to say, 'Shut the door, or the germs will be getting in.'" Joe Bell tells us that Dismal Jeemy Spence used to holler (always in Baron Lister's presence) "Shut the door; ye'll let the germs oot!"

If there is anything in the idea that Arthur Conan Doyle projected himself into many of his literary creations, not much effort was required when he wrote "The Croxley Master" in 1899. A medical student, strapped for funds because of a fouled-up bursary (scholarship), takes a job with an established practitioner in Sheffield. Conan Doyle suffered the same financial problem as a student, and his first assistantship was with a Dr. Richardson in Sheffield. Like Conan Doyle, the student is trying to cram five years' work into four, and is overworked by his mentor. To make ends meet, the husky young fellow agrees to box a local dreadnought, the Croxley master. Conan Doyle did not earn his tuition with his fists, but as a student sailing as ship's surgeon on the Greenland whaler *Hope* he put on the gloves more than once, and his fists won him many admirers. Conan Doyle's account of the young student's relationship with the parched Dr. Oldacre matches his own unillustrious three-month stint with Dr. Richardson in Sheffield. Both young men found little time for themselves; rolled countless pills; lived on skimpy diets; prided themselves on their cricket game; and removed themselves from the unpleasant situation as soon as possible.

At this juncture it may be well to mention briefly four works by Conan Doyle dealing with the occult. His first published non-Holmesian novel, *The Mystery of Cloomber* (1889) demonstrates how interested and sympathetic toward Spiritualism Conan Doyle already was by this early date, twenty-eight years before his final conversion. His 1894 novella, *The Parasite*, and a short story of the same year, "John Barrington Cowles," show similar but less sympathetic interest in the occult, since in both tales young Edinburgh medical students come under the diabolical influence of female mesmerists. And one of Conan Doyle's most powerful early short stories, "The Captain of the Pole-Star," is an eerie tale of the sea: the Arctic setting, the life aboard the whaler, were straight from his six-month voyage on the *Hope* in 1880.

4. Drs. Joseph Bell and Patrick Heron Watson were, of course, trained by surgeons who grew up before the invention of anesthesia. Their motto: "Get the patient off the table." Watson could remove an arm from the shoulder in less than nine minutes and felt that no surgeon should take more than two minutes to remove a stone from the bladder.

The next stage in the search for authentic autobiographical elements may be summed up as the Curious Case of the Two Neglected Domestic Novels. Conan Doyle tells us he agreed with the critics that *Beyond the City* and *A Duet* left much to be desired. He also said they contained much fact among the fiction, and they do comprise an excellent montage of his first few years of marriage in the 1880s and his subsequent move to London's South Norwood suburb in 1891.

While Frank Crosse's courting of Maud Selby in *A Duet* is not an account of Conan Doyle's courting of Louisa Hawkins, the two newlyweds settle in Southsea and live at the Lindens (Bush Villas in real life). Frank "had inherited nothing from his parents save a dash of artist from his mother. It was not enough to help him earn a living, but it transformed itself into a keen appreciation of some ambitions in literature." Modern readers may find the courtship chapters and the maxims drawn up for a happy married life a bit saccharine. They reveal a different Conan Doyle than we are used to, and an interesting one.[5] One of the first places Frank takes his fiancée is "England's Valhalla," Westminster Abbey. She realizes how much it means to Frank. He, in turn, tries to convey to her his love for what the shrine represents in his heart and mind. He tells her of the Middle Ages as they stand before the tombs of Edward I and his Eleanor. He waxes rhapsodic over Scott, Burns, Macauley, and Dickens in the Poet's Corner. (Conan Doyle's favorites, of course.) They spend hours there, she doting on his every word.

After their wedding, Frank tells her more about his literary favorites (again, Conan Doyle's): Holmes' *Autocrat*, Gibbons' *History*, Macaulay's *Essays*, Carlyle's *Life*, and Pepys' *Diary*.[6] The two chapters devoted to Pepys are exquisite. The couple's conversation about the great diarist is something like a Burns and Allen routine at first, but as Dr. Johnson said about great literature, it instructs while it pleases, and it pleases while it instructs. We know that Conan Doyle did take Louisa to Pepys' burial site in London and to Carlyle's home in Cheyne Row. He devotes a chapter apiece of *A Duet* to each visit, and the tours, the guides (some very funny), the awe, and the aura are quite moving. One final domestic scene, played out earlier by Conan Doyle in Southsea, is joining the local

---

5. However, in contrast to the saccharine, Frank's confrontation by his former mistress in *A Duet* was considered by some to be in bad taste—a charge that an unimpressed Conan Doyle shrugged off prior to the novel's publication, insisting on leaving the incident intact in the book for the sake of realism. See Richard Lancelyn Green and John Michael Gibson, *A Bibliography of A. Conan Doyle* (Oxford: Clarendon Press, 1983), pp. 114–15.

6. Conan Doyle devoted an entire book to his favorite literature: see *Through the Magic Door* (London: Smith, Elder and Co., 1907). Very early in their friendship, which began in 1897, Conan Doyle had drawn up a reading list for Jean Leckie.

literary society. (Seeking culture, a few characters decide to form a Browning Society; their attempts to come to grips with the poet at a reading of "Caliban Upon Setebos" is hilarious. They decide, finally, that Browning is too much for them, Tennyson too obvious, and so it is every reader for himself.)

Beyond the City is an early-day glimpse of suburbia, written when the Conan Doyles moved from lodgings in Bloomsbury to larger quarters in South Norwood, shortly after his decision to give up medicine for literature. The story of several families new to the suburbs, it speaks of young love, Dickens-like money problems, and an early view of woman's rights, for the overriding character is a champion of that cause: Mrs. Westmacott, a tall, powerfully built woman with a right hand like John L. Sullivan's, a tongue like a lash, and a mind that is her own. Two elderly sisters, original settlers of South Norwood, come calling, and find Mrs. Westmacott swinging a pair of dumbbells over her head. She offers the ladies some stout, which they refuse with blushes.

> "I am sorry that I have no tea to offer you. I look upon the subserviency of woman as largely due to her abandoning nutritious drinks and invigorating exercises to the male. I do neither." Then whipping the dumb-bells around: "You see what may be done on stout."
>
> "But don't you think, Mrs. Westmacott, that woman has a mission of her own?" asks one of the ladies.
>
> "The old cant!" she cries. "The old shibboleth! What is this mission which is reserved for woman? All that is humble, that is mean, that is soul-killing, that is so contemptible and ill-paid that none other will touch it. All that is woman's mission. And who imposed these limitations upon her? Who cooped her up within this narrow sphere? Was it Providence? Was it Nature? No; it was the arch-enemy. It was man."

Some Conan Doyle biographers have made much of his strong stand against the suffrage movement, but that was not until 1913, and it concerned the movement's violent tactics as well as the issue of voting rights. By contrast, Owen Dudley Edwards feels that Conan Doyle believed in the superiority of women, stemming from his admiration and respect for his mother. Mrs. Westmacott may be drawn by a broad brush, but it is her knowledge of men and her financial acumen that save the day for several of her male neighbors. She may hurl dumbbells around, strut in double-breasted jackets, and puff on one cigarette after another, but in the long run she is solid, resourceful, farsighted, and practical.

And when her nephew Charles mildly objects to her remarks, she yields not an inch:

> It was man, Charles. It was you and your fellows. I say that a woman is a colossal monument to the selfishness of man. What is all this boasted chivalry—these fine words and vague phrases? Where is it when we wish to put it to the test? Man, in the abstract, will do anything to help a woman. Of course. How does it work when his pocket is touched? Where is his chivalry then? Will the doctors help her to qualify? will the lawyers help her to be called to the bar? will the clergy tolerate her in the Church? Oh, it is close your ranks then, and refer poor woman to her mission! Her mission! To be thankful for coppers and not interfere with the men while they grabble for gold, like swine round a trough, that is man's reading of the mission of women.

Nearly every line could be found in slightly altered form in the *Scotsman*, Edinburgh's leading newspaper since the nonage of Sir Walter Scott, during the trial of Sophia Jex-Blake and her little band of medical hopefuls. Few doctors had wanted to admit them, and almost none to teach them; to Conan Doyle's credit, he seems quite liberal by contrast, and his defense of women's rights in professional life, in "The Doctors of Hoyland," *Beyond the City*, and in other work is strong and unambiguous, regardless of contradictory evidence of other kinds. Obviously Conan Doyle was wrestling with contradictions between his personal views of women, his mother's effective exhortations in favor of chivalry as a code of behavior, and the conventions of his era.

In 1895 Conan Doyle published his comic autobiographical master-piece, *The Stark Munro Letters*. (Twelve years earlier, he had published "Crabbe's Practice," a capsulized version of the story: a young medical graduate recounts his adventures with a former classmate, the latter being cunning, ferocious, ingenious, mercurial, and charming by turns.) *The Stark Munro Letters* is Conan Doyle's greatest piece of sustained comic writing. Basically, it is Conan Doyle's account of how he, a recent gradu-ate, came to work for a classmate, Dr. James Cullingworth (George Budd in real life). Prior to joining Cullingworth, Stark Munro had listened to his ailing father and taken a job with Dr. Horton in Yorkshire. But then Cullingworth's summoning telegram arrived: "Come at once."

It is a novel in epistolary form—a series of letters from Dr. Stark Munro (Conan Doyle) to an imaginary American friend. Heavily in debt from an earlier practice, Cullingworth and his new bride have fled to Bradfield: read Plymouth, whence Budd telegraphed Conan Doyle that his practice was lucrative, he needed an assistant, would make him rich for life, etc. Budd was a thick-necked soul, quixotic, erratic, irascible. In Plymouth he charged nothing for his services, but a small fortune for his quickly prepared prescriptions ("With him . . . the whole act of medicine lies in judicious poisoning"); he abused his patients ("Go out and knock down a policeman, then come back to me when they let you out!"); told them that tea was poison and never to touch the stuff; somehow cured most of them; and went home at night, often roaring drunk, jangling a sack full of coins—the better to infuriate his outraged professional colleagues in the High Street.

With the exception of an incident about a young mental case, the novel is essentially autobiographical. Nearly everything in *The Stark Munro Letters* was true to Conan Doyle's life: Stark Munro's mother's rage on hearing that the egregious Cullingworths are reading her letters to him; quarrels with his father over religion; violent boxing matches with Cullingworth; teaching his younger brother Paul (read Innes) boxing when Stark Munro brings him down to Birchespool (Southsea) after leaving Cullingworth; a fight with a wife-beater the night he arrives in Birchespool; his brother as his servant, housemaid, Buttons, and companion; 1 Oakley Villas (1 Bush Villas in real life); his great love of America and Americans; the case of a man who developed cancer of the cheek from smoking a short cutty pipe (one of the best-known anecdotes about Joe Bell's great diagnostic powers). All of this could be a second autobiography.

But while all that is of autobiographical interest—biographers like Hesketh Pearson have made much of the Budd episode in Conan Doyle's life, and of Budd's putative influence on his writings—so is much of the book invaluable to biographers because of its revelation of Conan Doyle's religious and philosophical *angst* in his early years. Conan Doyle considered this the important aspect of the book, though most have focused on the highly entertaining Budd. As Owen Dudley Edwards observes, it was not easy to be a young Irish Catholic in Edinburgh. Tack on a youth spent in devouring Romantic books, in strict Jesuit schools, then a four-year immersion in an agnostic atmosphere of science and medicine, and a newfound interest in psychic matters—and you have a young man with profound new questions about the universe.

Stark Munro, like Conan Doyle, had asked his questions and was developing some of his own answers:

Is religion the only domain of thought which is non-progressive, and to be referred forever to a standard set two thousand years ago? Can they not see as the human brain evolves it must take a wider outlook? A half-formed brain makes a half-formed God, and who shall say that our brains are even half-formed yet? . . . I respect every good Catholic and every good Protestant . . . [each] has been a powerful instrument in the hands of that inscrutable Providence which rules all things. . . . Catholicism is the more thorough; Protestantism is the more reasonable. Protestantism adapts itself to modern civilization. Catholicism expects civilization to adapt itself to it. . . . When first I came out of the faith in which I had been reared, I certainly did feel for a time as if my life-belt had burst.

From what we know of Conan Doyle's break with his family's religion and church, Stark Munro's thoughts mirror his exactly. And he did not find a new "life-belt" to replace it until many years later, when he embraced Spiritualism in 1916. But he foreshadowed that conversion to a new faith when he concluded, in *The Stark Munro Letters*, that "the last reformation simplified Catholicism. The coming one will simplify Protestantism and when the world is ripe for it another will come and simplify that. The ever improving brain will give us an ever broadening creed. Is it not glorious to think that evolution is still living and acting—that if we have an anthropoid ape as an ancestor, we may have archangels for our posterity."

So much for a novel from his heart and soul. There are countless little autobiographical traces in the Sherlock Holmes stories, and in the Professor Challenger stories. The extent to which Conan Doyle identified himself with Sherlock Holmes is a subject dealt with by a number of his biographers and is still being researched today. Little things like giving Holmes his initial London lodgings in Montague Street, whereas Conan Doyle had lived just around the corner in Montague Place when he was new to London, are interesting and indicative if not necessarily of great biographical weight. Of more importance, perhaps, are things like the death of the alcoholic brute who had cruelly mistreated his wife in "The Adventure of the Abbey Grange": Holmes and Watson trap the killer but, given the circumstances, pronounce a private verdict of not guilty and let him go without revealing his identity to the police—a reflection of attitudes wrought by the author's upbringing in a household marked by similar, if less severe, problems. In "The Adventure of the Missing Three-Quarter"—one critic has perceptively suggested—Conan Doyle merged his wife Louisa and his great love Jean Leckie into a single character: written while Louisa was slowly dying from consumption, and when Conan Doyle's romantic (if platonic) relationship with Jean Leckie was well advanced, the plot turns on a young woman whose liaison with the missing athlete is a close-kept secret, and whose death from illness frees her bereaved husband from his painful and complicated double life.[7]

Even if Conan Doyle did identify himself with Sherlock Holmes to some extent, Professor George Edward Challenger, who first appeared in the 1912 novel *The Lost World*, was more a favorite creation of the author, who once made himself up as Challenger and set forth to scare the beejezus out of his brother-in-law E. W. Hornung, the novelist and creator of Raffles. Conan Doyle modeled the bull-chested, Assyrian-bearded Challenger—an iconoclast, a dauntless pioneer in uncharted scientific territory, and a terror unto orthodox colleagues and sensation-seeking reporters—on another of his instructors at Edinburgh University's medical school, Professor William Rutherford, "the ruthless vivisector" (and perhaps also, some believe, on George Budd). It was Challenger and his Anglo-Irish journalist associate Edward Dunn Malone whom Conan Doyle chose as literary symbols for the triumph of Faith in the Spirit in his 1926 novel *The Land of Mist*. "I have for years had a big psychic novel in me," he had written to his *Strand Magazine* editor, H. Greenhough Smith, "which shall deal realistically with every phase of the question, pro and con. I waited, I knew it would come. Now it has come, with a full head of steam, and I can hardly hold onto my pen it goes so fast." *The Land of Mist* gives "a detailed picture of the author's later years as a spiritualist,"[8] with Malone running the entire gamut of Spiritualist experience in an increasingly nonimpartial newspaper investigation and Challenger symbolizing the author's own intellectual conflict between the claims of Science and Faith. Professor Challenger, like Sherlock Holmes, represents a corpus of Conan Doyle's literary work that has not yet been thoroughly mined for autobiographical content.

Arthur Conan Doyle, this amazing man with a near-photographic Romantic memory, drew events, attitudes, people, and places for his fiction from his life—from his days at his mother's knee, his fondest memories of books, his school days, his education and practice as a doctor, his investigation of psychic matters, his family relationships and problems, and his religious quandaries, culminating in his wholehearted conver-

7. See Don Richard Cox, *Arthur Conan Doyle* (New York: Frederick Ungar, 1985), pp. 124–25. Cox notes that the young rugby player "keeps a woman in a secret cottage in the woods and visits her when he can—a situation that veils Doyle's own circumstances about as thinly as one might dare. . . . the death scene in the cottage . . . may have reflected Conan Doyle's mixed feelings about his own marriage. This is not to say that Doyle wanted to see his wife die; the story contains a strong mixture of the love, loyalty, and grief Doyle no doubt felt. Still, in this story (and in the general theme of this collection of stories [*The Return of Sherlock Holmes*]), there is a remarkable fictionalizing of the romantic unrest the author was experiencing for a ten-year period."

8. Green and Gibson, *A Bibliography of A. Conan Doyle*, p. 198.

sion to Spiritualism. One could say that Conan Doyle threw in everything but the kitchen sink—but he included that, too, in the domestic tale of *A Duet*. He told things about himself in his fiction that he never mentioned in his autobiography, *Memories and Adventures*, which was heavy on the Adventures and very selective in the Memories it presented. Scholars have made use of autobiographical content in Conan Doyle's fiction—but incompletely, sometimes uncritically, and too often without enough knowledge of Conan Doyle's life to obtain full benefit from the clues he scattered throughout his literary output. The latter is indispensable, for without the navigational assistance afforded by a sound working knowledge of Conan Doyle's life, uninformed biographical mariners can all too easily sail past items of interest in his fiction or run aground on the reefs of his undeniably fertile sense of creativity.

2 ° His Final Tale of Chivalry

Richard Lancelyn Green

Memories and Adventures
by Sir Arthur Conan Doyle

In the preface to the revised edition of his autobiography, Sir Arthur Conan Doyle spoke of the variety and romance of his life that he thought could hardly ever have been exceeded: he had known what it was to be poor and "fairly affluent"; he had sampled "every kind of human experience"; he had known many of the most remarkable men of his time; he had had a long literary career after a medical training; he had tried his hand at various sports; he had traveled as a doctor to the Arctic and the west coast of Africa; he had seen something of three wars; he had had adventures of all sorts; and finally he had been "constrained" to devote his latter years to the subject of the "occult." "Such," he says, "is the life which I have told in some detail in my *Memories and Adventures*." [1]

i

Its first three chapters, which opened the *Strand Magazine* serialization in October 1923, deal with the first twenty years of his life. He was born in Edinburgh, in flats that were then "of good repute"; he speaks of his distinguished grandfather, John Doyle, whom he could just remember, and of his uncles Henry, James, and Richard Doyle, and then, for almost the first time in print, he mentions his own father, Charles Doyle, recalling that he had been sent to Edinburgh at the age of nineteen. There follows a history of his mother's forebears ending with his grandmother, who had moved to Edinburgh from Ireland in her widowhood. Charles Doyle had lodged with her and subsequently married her daughter Mary.

1. British publisher, London: Hodder and Stoughton, 1924; American publisher, Boston: Little, Brown, 1924; revised edition, London: John Murray, 1930.

Conan Doyle's description of his father is vague. He had, he says, been thrown at a dangerously early age into heavy-drinking Scottish society, and the environment was a hard one. His salary was limited, he was unambitious, and his artistic work was spasmodic. The result was that the family "lived in the hardy and bracing atmosphere of poverty," and though he and his sisters helped, his mother bore the "long, sordid" strain. "My father, I fear, was of little help to her, for his thoughts were always in the clouds and he had no appreciation of the realities of life."

Conan Doyle then turns to the local school he attended, where, being among rough boys, he "became a rough boy, too." Three Jesuit institutions followed. His memories of Hodder were happy, but he felt he had wasted his time at Stonyhurst learning the classics and mathematics, which had been of little or no use to him in later life. Corporal punishment was severe and he endured more of it than other boys—not because he was vicious, but because he "had a nature which responded eagerly to affectionate kindness (which I never received), but which rebelled against threats and took a perverted pride in showing that it would not be cowed by violence. I went out of my way to do really mischievous and outrageous things simply to show that my spirit was unbroken." Conan Doyle recalls realizing "that I had some literary streak in me which was not common to all. It came as quite a surprise, and even more perhaps to my masters, who had taken a rather hopeless view of my future prospects." Despite her "struggle to keep up appearances and make both ends meet," his mother found sufficient money for him to spend a year at Feldkirch, in Austria, where he ceased to be "the resentful young rebel" and became a "pillar of law and order."

Back in Edinburgh the family affairs were "still as straitened as ever" and his mother had "adopted the device of sharing a large house, which may have eased her in some ways, but was disastrous in others." Conan Doyle was to study medicine, "chiefly, I think, because Edinburgh was so famous a centre for medical learning." He entered Edinburgh University as a tall, strongly framed, but half-formed young student in October 1876 and received a bachelor of medicine degree in July 1881. During that time he lived at home. Though enjoying no close friendships with his professors, he was impressed by them—not least by Joseph Bell whose powers seemed miraculous to his "audience of Watsons." "It is no wonder that after the study of such a character I used and amplified his methods when in later life I tried to build up a scientific detective."

As a student Conan Doyle considered he won no distinction. "I was always one of the ruck, neither lingering nor gaining—a 60 per cent. man at examinations." The reason was that he needed to earn money and so compressed a year's classes into half a year. In the summer of 1878 he spent three weeks with a doctor "running a low-class practice in the poorer quarters of Sheffield," and then he visited his Doyle relatives in London—finding them too conventional, while they considered him too Bohemian. Four months were later spent with another doctor, and after that his next student assistantship was with Dr. Hoare, a well-known Birmingham physician, where Conan Doyle's position was soon that of a son rather than an assistant.

His literary career may be said to have started during this period: the general aspiration was strong, so he wrote a slight tale entitled "The Mystery of Sassassa Valley," and to his surprise it was accepted by *Chambers's Journal*.

Conan Doyle's account of his first twenty years follows the line of earlier interviews, but it is incomplete, omitting a number of important details. Conan Doyle did not wish to draw attention to the nature of his father's "illness" and so could not refer to people who had been intimately involved with the family at the time. Charles Doyle had caused a great deal of suffering and embarrassment to his family, leading to divisions within it that were never resolved. He had cast a shadow for nearly forty years over his son's life, and it was only after his mother's death that Conan Doyle was able in part to exorcise the ghost. Even so, he never wrote openly about his feelings and appears to have suppressed them entirely.

More details about Arthur Conan Doyle's father are now available. Born in London in 1830, he inherited the artistic abilities of his family. London in the late 1840s had many attractions, and he was happy and carefree when, in October 1849, he was told that he must go to Edinburgh to take a post at the Scottish Board of Works that his father had accepted on his behalf. His enthusiasm for the job did not last long. He was lonely and appears to have started drinking heavily soon after he arrived.

His wife and mother-in-law reinforced the Doyle family's Irish Catholic connection. After his marriage, Charles Doyle worked well for a number of years, while also doing illustrations for periodicals and for local Edinburgh publishers. The first child, Annette Conan Doyle, was born in 1857, and Arthur Conan Doyle followed two years later. But Charles was becoming more dependent on alcohol and by the mid-1860s was given to periods of morbid introspection and prolonged bouts of depression. The Doyles migrated from address to address in Edinburgh and, with the help of a friend, to Liberton Bank outside town.

The help came from Mary Burton, sister of the distinguished Edinburgh bibliophile, John Hill Burton. Of importance to Arthur Conan Doyle was his friendship with John Hill Burton's sons, especially William Kinnimond Burton. "Willie" appears to have introduced Conan Doyle to photography and to have recommended his work to the *British Journal of*

Photography that between 1880 and 1885 published his series of descriptive and technical articles.[2] They kept in close touch when Conan Doyle moved to Southsea in 1882, and both began writing novels at the same time; Conan Doyle's 1890 *The Firm of Girdlestone* is dedicated to Burton. The early photographic articles provide details about Conan Doyle's life at that period. It is strange that he does not refer to these articles, but stranger still that he does not mention the Burtons.

Other omissions are no less remarkable. The strangest of all, considering his undoubted importance, is Conan Doyle's failure to mention the man who had coached him in his exams and encouraged him in his work, who had shared the same house, and on whose estate Conan Doyle's mother spent over thirty years of her life: Bryan Charles Waller, born at Masongill, Yorkshire, in 1853. Waller graduated from Edinburgh as M.B. in 1876 and M.D. with Gold Medal in 1878; between 1879 and 1882 he was lecturer on pathology.

It is not, however, Waller's academic career but his private life that is of interest. In 1875 he shared a house with the Doyle family and therefore witnessed the serious decline in Charles Doyle's condition: pensioned off from his job in June 1876, he was admitted to Fordoun House, a nursing home specializing in the treatment of alcoholics, in 1879. In 1877 Waller had taken the lease on another house that he shared with the Doyles, and they remained there until 1881 when they went to yet another house where Waller paid the rent. The following year Mary Doyle left Edinburgh and moved to Masongill Cottage on Waller's estate, remaining there until 1917. Charles Doyle was to spend the remainder of his life in various nursing homes and asylums. He broke out of Fordoun House in May 1885 and was soon afterward committed to the Montrose Royal Lunatic Asylum where he remained until January 1892; after three months in the Edinburgh Royal Infirmary, he was moved to the Crighton Royal Institution, where he died on October 10, 1893.

In saying that his mother's device of sharing a large house was disastrous in some ways, Conan Doyle left the disastrous consequences unsaid. It is unclear why Waller had chosen to befriend Mary Doyle, but the likelihood is that he had felt he would be able to help her husband. His failure probably soured his relationship with Arthur Conan Doyle, who also no doubt felt that his position had been usurped. Waller had coached him for his medical exams and had advised on his education, but any warmth that existed between the haughty, stuttering Dr. Waller and the young Arthur Conan Doyle quickly evaporated. The relationship between Waller and Mary Doyle and the rest of the family, however,

---

2. See *Essays in Photography* by Arthur Conan Doyle, ed. John Michael Gibson and Richard Lancelyn Green (London: Secker and Warburg, 1982).

remained cordial, and for the next thirty years the family revolved around Masongill. Conan Doyle never, so far as is known, referred to Waller in print, but he had been a regular visitor to Masongill in the 1880s and made oblique references in his fiction.[3] There were also the family weddings, many of which took place at the local church—including Conan Doyle's own, in August 1885, to Louisa Hawkins.

Conan Doyle also lost his faith in Roman Catholicism during these years. He gives the reason as the "uncompromising bigotry of the Jesuit theology" that made "difficult for the man with scientific desire for truth or with intellectual self-respect to keep within the Church." His doubts first arose at Stonyhurst when he heard "a great fierce Irish priest" declare that all non-Catholics were hopelessly damned. "I looked upon him with horror," Conan Doyle says: "all that was sanest and most generous in my nature rose up against a narrow theology and an uncharitable outlook upon the other great religions of the world." The drift away from the Catholicism of his youth began at university, when he came under the influence of philosophers like Huxley, Darwin, Spencer, and Mill: "even the man in the street felt the strong sweeping current of their thought, while to the young student, eager and impressionable, it was overwhelming." Conan Doyle therefore broke with the Catholic church, and adopted agnosticism. This "never for an instant degenerated into atheism, for I had a very keen perception of the wonderful poise of the universe and the tremendous power of conception and sustenance which it implied." He suggests that his decision was accepted by his mother, who herself later turned Anglican, but does not comment on the adverse reaction of his uncles and aunts who were so staunchly true to their faith. In *The Stark Munro Letters*, he also refers to discord over religion with an unsympathetic father but gives no hint of this in his autobiography.

Unlike many other autobiographers, Conan Doyle does not deal at length with his childhood, with the mysteries and pleasures of learning. He is factual and without sentiment, offering no psychological explanations. The characters are not fully rounded: his great-uncle and godfather Michael Conan, for example, is "volcanic" and has a "dicky-bird" of a wife. Conan Doyle calls himself rebellious and Bohemian, yet the reader must take it all on trust. With Joseph Bell, he does give an example of his powers of observation, but leaves the man an enigma. Neither here nor in the subsequent chapters are there any intimate portraits

3. There is, for example, "B. C. Haller" in the 1885 story "Uncle Jeremy's Household" (published in 1887), or there is "The Surgeon of Gaster Fell" (1890) that provides evidence the surgery outbuilding Waller constructed on his return to Masongill may have been intended for the use of Charles Doyle, or again there is the 1904 Sherlock Holmes story "The Adventure of the Priory School" that, the manuscript shows, is set in the area.

of friends or associates that would enable the reader to know them as Conan Doyle presumably did. It is as if Conan Doyle—whose character suggested kindliness and trust—had a fear of intimacy. When he describes his life, he omits the inner man. There are no revelations, no great pangs of remorse, and no sense of personal injustice. It is very much a drawing-room book without gossip or scandal—and without the truth that often lies behind them.

ii

The "first real outstanding adventure" of his life, Conan Doyle says, was his visit to the Arctic in 1880 when at short notice he occupied a berth on the Greenland whaler *Hope*, with a crew of fifty Scots and Shetlanders. Throughout the voyage they received no word of the outside world, and instead Conan Doyle experienced the haunting other-worldly quality of the polar regions. His mind may have become stagnant, he says, but his health had never been better, and the big straggling youth who had gone on board came off a powerful, well-grown man. The *Hope* sailed in late February 1880, returning in mid-August with sixty-six tons of seal and whale blubber. The voyage gave Conan Doyle firsthand knowledge of the sea and ships, and many of his best short stories during the 1880s made use of it. Also, though his mind may have been stagnant during the voyage itself, it left him with many vivid memories, of an almost epic grandeur. It was an ideal "adventure" for a young man whose *wanderlust* was constantly urging him to break out from the straitjacket of youth.

The fifth chapter, "My Voyage to West Africa," passes quickly over his leaving Edinburgh University with his M.B. in July 1881. His plans for the future were fluid, he says, and he was ready to accept any position that was offered. At the beginning of October he found himself as medical officer on board the African Steamship Company's *Mayumba*. It was a monotonous journey and the landscape of the Ivory Coast, the Gold Coast, and the Liberian shore was unchanging, while the ports at which they stopped became a blur. The heat was stifling and the conditions enervating. The impression made on him was of a dead and putrid land. He vowed to "wander no more," and though he drank "quite freely" at the time, he swore off alcohol for the remainder of the voyage.

The "most intelligent and well read man" he met was the American consul in Liberia, who came aboard at Monrovia: this black man did him good, he recalls, though he could not think that the voyage itself had contributed to his mental or spiritual advancement. The omission of the name of the American consul, Henry Highland Garnet, is strange. Garnet had been born in 1815, the son of a slave; by the 1840s he had become a leading advocate of abolition. Garnet's views should have had an influence, and Conan Doyle does say that he was impressed, "for a man's brain is an organ for the formation of his own thoughts, and also for the digestion of other people's, and it needs fresh fodder." This suggests that Garnet drew Conan Doyle's attention to his own prejudices, and that he opened a new avenue of thought. Though the Sherlock Holmes story "The Adventure of the Three Gables" does contain a description of a black man that could be considered offensive, Conan Doyle can rarely be accused of having reinforced racial prejudice in his works.

Conan Doyle was footloose and fancy-free, and he admits that he was quite taken with some of the younger ladies aboard ship. He refers to his physical and sexual development, though only indirectly, for he says that he was "a strong full-blooded young man": "I was a man among men. I walked ever among pitfalls and I thank all the ministering angels that I came through, while I have a softened heart for those who did not." Reading between the lines, it is quite possible that temptation was there, and that with the "unbounded cocktails of West Africa" to cloud his judgment, he may have come perilously close to satisfying his sexual appetite in a way that he would afterward have regretted. When he says that he drank "quite freely" at the time, it may be that he drank too freely and had some experience that would explain why he "swore off alcohol for the rest of the voyage." The early sexual development of Conan Doyle, however, is not a subject on which the author provides any information in his autobiography or other memoirs.

A stronger contrast could hardly have been found between the Arctic with its glamour, ice, and blood and the African coast with its putrefaction, malarial swamps, and oil-brown rivers; between the hardy whalers pulling in their catch and gutting it on the decks and the missionaries on board the steamer with the crew unloading mail, sacks of salt, and other merchandise from England and stowing aboard the palm oil, cotton, and benniseed; or between the eerie silence of the polar regions and the noise at the Equator, the chatter of the natives crowding the decks, and the constant buzz of the mosquitoes. And there was the difference between the bunk and cramped quarters of the first and the well-appointed saloon and comfortable cabin of the second.

iii

The voyage to West Africa made up only one chapter of the autobiography as serialized in the November 1923 *Strand*, and readers learned there for the first time that *The Stark Munro Letters* was based on personal experience and that "Cullingworth" was in reality George Budd.

Conan Doyle had first met Budd in Edinburgh early in 1881. That September Budd sent Conan Doyle a telegram asking him to come to Bristol, where Budd's father had been in practice. Despite an impressive mansion, Budd was on the verge of bankruptcy, and after two "riotous days" Conan Doyle returned home. The following March he received another telegram inviting him to come to Plymouth where Budd said he was having a prodigious success. Conan Doyle discovered that his claims were justified and that by unconventional means he had built up a practice worth several thousand pounds a year. Conan Doyle went into partnership with him. After six weeks there was a violent quarrel and he left. He says that his mother opposed the association and that Budd had read her letters and had started "scheming his ruin."

Budd told Conan Doyle that he must leave and set up on his own but offered to send him a pound a week, so Conan Doyle departed, arriving in Portsmouth with less than ten pounds. Budd soon "hurled his thunderbolt." He admitted that he had read Conan Doyle's mail and said he would make no further payments. For a moment Conan Doyle was staggered, but he sent Budd a derisive reply and "put him out of my head for ever." He heard nothing more of him until he read of Budd's untimely death some years later. In spite of it all, he had "liked Budd . . . I admired his strong qualities and enjoyed his company and the extraordinary situations which arose from any association with him." He was "a remarkable man and narrowly escaped being a great one."

The account deftly skates over what had been a turbulent and significant period of Conan Doyle's life, for it was during the five years before his marriage that his character was formed, and that he sowed the seeds that flowered throughout his life. In his youth he had had the guidance of Dr. Waller and of Dr. Hoare and had taken whatever came his way without thought for the future, but from the end of 1881 he was his own master. It was a period of intense uncertainty and doubt during which he came perilously close to ruin.

What Conan Doyle does not mention is that Dr. Hoare and others had tried very hard to dissuade him from going. Though Budd came from a distinguished medical family, he was unscrupulous, and his contributions to the medical journals did not inspire confidence. He was deemed precocious but shallow, and his unethical behavior antagonized the profession. Worst of all, he had left Bristol a bankrupt and showed no inclination to settle with his creditors. Conan Doyle was told that people associated with Budd would compromise themselves and damage their own prospects. His stubborn decision to join Budd in Plymouth was a major step in his life. It would be his first experience in practice and he refused to believe the warnings. He was determined to go, and the more Budd was criticized the more he defended him.

There was a battle for his soul that for a time it seemed his mother and friends had lost, for he was resolved to reject the advice of those closest to him. They redoubled their efforts to show that Budd was a charlatan and they did not mince words. When Budd told Conan Doyle to go, it "staggered" him, because he was quite unaware that Budd had read his mail, and he was settling happily into his job with the promise of three hundred pounds a year. Conan Doyle's world had collapsed and his first attempt to establish himself in practice had failed. When he arrived in Portsmouth, it was with the aim of freeing himself from his past, from the restraints of his Edinburgh connections. He chose a place where he was unknown in order to create himself anew as an unostentatious middle-class professional. The swagger of his youth would give way to conformity; he would curb his Bohemian habits and pay greater heed to "points of etiquette." It was the moment at which dreams thinned and he awoke to hard reality.

He began *The Stark Munro Letters*, which describes this period, at the end of 1893. His memories of it were still vivid, and he felt he was breaking new ground by being honest about the problems that had beset him. He might have done so if he had been true to his intention and shown the inner life of a young man from the age of puberty to the time he finds his feet: "The shrinking, horrible shyness, alternating with occasional absurd fits of audacity which represent the reaction against it, the longing for close friendship, the agonies over imaginary slights, the extraordinary sexual doubts, the deadly fears caused by non-existent diseases, the vague emotion produced by all women, and the half-frightened thrill by particular ones, the aggressiveness caused by fear of being afraid, the sudden blacknesses, the profound self-distrust." Unfortunately the finished book failed to live up to its promise. And although it reveals a great deal about his character, he had not set out to describe his experiences with Budd in exact detail. It would have come as a shock to him (despite what is virtually an open invitation in his autobiography) to find his biographers quoting from it as if it were fact, and as if he had reproduced direct transcriptions of the original conversations.

iv

The chapter devoted to Budd ends with Conan Doyle's arrival in Portsmouth, and he divides the following eight years into two chapters, covering the years before and after his marriage. He recalls how pleased he was to have a house of his own, how he lived on only a shilling a day, bought drugs on credit to treat the trickle of lower-class patients that came his way, how he joined a circulating library, and took long walks in the evenings. There were moments of loneliness that after a few weeks became so acute that he suggested his younger brother Innes might join him and so relieve his mother of the responsibility of looking after him.

Although it has become so familiar, Conan Doyle's description of his arrival in Portsmouth and of the years that followed is not as complete as the reader would wish nor, perhaps, is it absolutely accurate. He arrived in the city on June 24, 1882, and by July 1 had installed himself in 1 Bush Villas, Southsea. Though he wished to be self-supporting, his earnings were not sufficient for his needs, and when Budd stopped the payments, he was uncertain how he could pay the rent and taxes. At this point his mother, who felt partly responsible for the break with Budd, offered a solution. His brother would join him and she would make up the one pound a week by paying for his board and lodging. (In 1885, Innes was sent to Richmond Public School at the instigation of Dr. Waller who was himself an old boy. The fees were paid by Innes' eldest sister Annette, whom Conan Doyle was to call the "prop" of the family, for she was a pillar of strength in adversity and worked quietly and unselfishly to give her brothers and sisters the benefit of good educations at a time when Arthur himself was hardly able to help.)

In 1883 Conan Doyle began to make his mark as a local figure in a milieu that exactly suited him. There were other doctors, the members of the football, cricket, and bowls teams, patients who became friends, and fellow members of the Portsmouth Literary and Scientific Society. Although socially active, he still considered his life Bohemian as he knew so few ladies. He tried to meet more. He was also reading widely and writing articles and fiction. The stories showed a marked advance on his earlier work and reached a peak in July 1883 when one about the *Mary Celeste* mystery, "J. Habakuk Jephson's Statement," was accepted by the *Cornhill Magazine*.

Although Conan Doyle makes a distinction between the years before and after his marriage, his bachelor days are perhaps most important because the life-style of Sherlock Holmes is based in part on them. The name and framework came later, but the essence of the relationship between the detective and Dr. Watson is almost certainly to be found in what existed between Conan Doyle and his brother and the household they kept. Conan Doyle's Bohemian ways were very similar to those of Sherlock Holmes, and Watson's apparent naiveté and good humor derive from Innes. Stark Munro was to say of his younger brother: "He shares the discomforts of my little menage in the cheeriest spirit, takes me out of my blacker humours, goes on long walks with me, is interested in all that interests me." And he adds in parentheses: "I always talk to him exactly as if he were of my own age." It is surely the explanation of the very special quality of the friendship between Holmes and Watson. Underneath the high gloss, Holmes is an elder brother, which in part explains Watson's undiluted admiration.

Conan Doyle married in 1885. He first met his future wife when he agreed to look after her brother who was suffering from cerebral meningitis. At the suggestion of another doctor, he accepted him as a resident patient. Within a short while, the boy was dead and a hearse stood outside the gates of Conan Doyle's home—the worst possible advertisement for a young doctor. Fortunately Conan Doyle had had a second opinion the evening before the boy's death, but even so it was a time of great anxiety. He was worried on his own account and did what he could to reassure the mother and her daughter, and they also felt concerned at having involved him. The upshot was that Conan Doyle and the "very gentle and amiable" Louisa Hawkins became engaged and soon afterward were married, the same summer he earned his M.D. degree. Their life together, though marred by her subsequent illness, was happy and there was never a "serious breach or division" in their relationship.

Conan Doyle's marriage provided a new sense of responsibility, but it had less effect on his literary work than he claims, for he had done good work before. It was, however, in the first year of his married life that he wrote the book that was in time to alter the course of his life and provide a solid basis for all his future work: *A Study in Scarlet*. On the surface it was what James Payn of the *Cornhill Magazine* called it in turning it down, a "shilling shocker." It was clumsy in construction, with a format copied from Poe and investigative techniques lifted verbatim from Gaboriau. But the book is far greater than anything by Poe or Gaboriau. Conan Doyle had added further ingredients and transferred the methods of medical diagnosis to detection; he also used a style where clichés and commonsense details give an aura of clarity and veracity. Holmes inhabits a world with stockbrokers and governesses, tradesmen and clerical workers. It is the world of the average doctor, and Holmes is what E. W. Hornung called a "crime doctor." He waits in his consulting room for patients or visits them in their homes. Conan Doyle was to say later (in a lecture at St. Mary's Hospital in 1910) that medicine "tinges the whole philosophy of life and furnishes the whole basis of thought." It unmasks the "villain" of disease and by so doing renders it innocuous.

Conan Doyle gives much of the credit to Joseph Bell, who had inspired him with curiosity about people and trained him to notice the small peculiarities that distinguish one person from another. But though Bell was undoubtedly the "model" for Sherlock Holmes, he had many students and no other student was similarly inspired. It is therefore impossible to reduce the argument to a simple one as to whether it was Bell or Conan Doyle himself who was the "original." What is beyond question is that with Sherlock Holmes, Conan Doyle has a major claim to fame, and the faults of the author's character, the imperfections of his literary style, the limitations evident in his other work, conspired together to produce something unique. Conan Doyle would never have claimed that he was a genius, but there is genius in Sherlock Holmes, for the stories create the illusion of an ideal detective. They are works of art that are exactly calculated to impress and please and amuse.

Conan Doyle never understood why the stories had such a universal appeal. To him they were "police romances" that came easily and could not stand comparison with his historical novels that had involved extensive research and that he assumed must be the greater books. He did not believe that skill is innate, he thought that any subject could be mastered in the way that he had mastered *Gray's Anatomy* as a student. But in fact his skill was based on long experience; when he immersed himself in an unfamiliar historical period, he only showed that he lacked true historical feeling. Conan Doyle had no outstanding vision, no deep understanding of the subtleties of the human psyche. Many of his novels dated quickly. But Sherlock Holmes never will, for though the stories are period pieces doing for London of the 1880s and 1890s what Dickens had done for the city thirty or forty years before, they are also timeless. The areas in which Conan Doyle was weakest are irrelevant in this form of fiction, so while Conan Doyle is still ranked as a minor author, Sherlock Holmes is and has always been acknowledged as one of the very greatest fictional characters of his or any age.

v

Spiritualism opens the next chapter. Conan Doyle had attended a lecture in Birmingham in 1880 called "Does Death End All," but he appears never to have referred to it afterward, and his interest seems to have started in earnest in Southsea. At the outset, he says, he had the usual contempt for the subject, but he became interested and made various experiments and had a notable experience in 1887 when a psychic warned him not to read a book by Leigh Hunt. As he had been considering doing so, he was sufficiently impressed to write to the psychic paper *Light* giving an account of the seance, thereby putting himself on record as a student of the subject.[4] But his enthusiasm waned after the exposure of the notorious Madame Blavatsky, who made no secret of her fraudulent methods and seemed to treat the subject with scorn while retaining

4. "A Test Message," *Light*, July 2, 1887, reprinted in *Letters to the Press* by Arthur Conan Doyle, ed. John Michael Gibson and Richard Lancelyn Green (London: Secker and Warburg, 1986).

the faith of her followers. Although Conan Doyle's confidence in the subject was shaken, he was not convinced that the whole subject was bogus, and his interest remained strong, extending to every aspect of the occult.

Life in Southsea meanwhile was pleasant. His daughter Mary was born in 1889, and his literary work met with increasing success. He says that as he had no great personal ambitions, he might have stayed there forever, had not a great urge come upon him to visit Berlin and witness the new consumption cure of Dr. Koch. The journey proved important, as he met a distinguished physician on the continental express who advised him to establish himself in London as an eye specialist. Conan Doyle came to London in early 1891 and took a consulting room at 2 Devonshire Place. It was while waiting for patients that he wrote the first Sherlock Holmes short stories, which the new *Strand Magazine* accepted without hesitation. Conan Doyle returned to his lodgings each evening carrying his latest literary efforts, until one day he suffered a virulent attack of influenza. While recovering, he decided to give up medicine for good.[5]

Following his decision, Conan Doyle found a house for himself and his family in the London suburb of South Norwood. He mentions two events standing out in his memory from the Norwood period, the birth of his son Kingsley and his service as a war correspondent in Egypt. He was also busy as a writer, he joined the Society for Psychical Research, he was introduced to the London literary world, and he had his first venture in the drama with *A Straggler of '15* that he sold to Henry Irving. His most notable achievement during these years was the writing of the Sherlock Holmes stories that established his reputation. In many ways he was at his peak, and when Jerome K. Jerome called him "Big-Hearted, Big-Souled, Big-Bodied," he was expressing the opinion of many. For though Conan Doyle was a rising star in the literary firmament, he remained modest and unassuming, and few people could have imagined that he would one day put himself forward as the leader of a Spiritualist

5. But a mystery remains. Later in Conan Doyle's life it became a standing joke that his waiting room had been a room in which *he* had waited, that "not one single patient had ever crossed the threshold of my room," but he gave a different account to the *World* in July 1892: its interviewer reported the following month that Conan Doyle had been working at the Westminster Eye Infirmary, "compelled to attend to his patients in the morning and spend most of the afternoon at the hospital, so that no time remained for his writing but a portion of the night. For months he struggled to combine the two wholly dissimilar avocations; but in the end his health began to give way, and, after mature consideration, he resolved to 'throw physic to the dogs,' and to rely entirely on the profits of his books and articles."

movement. Even then, however, his interest in Spiritualism was evident.

But it was Sherlock Holmes who dominated the thoughts of the general public. *The Strand* was anxious for more, but Conan Doyle was wary as he did not wish to have his hand forced. Instead, he wrote *The Refugees* and *Beyond the City*. But Sherlock Holmes was what the public demanded, and his only means of escape was to engineer the detective's demise. Although there was an outcry, he was utterly callous and "only glad to have a chance of opening out into new fields of imagination." But throughout his life, Conan Doyle found himself unable to escape from Sherlock Holmes, and would have found the ground cut from beneath him if he had done so, for everything he turned his hand to, and every book he wrote, of whatever kind, had the success of Sherlock Holmes underpinning it. In 1893 he felt confident that he could repeat the success in a different way, but time was to show that this was not possible, neither Nigel Loring nor Brigadier Gerard nor Professor Challenger ever really left the pages of their books, so Conan Doyle returned again and again to Sherlock Holmes.

It was at this time that Conan Doyle discovered that his wife was suffering from consumption. They spent that Christmas at Davos where Conan Doyle wrote the first of the Brigadier Gerard stories. His sister Lottie had joined the family group, enabling him to make occasional trips back to England and, at the end of 1894, a speaking tour of America with Innes. Conan Doyle's fascination with America and his very warm feelings for Americans and their literature was a feature of his character; but though he enjoyed the company of the American literary circles who lionized him and was able to repay a few debts to his former literary idols, he was not greatly influenced by what he saw. The American influence had already reached him before he ever set foot in the country, through the pages of Fenimore Cooper, Edgar Allan Poe, Bret Harte, Mark Twain, Oliver Wendell Holmes, and others. And his grueling schedule in America and the lavish hospitality left him with little time for thought.

He rejoined his wife in Davos before Christmas, and in the early months of 1895 "developed ski-running in Switzerland." He made several more trips to London and met Grant Allen who, though a consumptive like Louisa, had chosen to live at Hindhead, near the sea. Conan Doyle decided to do the same. He bought a plot of land and chose an architect and a builder. He then rejoined his wife and sister and they traveled to Egypt. There they found, after a Nile cruise on which he based his 1898 novel *The Tragedy of the Korosko*, that the British reconquest of the Sudan was about to begin. With the first advance in the spring of 1896, Conan Doyle suddenly found himself at the "storm centre of the world." Anxious to witness the war at first hand, he applied to the *Westminster Gazette* to act as a special correspondent.

Conan Doyle saw only the advance on Dongola, which was in some respects less important than subsequent stages of the campaign, especially the climax reached in 1898 with the Battle of Omdurman and the final destruction of Dervish power. After writing his first dispatches in Cairo, Conan Doyle joined other correspondents for the advance; but no sooner had he arrived than it was time for him to leave, and despite the initial enthusiasm, he had witnessed nothing except troop movements.

Conan Doyle passes rapidly over the "Interlude of Peace" from his return to England to the outbreak of the Boer War. In the meantime he was busy writing—*Korosko*, *Rodney Stone*, *Uncle Bernac*, *A Duet*, and a large number of short stories. As well as those, he also wrote a play about Sherlock Holmes, which the American playwright/actor William Gillette soon took up and rewrote completely as his theatrical masterpiece. Conan Doyle's wife was holding her own, and their two children were "passing through the various sweet stages of human development" that added to their contentment. Also mentioned is his continuing interest and experiments in psychic research.

Where Conan Doyle suggests drama and adventure, the truth is often more mundane, but here, where he suggests a period of quiet, there was a real drama that had a profound effect on him—though he says next to nothing about it in *Memories and Adventures*. It occurred in March 1897 when he met the twenty-four-year-old Jean Leckie, with whom he soon fell in love. As their affection for each other grew, so he became ever more conscious of the difficulty of his position toward his wife, for whom he retained an affectionate regard.

Conan Doyle was also becoming more self-assertive. His opinion of himself can be seen in a questionnaire that he filled out late in 1899.[6] He gave "unaffectedness" as his favorite virtue; "manliness" as his favorite virtue in another man; "work" as his favorite occupation; "time well filled" as his ideal of happiness; "men who do their duty" as his favorite heroes in real life; and "affectation and conceit" as his pet aversions. But admirable though the latter are, it was no longer quite as true as it had been earlier in his life. "What I believe," he told his mother at the end of 1899, explaining why he would have to go out to the war in South Africa, "is that I have perhaps the strongest influence over young men, especially young athletic sporting men, of any one in England (bar Kipling)." It was a claim perhaps justified only in a private letter to his mother, as his fame rested mainly on his work as an author, for he had not yet been

6. Apparently never published, it is part of the "Conan Doyle Spiritualist Collection" at the Humanities Research Center of the University of Texas.

much in the public gaze or held any positions of great responsibility. It was more of an aspiration, and a harbinger of what was to come, than a fact.

Conan Doyle was neither the first nor the last author to have an exaggerated idea of the power behind the pen, but he went further than most. He had inherited from his father a creative power that inclined to the bizarre and hovered on the dream fringes of the real world, and from his mother, who had sustained herself through a difficult period, there came embattled pride and a rigorous code of honor. He had imagination, but also a strict sense of justice, and his blood would boil and he would burn with indignation when confronted by injustice, or by what he saw as injustice (the two not always the same). He was on occasion precipitous and rash in running to a person's defense, only to realize when it was too late that appearances sometimes belied the truth.

An author has the power to create characters at will but may be left with no identity of his own, and Conan Doyle perhaps envied those, whether in the army or in politics, who had power and importance, and whose path of duty was clearly marked. He had to find his own way, and felt that his success as an author was not the ultimate purpose for which he had been put on earth. The Boer War seemed to offer a chance to find a new role.

Although no longer in the first flush of youth, he was energetic and prepared to jump at any opportunity that promised excitement. The use to which he put such experiences shows authorial skill of a high order, for however slight they were in reality, they assumed epic proportions in print—and often in the eyes of those who had been present. Many people, for example, won glory on the Dongola advance, and many correspondents spent months in the desert, whereas Conan Doyle spent only a few days; and yet it was to him that somebody wrote shortly afterward asking if he had received a medal for his war services. He may not have realized how potent were his descriptions, for he was always modest and was not amused when others engaged in flattery, but his own descriptions were often to blame.

vi

In December 1899, when Britain suffered its most serious setbacks in South Africa, Conan Doyle felt that he should enlist. His age was against him, but he was determined to reach South Africa, and by Christmas had decided to accompany a civil field hospital. He arranged for his family to stay in Naples, and then, with his affairs settled up, he reached Bloemfontein on April 2, 1900. The hospital was made ready, with the staff camped on a cricket ground and its pavilion serving as the main ward. At first they had a trickle of wounded soldiers, but enteric fever quickly set in and they were overwhelmed with patients. The conditions became frightful. The epidemic lasted four weeks, a number of the staff died, and Conan Doyle's own health was deteriorating. Relief came when the army moved on and captured vital waterworks. Conan Doyle joined the main advance for a time, before leaving for England in mid-July.

Conan Doyle's main reason for going out to South Africa was that he had taken upon himself the task of writing an "interim" history of the war. During the autumn of 1899 he had been buying all the newspapers and using them as the basis for his work. It was already well under way when he sailed and was within four chapters of completion when he returned to England, or so he thought, but as the war dragged on he had to revise and expand what he had written to take account of it. He had at the outset agreed to pay his own expenses and probably imagined that the demands made upon him would be slight, but the epidemic meant that he was called on to work hard, and for the first time in many years had a real sense of achievement and a deep inner satisfaction.

Those who met Conan Doyle in South Africa were struck by his good nature and geniality. He was, one correspondent wrote at the time, "a large, loosely-made man, with big grey eyes that turn on you when you speak to him with a trustful friendliness like a big dog's";[7] but the correspondents also recognized that this "trustful friendliness" tended to weaken his power to judge evidence and to resist the wiles of conscious and subconscious deceivers. Conan Doyle was too easily influenced and tended to oversimplify complex subjects. Many correspondents were aware of the failings of the British army, and had witnessed at close quarters the guerrilla tactics of the Boers, and suggested reforms. Nevinson and Donohue of the *Daily Chronicle*, for example, published an article on the "Lessons of the War" in June 1900. Much of what they said was to be repeated by Conan Doyle, but being more easily convinced of the merits of reforms that worked well on paper, he was impatient of those who pointed out that they could not work in practice.

At heart Conan Doyle was an armchair strategist typical of other clubmen of his day, but he did have an advantage over them in that his name was widely known because of Sherlock Holmes, and he wrote well, therefore his letters were published and his views received an airing. It was perhaps inevitable that he should go a stage further and put his name to a propaganda pamphlet. It opened a new chapter in his life that

7. See Henry W. Nevinson, *Changes and Chances* (London: Nisbet, 1923), p. 287.

culminated in the Spiritualist crusade. Conan Doyle was to achieve two things in his life: he was a successful author (who achieved greatness in his detective stories) and he was a prolific propagandist. The first, which he played down, is the reason why his name is known today, but his efforts and energy were largely devoted to the other. His autobiography does not dwell on the stories that made him famous, on his method of work, on his system of note-taking, or on the personal and domestic details that were worked into his stories but concentrates instead on his public career, on actions that were at best noble gestures.

The chapter "An Appeal to the World's Opinion" deals with his 1902 pamphlet, *The War in South Africa: Its Cause and Conduct*. Conan Doyle felt that the episode was one of the "most pleasing and complete" of his life. He started work on January 9, 1902, and with enormous energy and enthusiasm he had finished it by the seventeenth. Considering its length and the fact that he had had to check every detail, he was proud of his achievement. It had a marked effect on the tide of world opinion, which thereafter was more favorably disposed to the British side.

Conan Doyle referred to the venture as a "small unauthorized incursion into amateur diplomacy." His qualifications, he said, were negative ones: he was not connected with the government or the army and so could not be considered a "mere official mouthpiece," and the only thing against him was the fact that he was best known as a writer of fiction. In fact it may have been that the reverse was true. Because the pamphlet was to be distributed free and did constitute propaganda, and because it was stating the British position, he was seen as an official mouthpiece; on the other hand, the fact that he was widely known as an author, particularly the author of *The Hound of the Baskervilles* that was appearing in tantalizing monthly installments at that time, was in his favor.

To the public, it did not matter so much what Conan Doyle said, as the fact that he took the trouble to say it. They in their thousands read Sherlock Holmes and thought well of his creator as a result. But to be thought well of was not in itself sufficient. He realized that he had achieved something remarkable when he wrote the Sherlock Holmes stories. He did not need to say so, as it was self-evident, and others in a wide variety of ways said it for him; but he also believed that he could achieve similar results in other fields. He thought time and again that he was on the point of doing so: that *The Stark Munro Letters* was to break new ground, that *Rodney Stone* represented a new departure in literature, that the Brigadier Gerard stories were more original than Sherlock Holmes, or that high-angle fire in warfare was epoch making, or that with his pamphlet he had personally turned the tide of world opinion. Fame had come unsought, but fame of the wrong kind, he felt, and every new adventure was an attempt to change the popular perception of himself. And the more that others praised Sherlock Holmes, the more he felt inclined to draw attention to the wide variety of his other achievements that failed to win the same popular acclaim.

There was a gulf between the public perception of Conan Doyle and his own private perception of himself. He was more ambitious than the public realized, and his estimation of himself had grown. That he should choose to stand for Parliament was well in character, even if it surprised those who knew him only as a novelist.

vii

Conan Doyle twice stood for Parliament, in 1900 and 1906, and was defeated on both occasions. He found it hard to say why he had stood, as he had no real desire to enter Parliament and no wish to be fettered to a party. He had deliberately chosen seats judged impossible for a Liberal Unionist like himself to win. The first was a Central Edinburgh seat, in the city of his birth. He felt, he says, deep in his bones that he was on earth for "some big purpose," and he allowed Providence to guide him: his failure was a sign and also a form of preparation for his "ultimate work," for it had taught him to face hecklers and remain cool under attack—something of use to him later when lecturing on Spiritualism.

Conan Doyle recalls that the Edinburgh constituency was a "premier radical stronghold" and, though he considered himself Radical in some ways, his campaign was restricted to one issue, the need to win the Boer War. He would have won, he says, had not his opponents realized that he was getting "dangerous" and taken alarm. On the day of the election, placards were posted up denouncing him as a Jesuit-trained Catholic, and this interference cost him the election. In 1903 he agreed to contest the Border Burghs on the issue of tariff reform. He acquired a working knowledge of the subject and put in many hours of work in the constituency over the next two years, but unfortunately when the election arrived in January 1906, tariff reform arguments had lost much of their appeal and he was defeated again.

He considered politics a vile business but chastening in its effect. His propaganda work had made him feel that if he chose to stand for Parliament, he would have a better than average chance of being elected. To discover differently was disheartening. He realized that the public does make a distinction between an author and his work, and he felt that what he took to be his versatility was not properly appreciated. He justified his failure by saying a political career would have been a sidelining that would have restricted his freedom to speak his mind, whereas his failure meant that his utterances in the press afterward carried more weight with the public, as he was dissociated from any political interest which would have swayed his judgment.

The next two chapters are both entitled "The Years Between the Wars" and deal with a variety of subjects. One memory that stood out was meeting the distinguished physicist Oliver Lodge at Buckingham Palace in 1902 when the two men were knighted (Conan Doyle, reluctantly, for his services on behalf of the British position in the Boer War) and discovering a mutual interest in Spiritualism. Conan Doyle's romance with Jean Leckie was growing more obvious, to outsiders if not to his progressively infirm wife; his mother took his side, but when he had escorted Jean Leckie to Lord's cricket ground in August 1900, he had been hurt by his sister Connie and brother-in-law E. W. Hornung taking offense at what they saw as a disregard for good form. But Conan Doyle's only genuine sadness during these years was the death of his wife in 1906, and his only genuine disappointment the failure of the public to appreciate *Sir Nigel*, which he considered his "high water mark in literature."

The case of George Edalji, the half-Parsee lawyer convicted of cattle maiming, is then described. There was no doubt in Conan Doyle's mind about the man's innocence. He says Edalji was of irreproachable character and therefore incapable of committing the crimes. He had the highest references and was a total abstainer, and there was no indication of eccentricity in his character. Furthermore, he was so blind that he could not recognize anyone at a distance of six yards, and as he shared a room with his father that had been looked into at the time the atrocities were committed, his innocence was clear.

As a result of his *Daily Telegraph* articles about the case, Conan Doyle continues, there was a storm of indignation, others joined in the good work, and a committee was set up. Unfortunately it was mishandled and Edalji was not cleared. The main problem Conan Doyle faced was that, in order to prove innocence, he had to prove the guilt of another party. He thought he had a direct clue as to the author of anonymous letters that had been sent in connection with the cattle maimings, but his evidence was ignored, and he "mentally began to class the Home Office officials as insane." Much of early 1907 was taken up with this barren business, but it was not wasted, as it ended after much labor "in partially rectifying a very serious miscarriage of justice."

After mentioning his marriage to Jean Leckie later in 1907, he passes to the Oscar Slater murder case. Although Slater was a less desirable character, his case had been a "dreadful blot upon the administration of justice" and Conan Doyle felt called upon to act. He started a newspaper agitation and wrote a small book. Eventually there was a commission, but once again it was mishandled by those responsible and did not lead to Slater's release.

It now seems clear, from the as yet unpublished discoveries by Michael Harley, that George Edalji was not the innocent and respectable man that Conan Doyle thought.[8] He was actually a bankrupt who owed large sums of money and had stolen funds entrusted to him. Despite his pleasant manner, he was crafty and malicious and there was more evidence against him than Conan Doyle realized. But having taken up the case, Conan Doyle felt duty-bound to continue with it, though he began to grow frustrated at his inability to settle the matter as the public now demanded. His relationship with the police deteriorated, they feeling that he had been far too impetuous in his initial support for Edalji and so had worked himself into a corner.

True crime rarely has the neatness of its fictional counterpart, and Conan Doyle was unhappy with the outcome, though posterity has always viewed his involvement in the best possible light. The Slater case was if anything even more tiresome, dragging on throughout Slater's long imprisonment that only ended in 1927. Here again Conan Doyle achieved less than he wished and regretted that he had ever become involved. His aim was to draw attention to the miscarriage of justice and let others follow it up, but he found he could not walk away from it, and having expressed doubts, he felt it his duty to continue until Slater was released.

These two cases probably brought Conan Doyle more unwelcome publicity than any other cause to which he turned his hand, for the public insisted on identifying him with Sherlock Holmes; instead of treating these matters as miscarriages of justice, they became mysteries calling for solutions, and Conan Doyle was expected to perform as a real-life Sherlock Holmes. But here he could not oblige. Despite the brilliance of his stories, Conan Doyle had never professed to have any ability as an amateur detective himself and had shown in a 1901 series of articles about true crime (*Strange Studies from Life*) that he had no great understanding of the criminal mind. But unsettled as he was by his wife's death, he had plunged into the Edalji case with the zeal of a defending counsel. Within these later chapters of his autobiography, as in the later years of Conan Doyle's life, there is a certain weariness. The earlier adventures had been complete in themselves, but many of the later crusades were not fully resolved. He worked hard, but to little effect.

Conan Doyle refers to *Sir Nigel* but does not mention his other important book of the period, *The Return of Sherlock Holmes*. He also skates

8. To be published soon in Great Britain in a book about the Edalji case, provisionally titled "The Terror That Walked by Night."

lightly over his wife's death. To say that he had been praying for it would be grossly unfair, but during his long courtship of Jean Leckie, he must occasionally have wished that his wife could be spared further suffering. Their children also had had a difficult time. But her death led to a period of intense depression and the Edalji case was in some ways the antidote. It is unlikely that he would have become involved had it not been for these special circumstances.

Other matters with which Conan Doyle deals in these chapters are his memories of the 1908 Olympics and his work for the British Olympic Committee; his effort to establish Rifle Clubs throughout Great Britain as a military reform; his four plays of this period, *Brigadier Gerard, The Fires of Fate, The House of Temperley,* and *The Speckled Band*; his two years' work concerning the Belgian Congo atrocities; and his presidency of the Divorce Law Reform Union. He ends, after describing some seances, with an account of his various financial speculations, few of which met with success, though his role as a director of the Raphael Tuck publishing concern resulted in mutual satisfaction for himself and the company.

viii

The discussions of the Edalji and Slater cases had been serialized in Max Pemberton's *Great Stories of Real Life* in March and April 1924; *The Strand* in April, May, and June 1924 serialized chapters on "Some Notable People" and on sport.

Although Conan Doyle had met a wide range of public figures during his life, he limits his recollections to only a few. These include President Roosevelt, who had "all the simplicity of real greatness" and the mischievousness of a boy, and Arthur Balfour whose "mind was so subtle and active that he would always see the two sides of every question and waver between them." The authors mentioned are also only a few of those he had known. They include George Meredith, an early cult figure of his, and James Barrie, one of his oldest literary friends. Conan Doyle saw a limited future for Meredith, explaining why by giving what he considered to be the three requisites of an author, intelligibility, interest, and cleverness—for Meredith only fulfilled the last. He says Barrie should have restricted himself to novels, as his prose had a chaste clarity that was the "great style," though appreciation of it had been debased by a generation of critics who confused what is clear with what is shallow, and what is turbid with what is profound. Henry Irving had been another great man he had known, and there was Bernard Shaw who had shown so little regard for human feelings after the sinking of the *Titanic*: superhuman in intellect, he was subhuman in emotion. Conan Doyle also mentions Kipling, Wells, Jerome, Hornung, Stevenson, and others.

The pen pictures of the great and good are of most interest as reflections of Conan Doyle's own ideals. His description of Roosevelt could, for example, be a description of himself, a simple outlook and a great deal of the boy in his character, while his criticism of Meredith and his praise for Barrie encapsulate his own view of the art of fiction. Conan Doyle did have a great sense of humor, but he was not a great critic or thinker. Those subjects on which he could speak with authority were not the ones he wished to talk about; his temperament was such that if he met a leading politician, he spoke about politics, never appreciating that what most interested the statesman was the fact that he was the author of Sherlock Holmes. Although Sherlock Holmes had a profound influence on his own and subsequent generations, Conan Doyle himself did not directly influence anybody or actively contribute to the literary movements of his day. He was invariably wrong when assessing merit in young writers and, having come to literature with a rather narrow base, never appreciated the modern movement. He viewed it and other modern movements as degenerate, indeed in an interview in 1912 he dismissed them as madness—as part of a "wave of artistic and intellectual insanity."

His sporting recollections follow naturally from the chapter about famous people, as the two were often combined. Sport had taken up an appreciable part of his life and though he judged himself to be "a second-rater in all things," he had tried his hand at many. He disapproved of racing that depended most on the horse, and of blood sports that blunt "our better feelings" and could be done as well by a coward as by a brave man, but there was a long list of sports in which he had engaged. His fondness for boxing provides the best clue to his character, for he saw it as a manly, commendable sport instilling in people a "combative spirit and aggressive quickness," while its roughness prevented the risk of effeminacy. Sport, he says, gives a certain balance of mind. "To give and take, to accept success modestly, and defeat bravely, to fight against odds, to stick to one's point, to give credit to your enemy and value your friend—these are some of the lessons which true sport should impart." Conan Doyle had learned to box while still a boy, and his aggressiveness was dissipated through it. His fighting spirit was integral to his character—the verse at the head of *The Lost World* about the "boy who's half a man, or the man who's half a boy" reflects his own makeup. He had missed many of the pleasures of childhood and had assumed the responsibility of a man without going through the various stages of adolescence. In later life, when the pressures had disappeared, he was able to make up the lost ground, but he always remained a boy at heart with an undiminished sense of fun, and a naïvete which could be disconcerting in a man who was so solidly built.

ix

The last chapters of *Memories and Adventures* may be passed over quickly. There are some eighty-four pages devoted to the Great War as "the physical climax of my life." It was a period during which he repeated his earlier propaganda efforts, wrote many letters to the press suggesting reforms, and once again took it upon himself to write an unofficial history of the war. The chapters describing his visit to the war fronts are a reprint of his booklet *A Visit to Three Fronts*, and though of interest, they are perhaps too detailed in this context. Conan Doyle had wished to complete his autobiography before sailing to America for a speaking tour, and he relied at the end on articles that were already written.

He ends with a short account of his Spiritualist faith, which he says had become "the most important thing in my life," for which everything that had gone before had been a training. God himself, he realized, had placed him in a special position to convey to the world this great truth. "All modern inventions and discoveries will sink into insignificance beside those psychic facts which will force themselves within a few years upon the universal human mind." His last fourteen years, of which half remained when he wrote his autobiography, were devoted to this cause. He spent considerable sums of money and he damaged his health, but though he lectured to thousands, the "universal human mind" that he hoped to convert rejected his message, and the phase that had brought comfort to the bereaved of the Great War has faded into oblivion.

Conan Doyle had used the words "queerness" and "madness" when talking about trends in modern art, and while one may sympathize with his motives and admire his determination and conviction, the same words can all too easily be applied to Spiritualism. It is difficult not to feel that in his care not to discredit evidence, he became unduly credulous. It is hard to understand how a man who had stood for sound common sense and healthy attitudes could sit in darkened rooms watching for ectoplasm or be convinced by psychic photographs or fairies. And some of the Spiritualists with whom he came into contact have far less to commend them than those people with whom he had associated during the earlier phases of his life.

Conan Doyle's Spiritualist leanings were an integral part of his being and not an aberration, but his declaration of faith came as a profound shock to many people, including his mother. It is hard to know how best to deal with it, for the reasons he gives in his autobiography for his belief are so unconvincing and so far beyond mere "spirit." They are physical phenomena. He has heard voices, felt spirit hands, and so forth. Many people at the time considered them fraudulent, and little credence can be given to the spirits who came over, as they are so selective as to suggest the hand of the living. There is no logical defense. Conan Doyle was deluding himself. He was too anxious to believe, too honorable in many ways to accept the possibility of fraud.

x

Arthur Conan Doyle's greatness lies in Sherlock Holmes and to a lesser extent in his other fiction. He left no mark on history, but he remains a larger-than-life figure, and his career has a certain glamour enabling him to be named in a variety of other contexts. There is also a world set apart from the real one in which Conan Doyle holds center stage as the "big man" of his own dreams: the champion, the lover of justice, the man of action, the friend of the oppressed. It is the world he created around himself, and it was not purely a dream. His autobiography becomes the sequel to his historical novels, for here Sir Arthur vanquishes his foes and wins glory for himself. His life becomes a romance. Indeed many of the illustrations in *The Strand* serializations were drawn as if for an adventure story. It is the world in which his fellow Spiritualists reveled as it brought an aura of color and respectability to their proceedings. And it is the world beloved of his biographers, who have seen events through his eyes and have been more impressed by the uncritical admiration akin to flattery that Arthur Conan Doyle's friends bestowed on him than by his own endearing modesty. He was not born great, and other than with Sherlock Holmes, he did not achieve greatness, but he has had greatness thrust upon him.

Throughout his autobiography, Conan Doyle both implicitly and explicitly asks the reader to decide whether his judgment is sound or unsound, for it was written at a time when his reputation was under attack. No one who reads it can fail to like the author, though he may feel that Conan Doyle is too reticent about his literary achievements and dwells too much on his other activities. The importance of the latter has been exaggerated as a result of the public criticism against him in the 1920s, when friends sprang to his defense and stressed the finer points of his character and built up a picture that at times suggested a rather pompous knight-crusader and champion of the underdog.

It was a veneer, for underneath there is a far more likable and human man: the Southsea doctor, the aspiring young author, the spectator on the fringes of war; one who could be rash and impetuous; who could be generous, kind, humorous, ingenuous, impatient, controversial; and who could fight with his fists and act as a peacemaker. He is all these and more. Most particularly he is a writer who has contributed more happiness to his fellow men through the pages of his detective stories than any of his contemporaries. Maybe it is to do him a disservice if his autobiography is discussed in a too critical way, for his reward for writing Sherlock Holmes should be uncritical and unquestioning admiration, and the praise for the creator should at least equal that given to his creation. One would not have Arthur Conan Doyle other than he was, and if in his autobiography he plays Dr. Watson to his own Sherlock Holmes, then so be it, for he is entitled in such a book to do as he pleases.

3 ○ COMMITMENT TO GREAT CAUSES

Andrew S. Malec

Conan Doyle's Other Autobiographical Works

☙ *Memories and Adventures*, Arthur Conan Doyle's autobiography, is the starting point for anyone contemplating a biography of the author. Less well known, but still important for a full understanding of Conan Doyle's life and accomplishments, are his several other autobiographical writings.[1] Some of the occurrences recorded in them were subsequently incorporated into *Memories and Adventures*, but Conan Doyle often shortened his descriptions of events in order to keep that volume to a reasonable length, so that one must turn to the earlier works for the complete story. Just as important, the others were written at the time or immediately after the events they record, and therefore possess a greater immediacy than *Memories and Adventures*.

i
Western Wanderings and *A Visit to Three Fronts*

In 1914, Sir Arthur and Lady Conan Doyle were invited to take a rail journey across Canada as guests of the government. Conan Doyle's account of their experiences, *Western Wanderings*, was serialized in the *Cornhill Magazine* in early 1915 and published in the United States later that year. A revised version forms a chapter of the 1924 edition of *Memories and Adventures*, but it was omitted from the 1930 edition.

The Conan Doyles arrived in New York in late May, spending several days there before proceeding to Canada. A disproportionate amount of the book is devoted to this part of their visit, and it is the most interesting part. Conan Doyle compared the city with the New York he had first seen

---

1. Discussion is necessarily limited here to the more substantial works. A comprehensive list of Conan Doyle's shorter autobiographical writings is provided in Richard Lancelyn Green and John Michael Gibson's *A Bibliography of A. Conan Doyle* (Oxford: Clarendon Press, 1983).

in 1894: though impressed by the growth and energy of the metropolis, he felt its residents would someday "bitterly regret" that so many historical landmarks had disappeared to make way for new developments. He formed a lasting friendship with the famous private detective William J. Burns, sometimes known as the "American Sherlock Holmes." He visited two well-known American prisons, the Tombs and Sing Sing, finding the former "a pleasant, bustling, companionable place . . . in spite of its sinister name," but feeling that the latter, with its small, crowded, ill-lit cells, should "be swept utterly away . . . and the latest and best model placed on its site." Though he found brutal prison conditions both offensive and counterproductive, he did not sympathize with the habitual offender and suggested that "when a man has thrice been convicted of a penal offence he should forever be segregated from the community in a permanent seclusion."

More pleasant visits were made to Coney Island and a baseball game. Conan Doyle enjoyed the game and hoped it might catch on in England, but he realized even then that the amount of money infused into the sport detracted from its purity, since it meant that "the largest purse had the best team." He also encountered, and fared badly with, the New York press, which misinterpreted his unfavorable remarks about suffragettes to mean that he advocated starvation or lynching for them.

Leaving at last for Canada, Conan Doyle entered what he called "Parkman land," a reference to the historian whose books had been his sources for *The Refugees*, his 1893 novel about the Huguenots in North America. He set out from Fort William Henry, on Lake George, and traveled on to Montreal, Sault Ste. Marie, Fort William, and Port Arthur, and then to the Canadian Rockies, recalling to his mind the works of another boyhood literary hero, Mayne Reid. His enjoyment of the trip was somewhat diminished by Montreal's Canadian Club imposing upon him to deliver some luncheon lectures during the tour. But he did offer some advice to readers considering immigrating to Canada: he felt, for example, that the prairie west of Winnipeg offered excellent agricultural potential—but only for the man who came prepared with adequate capital. Closing with speculations about the future of Canada, Conan Doyle saw no prospect of unification with the United States despite the friendly relationship between the two countries, and as a loyal British subject, he saw no need for complete independence from England, since Canada was already free in "all important things."

Conan Doyle returned home to find Britain preparing for war. He spent parts of his life on the fringes of great conflicts, but his age always prevented him from entering his country's armed services. He satisfied his zest for adventure and fulfilled what he regarded as a moral obligation to contribute to the cause through a wide range of private activities.

65

During the Boer War, he had served in a volunteer hospital at Bloemfontein and had written his history of *The Great Boer War* and *The War in South Africa: Its Cause and Conduct,* his propaganda pamphlet defending Britain against charges of atrocities. Conan Doyle fell into a similar pattern immediately preceding and following the outbreak of World War I. He formed a civilian rifle corps for home defense and wrote several more rallying propaganda pamphlets, such as *Great Britain and the Next War* and *To Arms!* (both 1914). He then began his ambitious *The British Campaign in France and Flanders,* a six-volume history published during 1916–20 which he felt never received the credit it was due.

Conan Doyle was an understandable choice when Italy requested that an independent British observer be sent to their lines following their much criticized retreat from Trentino in May 1916. He agreed to go if he could first visit the British lines to obtain a standard of comparison. Through the *Daily Chronicle*'s intercession he also saw something of the French war effort. The trip resulted in three articles: "A Glimpse of the British Army," "A Glimpse of the Italian Army," and "A Glimpse of the French Lines," collected as *A Visit to Three Fronts* (1916). They later comprised three chapters of *Memories and Adventures.*

This slim volume's chapters are aptly titled, for given time constraints and wartime security, Conan Doyle was able to see or relate little more than glimpses of the sites he visited. The book carries the reader along in a blur of walks through trenches and hazardous motor trips, during which the occasional shell had to be dodged, and it is evident that Conan Doyle realized that his chief function was to help patch up any ill feelings among the allies. He obliged and was full of praise for the British tommies and their Italian and French comrades. At the same time, Conan Doyle was subdued and profoundly disturbed by the awful carnage that confronted him at every turn. Like many other British families, Conan Doyle's suffered heavy personal losses from the war and would never again be able to look at the world with quite the same basic innocence and optimism.

ii
The New Revelation, The Vital Message, The Wanderings of a Spiritualist, Our American Adventure, Our Second American Adventure, Three of Them, and *Our African Winter*

Near the end of 1916, Conan Doyle announced his conversion to Spiritualism in an article in *Light,* the movement's leading British journal.[2] Conan Doyle had investigated psychic matters since the early 1880s, and his new belief represented the culmination of a lifelong search for a religion to replace the Roman Catholicism with which he had broken in his youth. In Spiritualism, Conan Doyle felt he had finally discovered a religion that offered rational, physical proof of its central principle: that human personality survives death and can communicate with the living. He thus embarked upon what he would henceforth regard as the most important phase of his life, to which he would devote more time, energy, and writing than to anything else previously.

Conan Doyle's wholehearted devotion to Spiritualism and allied paranormal pursuits has baffled most of his biographers, who could not reconcile Sherlock Holmes' creator with a man of, they felt, almost limitless credulity. It has often been suggested that Conan Doyle, like many others of his time, embraced Spiritualism in reaction to the horrors of World War I. Though Conan Doyle's most grievous bereavements, the deaths of his son and brother, occurred after his announced conversion, they may have made him all the more desperate to believe his loved ones were not lost forever, that he would be reunited with them someday and could stay in touch with them in the interim. But some recent biographers, noticing Conan Doyle's lifelong interest in the supernatural, have suggested that his troubled father, Charles Doyle, himself strongly attracted by the unseen world, had exerted a stronger influence on his son than had been allowed by earlier interpreters of Conan Doyle's life. To them, acceptance of Spiritualism might be seen as almost a natural development in Arthur Conan Doyle's case.[3]

2. "A New Revelation: Spiritualism and Religion," *Light*, November 4, 1916, reprinted in the *New York Times*, November 26, 1916. In it he wrote: "If anyone were to look up the list of subscribers to *Light* for the year 1887 I think that he would find my name. I am also one of the oldest members of the Psychical Research Society . . . I cannot be accused of having sprung hastily to my conclusions."

3. See Charles Higham's *The Adventures of Conan Doyle* (1976) for discussion of the morbid qualities of some of his lesser known fiction and Owen Dudley Edwards' *The Quest for Sherlock Holmes* (1983) for speculations about the darker side of his personality during his early years; both biographies are discussed at length elsewhere in this volume. In *Adventuring in England with Doctor Arthur Conan Doyle* (privately published, 1986), Alvin E. Rodin and Jack D. Key point out that artistic fascination with the supernatural ran strong throughout Conan Doyle's family: see *Richard Doyle's Journal, 1840* (Edinburgh: John Bartholomew and Sons, 1980); the catalogue of the exhibition on *Richard Doyle and His Family* (London: Victoria and Albert Museum, 1983), which notes both "the high Victorian delight in the escapist world of faery at its most developed form" and the Doyles' "vivid imaginative powers and . . . intense interest in fantasy and the supernatural"; and *Richard Doyle*, vol. 22 of *The Artists and the Critics* (Stroud,

Despite such insights, the Spiritualistic aspects of Conan Doyle's career remain very incompletely recorded and largely misunderstood.[4] To fully document, much less interpret, it would require familiarity with the numerous Spiritualist and psychic books, pamphlets, and periodicals published during the period when Conan Doyle was active, most of which have become rare. Equally critical would be access to the relevant primary materials, and though some of these are in public institutions, others are still locked away pending the resolution of litigation over Conan Doyle's estate or are scattered among private collectors.

Conan Doyle's own writings in the field comprise a starting point. Some of them contain substantial sections devoted to other subjects and thus are of interest to people who refuse to come to grips with the author's psychic side. Despite this, it is a tribute to Conan Doyle's determination and popularity as a writer that he was able to get many of them published at all. George H. Doran, the American publisher who had reason to be grateful to Conan Doyle (having published *The Lost World*, *The Poison Belt*, and the last three Sherlock Holmes books, among other works), spoke diplomatically on this point in his memoirs:

> Doyle was exceedingly restive over the fact that his books on spiritualism did not have as relatively large a sale in the United States as they did in Britain. He volunteered that all his royalty earnings from the sale of these books in America should be devoted to their wider publicity and sale. But it was difficult to persuade Americans to whom Doyle and Sherlock Holmes were synonymous to accept Doyle as the prophet of a new spiritualism.[5]

Conan Doyle's first two Spiritualist books, *The New Revelation* (1918) and *The Vital Message* (1919), are not wholly autobiographical, but in them he does briefly describe some of the experiences that led to his conversion, while laying out the framework of his own approach to the religion. Conan Doyle revealed even in these early contributions that his

Glos.: Catalpa Press, 1983), which discusses "the Doyle family's preoccupation with the spirit world, and Arthur's attempt to prove his father and his uncle's fairy preoccupations had been more than mere artistic whims."

4. Among the few who have approached the subject at all is Trevor Hall, "Conan Doyle and Spiritualism," in his book *Sherlock Holmes and His Creator* (London: Duckworth, 1977). Hall's survey of Conan Doyle's psychic writings and activities is useful for the novice, though marred by the inclusion of a lengthy and faulty argument concerning the date of authorship of some of the later Sherlock Holmes stories. A more satisfactory review of Conan Doyle's psychic career is Jeffrey L. Meikle's "'Over There': Arthur Conan Doyle and Spiritualism," *Library Chronicle of the University of Texas at Austin*, n.s., no. 8 (Fall 1974).

5. *The Chronicles of Barabbas* (New York: Harcourt, Brace, 1936), p. 240.

chief interest no longer lay in the psychic phenomena associated with Spiritualism. Rather, he felt that the central beliefs of Spiritualism had already been proven, freeing him to concentrate on the message the departed had for those who remained on this side and on the question of how one could best prepare for the life to come. Thus was set the tone for the bulk of Conan Doyle's subsequent work: though he continued to investigate mediums and other psychic occurrences, his chief contribution to the Spiritualist movement was as a propagandist.[6]

Conan Doyle proselytized through both his writings and a series of lecture tours throughout Europe and three other continents. He usually alternated between two basic presentations, the "photographic" lecture and the "philosophical" lecture. In the former he would display lantern slides of various physical "proofs" (such as ectoplasmic materializations and spirit photographs), which he hoped would lend credence to his assertions and create interest in the more important latter lecture, which was devoted to the ethical and moral precepts of Spiritualism. The content of the photographic lecture would change from time to time as new evidence came to hand, but the philosophical lecture remained unaltered in its essentials from the time that Conan Doyle wrote *The New Revelation* and *The Vital Message* to his death: the books thereby give a good idea of the text of these lectures.

More autobiographically relevant are the four books that Conan Doyle wrote about his lecture tours. These are almost entirely untouched upon by either edition of *Memories and Adventures*, though a number of the incidents related in the travel books have become familiar through some of Conan Doyle's biographies.

The first was *The Wanderings of a Spiritualist* (1921), about Conan Doyle's tour of Australia and New Zealand between August 1920 and February 1921. At the outset of the book, Conan Doyle showed he was aware that it might not be what his readers had come to expect from him: "This is an account of the wanderings of a spiritualist, geographical

6. Among the most noteworthy of these investigations is recorded in *The Case for Spirit Photography* (1922) in which Conan Doyle defended a psychic photographer accused of fraud. But eclipsing this and all of Conan Doyle's other encounters with the paranormal was the "Cottingley [Yorkshire] fairies" business in which he championed two young cousins, Elsie Wright and Frances Griffiths, who claimed to have seen and photographed fairies. The matter is recounted in Conan Doyle's book *The Coming of the Fairies* (1922) and in several periodical articles. He retained his belief in the girls' veracity to his dying day and remained active in promoting their claims, even though this episode in his career did more to harm his reputation than anything else. A comprehensive historical analysis of the matter is supplied by Geoffrey Crawley in his series of articles, "That Astounding Affair of the Cottingley Fairies," *British Journal of Photography*, December 24, 1982–April 8, 1983.

and speculative. Should the reader have no interest in psychic things—if indeed any human being can be so foolish as to not be interested in his own nature and fate—then this is the place to put the book down."

The Wanderings of a Spiritualist is the longest of the four travel books and the best written of them. Conan Doyle had a talent for describing locales, flora, and fauna that would have been exotic to the majority of his readers, a fact still contributing to the work's appeal today. Less interesting to present-day readers are his remarks about contemporary political and social problems besetting Australia, though awareness of these attitudes is of course important as an assessment of Conan Doyle himself. The later three travel books are similarly filled with comments on a wide range of topical concerns.

Following a voyage through the Mediterranean, the Suez Canal, and the Indian Ocean, the Conan Doyles arrived in Australia on September 17, 1920. Conan Doyle's forthcoming visit had been noted in high places, and he was greeted upon arrival by a "hospitable letter" from Premier Hughes; later he lunched with members of the government. Before departing on February 1, 1921, the Conan Doyles visited all the major Australian cities, and Conan Doyle himself had also gone alone to New Zealand, a trip involving a dangerous sea navigation during which a fellow passenger entertained him with tales of ships that had foundered during similar passages.

As he would do in the missionary trips that followed, Conan Doyle divided the time not devoted to his lectures or the related press controversies to a wide range of pursuits. Whenever he had the chance he visited local mediums, and other examples of psychic phenomena. Additionally, in this and his subsequent travels Conan Doyle had a penchant to become attracted to subjects of even more dubious validity: in the volume at hand, for example, he considered theories concerning Atlantis, and, when told of a fighter suffering from a tumor in the shape of a boxing glove, regarded the anecdote as another sign that the potential effects of mind over matter had yet to be fully explored. Conan Doyle's writings on mainstream psychic issues were frequently peppered with speculations of this sort, a fact that must have significant bearing upon any evaluation of his critical acumen in this area.[7]

7. Though admired for his sincerity and concern for humanity, Conan Doyle's essentially subjective approach to the study of the paranormal was decried by those of his contemporaries who were trying to establish psychic research as a legitimate science. Among the most important of these was Walter Franklin Prince, whose "Houdini and Conan Doyle," in *The Enchanted Boundary: Being a Survey of Negative Claims of Psychic Phenomena 1820–1930* (Boston: Boston Society for Psychic Research, 1930), is representative of the general view of Conan Doyle held by those who attempted to approach the subject with a genuinely scientific methodology.

Other visits were made to more traditional tourist attractions. Conan Doyle dropped in on the Maoris and did not know what to make of them, nor could they seem to understand the exact object of his visit. He enjoyed observing Australia's sheepherding industry, but when he visited a bee farm, he found the belief prevalent that he was already an expert on the subject, a misconception arising from his having consigned Sherlock Holmes to beekeeping in the detective's retirement. Conan Doyle also managed to take in an occasional sporting event; he was inconvenienced, however, when the mania surrounding the running of the Melbourne Cup virtually shut down the metropolis, and he admitted feeling that wagering on horse races tended to have a demoralizing effect on people.

Conan Doyle met with a variable press, and the degree of sympathy of his audiences differed, but on the whole the tour was a rousing success. He could boast of having spoken twenty-five times to audiences averaging 2,000 people each, and he quoted in *The Wanderings of a Spiritualist* the highly favorable assessment of the tour's impresario, Carlyle Smith: "For an equal number of lectures, yours proved the most prosperous tour in my experience. No previous tour has won such consistent success . . . I have known in my career nothing to parallel it." The tour was not without personal sacrifice, however, for when Conan Doyle returned to Melbourne from New Zealand, he learned that his mother, who had long been ill, had died during the family's absence. That Conan Doyle was prepared to leave her when she was in precarious health, and was then able to carry on in the face of this blow, is a measure of the firmness of his conviction in the vital importance of his mission—and of his belief that she had simply passed over to a far more pleasant existence.

His duty discharged to Australia and New Zealand, Conan Doyle was free to respond to the increasingly persistent invitations from America. In 1922 and 1923, the Conan Doyles made two lecture tours of the United States and Canada, detailed in *Our American Adventure* (1923) and *Our Second American Adventure* (1924) respectively. They arrived in New York to begin their first circuit on April 9, 1922. Prior to departing on June 24, Conan Doyle visited Boston, Washington, Philadelphia, Yale University, Buffalo, Toronto, Detroit, Toledo, Chicago, and Atlantic City. The second tour, necessitated by requests Conan Doyle received to lecture in cities missed in 1922, took place between April 3 and August 4, 1923, and found him traveling from New York City to Hydesville, New York (birthplace of the Spiritualist movement), and to nearly two dozen major cities in midwestern and western America and Canada.

During the New York portions of the tours, Conan Doyle had some experiences and expressed some points of view similar to those in *West-*

ern Wanderings (more baseball games, prison visits, and William J. Burns), and hence these sections of the two books are somewhat repetitive of both each other and the earlier work. As with his previous visits to the United States, Conan Doyle spoke and wrote at some length about Anglo-American unity, though now with greater urgency, since the former colonies were the starting place of what he hoped would eventually become a worldwide religion.[8] He now felt compelled to maintain a frenetic pace, and the style of *Our American Adventure* communicates the immediacy of his impressions very effectively. Both books were written in snatches whenever he had a free moment, and they read almost like diaries fleshed out to make a continuous narrative.

Conan Doyle was perhaps at the height of his celebrity when he arrived in the United States for the 1922 tour. He was swamped by the New York press, whose representatives were no doubt less interested in Spiritualism than in the man who had come to espouse it. Conan Doyle was particularly keen to stay on the reporters' good side, since Spiritualism and its practitioners had so frequently been subjected to ridicule and sensational exposures in the newspapers. He had little complaint, to start with, for his initial lectures met with an enormous response, the photographic one having to be repeated three times, for a total of seven crowded houses, in the New York area alone. Conan Doyle's success was more mixed as the tour proceeded, but still he had a full and demanding schedule. Relaxation was sometimes difficult because of Prohibition, but this impediment did not prevent at least some of Conan Doyle's hosts along the journey from having liquor on hand—and he confided that his party "carried two bottles of medical comforts with us all the way" in case of dry spells.

Conan Doyle managed some respite when he returned to New York at the conclusion of the tour. On June 2, Conan Doyle was guest of honor at a banquet of the Society of American Magicians, whom he delighted in mystifying by showing, after a cryptic introduction, scenes from a forthcoming motion picture of *The Lost World*, with convincing animation of dinosaur models. His friend Harry Houdini was among the conjurors present, and he subsequently visited the Conan Doyles in Atlantic City. While there, he agreed to a sitting with Lady Conan Doyle, who had developed powers as a writing medium. The session left her and Sir Arthur convinced that Houdini's mother had "come through" to communicate with her son—and certain that Houdini, too, had been convinced. But Houdini, famous for denunciations of fraudulent medi-

8. Howard Lachtman provides succinct accounts of all four of Conan Doyle's visits to North America in *Sherlock Slept Here* (Santa Barbara: Capra Press, 1985), a book useful to those who lack access to Conan Doyle's relevant autobiographical writings.

ums, later broadcast a different interpretation of the event, an incident that led to the disintegration of his friendship with Conan Doyle.[9]

The second American tour received an initial burst of publicity in New York when Lady Conan Doyle delivered a radio address on Spiritualism that her husband estimated reached 500,000 listeners. Among Conan Doyle's most interesting stops was Salt Lake City: he was impressed by the industry and tolerance of the Mormons, who extended him hospitality even though, as he recognized, they had legitimate reason to resent the "rather sensational and overcoloured picture" of the Latter-Day Saints' history that he had presented in *A Study in Scarlet*. Another visit was to Hollywood, where Conan Doyle was photographed with Mary Pickford and Douglas Fairbanks, and where he entertained child star Jackie Coogan with a "gruesome Sherlock Holmes tale."

Conan Doyle concluded this tour by swinging back through Canada in a journey recalling *Western Wanderings*. In the preface to *Our Second American Adventure*, which Conan Doyle described as the "third and last volume" of a trilogy encompassing *The Wanderings of a Spiritualist* and *Our American Adventure*, he noted with satisfaction that in the past three years he had "traversed at least 50,000 miles" and "addressed nearly a quarter of a million people" personally on behalf of Spiritualism. He was due for a rest, and for the next several years he restricted his efforts on behalf of Spiritualism to England and Europe. There his activities, if no less vigorous, at least did not involve as much travel.

Conan Doyle no doubt welcomed the chance to spend more time at home with his family, who had served and would continue to serve him well during his Spiritualist sojourn. Conan Doyle on the whole was fairly reticent about his home life, but he did provide at least a partial picture of the domestic scene in *Three of Them: A Reminiscence* (1923). The volume's seven essays are concerned with the thoughts and foibles of the young children of his second marriage (Denis, Adrian, and Jean) during their formative years, as well as with the various stratagems that their thoroughly sympathetic father devised to entertain them (and himself). Though the book is embarrassingly sentimental at time, particularly when Conan Doyle phonetically reproduces the children's manner of speaking, his willingness to so openly reveal his great affection for his family is a strong indication of his decent character.

9. Bernard M. L. Ernst and Hereward Carrington's *Houdini and Conan Doyle: The Story of a Strange Friendship* (New York: Albert and Charles Boni, 1932) is a fascinating record of the association between the two men, especially valuable for its inclusion of their correspondence. For Conan Doyle's views, see "The Riddle of Houdini" in his last book, *The Edge of the Unknown* (1930). Houdini told his side of the story in "Sir Arthur Conan Doyle," in *A Magician Among the Spirits* (New York: Harper, 1924).

In 1928 Conan Doyle was on the move again, this time to South Africa. The family arrived in Cape Town on November 12, 1928, and proceeded to travel through South Africa, Rhodesia, and Kenya, finally departing on March 13, 1929. Conan Doyle's account of the journey, *Our African Winter* (1929), was published by John Murray, the firm then emerging as the primary publisher of Conan Doyle's works in Britain. George Doran turned it down, however, because Americans were little concerned with "political and economic questions of Africa" and because "we can do almost nothing with Sir Arthur's psychic books."[10] The volume failed to find any other American publisher.

This tour also began with a radio broadcast. Sir Arthur spoke this time, from a Cape Town station with a transmission range of 1,000 miles. Major population centers were not nearly so numerous in these parts of Africa as they had been in the United States, so the actual number of lectures that he delivered was not large. But they were farther apart, and travel was usually difficult and occasionally perilous. During the rail trip from Salisbury to Beria the Conan Doyles inched precariously through the badly flooded and snake-infested Pungwe Marshes, eventually having to disembark and walk some distance to a train coming the other way when the water's depth made it too dangerous for the trains to meet on the track. Things did not improve much when they attempted to leave Beria for Mombasa—a cyclone struck, and they spent an anxious night waiting it out aboard ship in the harbor.

The comparatively light lecture schedule and extensive travel required to present them gave Conan Doyle the opportunity to engage in a great deal of sight-seeing. He also found time to pursue his interest in crime by mulling over the "Umtali Murder" in which an Englishman had been accused of killing a local woman. Conan Doyle dissected the affair, noting numerous inconsistencies in the case against the accused man. Unlike his experience in the Edalji and Slater cases, however, the deficiencies in the case were apparent even to the authorities, and by the time the affair came to Conan Doyle's attention the charges had been dropped.

As with his previous tours, Conan Doyle commented on numerous social problems in Africa, among them the continuing tensions in South Africa between the English and the Boers, and those caused by the persistent influx of laborers from Asia, when some were beginning to feel that they were no longer useful for the development of the continent. Conan Doyle stoutly defended the continuing British presence in Africa. His remarks on South Africa may be taken as representative of his general attitude:

10. Quoted in Green and Gibson's *A Bibliography of A. Conan Doyle*, p. 335.

The native question occupies a considerable place in the minds of thoughtful men in South Africa. There has been education and there has been Bolshevist teaching, and now there are dark swirls and eddies dimly visible down in the black depths. The whites in the country are under 2 million. The blacks are over 7 million. Then you have self-contained black countries such as Basutoland and the lands of the North. The present rate of increase is all against the whites. The danger is not immediate, but it is a very real one for the future. The only solution would seem to lie in greatly accelerated immigration.

This passage might have been written yesterday. Conan Doyle's opinions on such matters may not seem enlightened by our standards, but he protested with some feeling in his book against the ill treatment of the native population, in a manner reminiscent of the sentiments expressed earlier in *The Crime of the Congo* (1909), his indictment of Belgian colonial policy and misrule.

The literary construction of *Our African Winter* is more erratic than that of the earlier travel books. The style is variable as well, at times trite and lifeless, criticisms seldom made against Conan Doyle's writing. The book is clearly the work of a tired and elderly man, and there can be little doubt that the rigors of the African tour hastened Conan Doyle's death in 1930. Altogether the volume adds less to his reputation as a writer than the three which preceded it; though, like them, it is a vital resource to those interested in having as comprehensive a record of Conan Doyle's life as possible.

iii

The works surveyed in this essay add significantly to our knowledge of Conan Doyle's career, but even so his autobiographical record is far from complete. Conan Doyle remained almost entirely silent about his early, formative years, and it is only recently that scholars have begun to realize just how difficult and generally unhappy they must have been. There are shorter but nonetheless significant lacunae in the periods covered by the autobiographical books as well, and details on these often must be pieced together from secondary sources or the occasional Conan Doyle letter which escapes into the open market. Perhaps the ultimate authority for many of the unanswered questions in Conan Doyle's life are his diaries, which he never expected or intended to be seen by the public. It remains to be seen, if these documents someday become accessible to scholars again, whether they do indeed contain nuggets unmined by the few biographers who were able to make use of them. In the interim, any evaluation of Arthur Conan Doyle's statements about his life must to a certain extent remain problematical. It seems fitting, if not satisfactory, that the author of the greatest detective stories of all time should himself have left so many mysteries behind him.

The young Arthur Conan Doyle, in the mid-1860s, with his father, Charles Altamont Doyle. The secret of his father's tragic fate would lie like a shadow over Arthur's life for many years. Photo courtesy of Dame Jean Conan Doyle.

The fourteen-year-old boy, sent off to boarding school in the north of England. The Jesuit education there brought him to challenge his family's Roman Catholicism, beginning a spiritual odyssey that culminated decades later in his embrace of Spiritualism. Photo courtesy of Dame Jean Conan Doyle.

The young athlete (*top row, far right*), ca. 1875: Conan Doyle remained avid about sports his entire life, and their values strongly influenced his outlook, writings, and public crusades. Photo courtesy of Richard Lancelyn Green, all rights reserved.

Graduating from Edinburgh University in 1881: he went out into the world with an uncertain medical career before him, an unquenched appetite for adventure, growing ambitions as a writer, an uneasy agnosticism, and serious family problems to deal with. But in his mind now were the seeds of Sherlock Holmes. Photo courtesy of Richard Lancelyn Green.

Dr. Joseph Bell, the legendary physician-teacher and Conan Doyle's mentor at Edinburgh. Bell was the source for Sherlock Holmes' method, but the full extent of his contribution to Conan Doyle's greatest creation has been a troublesome biographical problem. Photo courtesy of Ely M. Liebow.

The young physician in Southsea, Portsmouth, Hants.—and the local sportsman, Literary and Scientific Society officer, struggling amateur author, and dabbler in psychic investigations as well. But he knew few young ladies, he complained. Photo courtesy of Richard Lancelyn Green, all rights reserved.

One young lady whom he did meet: Louisa "Touie" Hawkins, whom he married in 1885. In the early 1890s Touie would contract tuberculosis and finally die of it in 1906. By then, Arthur Conan Doyle had been in love with someone else for almost ten years, a secret that Touie never learned. Photo courtesy of Richard Lancelyn Green, all rights reserved.

The birthplace of Sherlock Holmes: the residence and consulting rooms of A. Conan Doyle, M.D., shown standing outside the gate. Conan Doyle wrote both *A Study in Scarlet* and *The Sign of the Four* here in the late 1880s, around the time of this photograph. Other members of his household can be seen at the windows. The house was destroyed in the Blitz in 1941. Photo courtesy of Richard Lancelyn Green, all rights reserved.

Jean Leckie, the striking and intelligent young beauty with whom Conan Doyle fell instantly in love upon meeting her in 1897. Despite their deep feelings for each other, they maintained a platonic relationship for ten years until their marriage in 1907, the year following Touie's death. Photo courtesy of Richard Lancelyn Green, all rights reserved.

Sir Arthur Conan Doyle (*rear row, center*) with his family ca. 1904—including his brother Innes (*rear row, left*), his sisters and their husbands and children, his wife "Touie" (*seated second from left*), their children Mary and Kingsley (*standing behind her*), and his mother (*seated second from right*), the redoubtable "Ma'am." But Conan Doyle's heart belonged now to Jean Leckie—a fact unknown to Touie, and a state of affairs dividing the family. While his mother supported the relationship, his sister Connie and brother-in-law E. W. Hornung (*rear row, left* of Conan Doyle) were censorious. Hornung's famous gentleman burglar *Raffles* had already been dedicated to a not altogether appreciative Arthur Conan Doyle. Photo courtesy of Richard Lancelyn Green, all rights reserved.

Jean Leckie as Lady Conan Doyle, around the time of their marriage in 1907. They would have three children, Denis (d. 1955), Adrian (d. 1970), and Jean, and she would survive her husband by ten years. While at first cool toward her husband's psychic interests, in time she too became a convinced Spiritualist and a medium herself. Photo courtesy of Dame Jean Conan Doyle, all rights reserved.

The world-famous author, and now an active social reformer as well, relaxing in Canada during his 1914 trip there. In the future his travels would be devoted to causes: the Allied effort in World War I and his Spiritualist missionary crusades around the world in the 1920s. Photo courtesy of Dame Jean Conan Doyle, all rights reserved.

Conan Doyle's final home, Windlesham, near Crowborough, Sussex, which he and his new bride took in 1907, was replete with the trophies and mementos of a varied and adventurous life. Photo courtesy of Dame Jean Conan Doyle, all rights reserved.

Sir Arthur in Home Guard uniform during World War I with his young son Denis. At the time he believed that he would never write fiction again, quite prepared to turn his back on it in favor of more "serious" commitments and writings. Photo courtesy of Dame Jean Conan Doyle, all rights reserved.

Sir Arthur with his son, Capt. Kingsley Conan Doyle,
during World War I. The deaths of Kingsley, his brother
Innes, and other relatives in the war would encourage an
allegiance to Spiritualism in 1916 that had merely been a
sympathetic, albeit strong, interest in it prior to that. Photo
courtesy of Dame Jean Conan Doyle, all rights reserved.

Sir Arthur and his second family after World War I: *seated left*, Lady Conan
Doyle (Jean Leckie); *in front*, their three children; *seated right*, Mary Conan
Doyle, his daughter by his first marriage. Photo courtesy of Dame Jean
Conan Doyle, all rights reserved.

The author in the mid-1920s: while still producing some fiction after all, including the final Sherlock Holmes stories, his writings were now overwhelmingly devoted to the Spiritualist cause—to the great disadvantage of his literary reputation and public stature. Photo courtesy of Richard Lancelyn Green.

Sir Arthur in 1929, the year before his death, at his Bignell Wood holiday house in the New Forest with his nearly grown-up sons Adrian (*left*) and Denis. The two sons, Adrian especially, would try to influence strongly what biographers would write in future years about their father and his varied and often controversial accomplishments. Photo courtesy of Dame Jean Conan Doyle, all rights reserved.

The author, public figure, and knight in his prime. Photo courtesy of Dame
Jean Conan Doyle, all rights reserved.

❧ *Part II*

BIOGRAPHY

4 ° A SPIRITUALIST CRUSADE

Philip A. Shreffler

Arthur Conan Doyle: A Memoir
by the Reverend John Lamond

That the first book-length biography of Sir Arthur Conan Doyle should have been written by an ardent and convinced believer in Spiritualism who knew Conan Doyle personally is hardly surprising, and in many ways is more appropriate than it might seem to the casual observer of Conan Doyle's life and works. John Lamond's *Arthur Conan Doyle: A Memoir* (London: John Murray, 1931) makes no attempt to present itself as other than an apologia for the Spiritualist movement and an examination of how the forces in Conan Doyle's life destined him to become one of the cause's chief champions.

During the span of Conan Doyle's lifetime, from 1859 to 1930, popular fascination with many areas of the occult ran high. This is particularly ironic in the face of the fact that the occult recrudescence occurred during the height of the nineteenth century's technological revolution and carried on nearly to the eve of World War II. In one sense, it may have owed its very existence to the technological, economic, and political upheavals of these times—much as it did in its most recent upsurge in the 1960s and 1970s.

Yet Conan Doyle was not swept along by the occult tidal wave. He had been interested in Spiritualism since the early 1880s, occasionally attending seances, discussing and reading on the subject, comparing its relative virtues with those of the organized religion he had rejected during his university days in Edinburgh. But it was only during the final fourteen years of his life that he at length cast away the last shreds of materialist skepticism and openly embraced the movement. When he did, however, he was as fervently committed to it as ever he was to any social, political, moral, or philosophical cause. In addition to his prodigious literary output in the Spiritualist field, Conan Doyle was an indefatigable public spokesman for the cause, lecturing throughout Great

Britain, across the Continent, and in the United States, Canada, Australia, New Zealand, and Africa. He aroused considerable public interest because of his religious ideas and garnered a great deal of press attention wherever he went, so that when he died the freshest memories of Arthur Conan Doyle in the world's mind were twofold: Sherlock Holmes and Spiritualism.

Moreover, when Lamond, the author of several books on religious, occult, and historical subjects, approached Conan Doyle's widow with the idea of doing Sir Arthur's biography, she wrote to him: "We feel convinced that you are the man we would choose for this task, and I think that is why you have been left on the earthplane, to do this work for the man I know you so greatly loved." Since Lamond's enterprise was fully authorized by Lady Conan Doyle, the former Jean Leckie, who was also devoted to her husband's propagandistic activities for the Spiritualist cause, this first biography could hardly have turned out other than it did. Conan Doyle had made Spiritualism a *cause célèbre*, and his survivors desired that he be remembered principally for that cause.

It is certainly for this reason that Lamond fails to deal in any analytical way with most of the elements of Conan Doyle's life that do not touch on Spiritualism. He races over issues like Conan Doyle's being the real Sherlock Holmes, for example, as if to say (and probably because he really believes) that Spiritualism is the one central biographical area that must be stressed. Therefore, readers coming to this book expecting probing critical analysis of biographical problems beyond the Spiritualist dimension of Conan Doyle's life will be disappointed.

A word or two about the nature of Spiritualism, at this point, perhaps, would be in order. Spiritualism, as Lamond is at great pains to repeat frequently throughout *Arthur Conan Doyle: A Memoir*, is based on two basic propositions: first, that upon death, the soul departs for various spheres or planes of nonmaterial existence beyond the so-called earthplane; and second, that a certain degree of communication between the living and the dead, among the various planes, is possible.

Spiritualism as a movement had its genesis in 1848 when the two daughters of a Methodist family named Fox heard inexplicable rapping noises in their Hydesville, New York, farmhouse. By and by, it developed that these rappings, which came now in code, originated with a ghost who wanted the living to know the truth about the existence of the spirit world. To Lamond, and other Spiritualists like him, the experience of the Fox sisters was a watershed event in the history of mankind. For the first time, there was contemporary "evidence" to suggest that the scientific materialism that was about to overrun the thinking of *fin de siècle* intellectuals was in error. The message was simple and reassuring: Man survives the grave.

However, in his effort to utilize Conan Doyle's life as an exemplar of Spiritualistic propaganda (a word from which neither Lamond nor Sir Arthur shrank), Lamond is careful to point out that Conan Doyle early abandoned the Roman Catholic church, adopted an agnostic posture, and clung to it until his Spiritualist conversion in 1916. That conversion, Lamond quotes Conan Doyle as remarking, was at least partly occasioned by Conan Doyle's loss of a son in the Great War and by his conviction that the mothers of many sons killed in the trenches would be similarly reassured by faith in a transcendent afterlife. Still, Lamond attempts to depict Conan Doyle as a philosophical inquirer whose own scientific skepticism required "proof" of Spiritualism's veracity rather than as a fool who rushed in to embrace a lunatic belief or who was gullibly duped by the charlatanism rampant in the occult community of the day. Nevertheless, Conan Doyle did become a Spiritualist, going so far in the mid-1920s as to establish in London a Psychic Bookshop in which he and his wife both worked from time to time.

But given the overall thrust of Lamond's *Memoir*, individual events like running the Psychic Bookshop seem to make solid sense. Lamond views Conan Doyle's life as a series of causes—almost as a kind of knightly quest—undertaken by a clean, brave, right-minded man who never buckled under adversity or injustice, but who positively thrived on it. This reflected, Lamond feels, the nobility and brilliance of the mind behind these activities. Conan Doyle's failing medical practice provided the opportunity for him to turn to literature, in which field, Lamond asserts, every word Conan Doyle wrote was golden. The Edalji and Slater cases in which Conan Doyle intervened on behalf of unjustly imprisoned men limned the doctor in his most altruistic raiment. Conan Doyle's defense of the British position in the Boer War, and his volunteer hospital work there, Lamond sees not so much as simple patriotism but as a noble conviction for a cause that to Conan Doyle transcended politics. Even as late as World War I, the now-famous and somewhat elderly Sir Arthur organized and drilled with a local militia unit called the Crowborough Reserve. To all these causes, like that of Spiritualism, Conan Doyle was committed, according to Lamond, not because of public sentiment one way or the other, but because Conan Doyle felt they were right.

Arthur Conan Doyle: A Memoir is, of course, a work of blatant hero worship. How much of this is derived from Lamond's genuine admiration for Conan Doyle, independent of Conan Doyle's Spiritualist activities, and how much because of them is difficult to discern. The major defect in this sort of biography, however, is that it tends to perceive each event in the hero's life as equally important. For this reason, a good deal of Conan Doyle's Kiplingesque poetry is quoted at length and more or less placed on a par with Sherlock Holmes, the Nigel Loring novels, and the Brigadier Gerard stories. The resultant critical myopia that affects Lamond's literary analysis presents Conan Doyle as a writer of first-rate serious literature rather than as a popular author whose works were merely meant to entertain.

Observers before me have noted that Lamond's *Memoir* is about half biography and half Spiritualist history. [1] This undoubtedly would have undermined the book as any kind of legitimate biography had it not been for the locomotive force—Conan Doyle's furious physical and intellectual energy—that Lamond sees as driving Conan Doyle through every moment of his life. From his early days as a medical student and ship's physician on an Arctic whaler to his final Crusade as a Spiritualist, Conan Doyle, as Lamond presents him, advances with a deliberate determination. In short, there is so much of this sheer power and energy packed into the book that Lamond's frequent and sometimes lengthy digressions into Spiritualism seem amply supported on the broad shoulders of Conan Doyle's accomplishments.

Moreover, from the purely Spiritualistic point of view, which does inform this book, it is necessary to return constantly to the occult subject matter in order to explain the beliefs that Conan Doyle ultimately adopted as well as why he adopted them. This, I suspect, as much as anything else, influenced Lamond's homogenizing elements of Conan Doyle's life and works in terms of their relative importance, since Lamond understands the spreading of the Spiritualist gospel to have been the work for which Conan Doyle entered the world, and that everything else was, in some sense, only a prelude and preparation for it.

To a modern reading public, which might wish the author of the Sherlock Holmes stories to reflect Holmes' scientific skepticism and logical positivism, virtually any author's account of the last years of Conan Doyle's life is likely to sound mildly absurd. For the man who invented Holmes to believe in ghosts, which Holmes most emphatically does not, is somehow disappointing. Yet for both Sir Arthur and Lady Conan Doyle such a belief was not only in earnest, it was of paramount importance to a world that, because of the increasing dissemination of the Spiritualist movement's message, might well stand at the very brink of a millennium. And because of Lamond's careful examination of Conan Doyle's evolution from agnostic to Spiritualist, Conan Doyle, even at what one might consider his silliest, sounds strangely logical and convincing. His simple question on the subject of the existence of fairies, "is it not time that our vision was extended to include the existence of be-

1. Donald A. Redmond, "A Reader's Guide to Doyle Biographies," *Baker Street Miscellanea*, no. 14 (June 1978): 32.

ings nearer it may be to the heart of Nature than we are ourselves?" is an example.

There is no question about Lamond's book being every bit as much Spiritualist propaganda as it is a biography of Conan Doyle. Yet, I think, both Lamond and Lady Conan Doyle considered these two elements to be well nigh inseparable. And that accounts for Lady Conan Doyle's staunch support for Lamond's project. While *Arthur Conan Doyle: A Memoir* contains no bibliography, it is obvious that Lamond had access to at least some of the Conan Doyle family papers, since a number of sympathetic letters received by Lady Conan Doyle upon Sir Arthur's death are included at her request as an appendix.

In fact, Lady Conan Doyle herself contributed to this book in the form of a fifteen-page "Tribute" to her late husband. That she approved wholeheartedly of Lamond's approach to Sir Arthur's life is evident in her final remark: "I will endeavour to work and fight for the Great Cause for which he gave his life, so long as there is breath in my body. So that when, in God's own time, my call comes to go to that wonderful other world, I can look into my Beloved's dear face, when he meets me at the Gateway of Death, and say, 'I have tried to keep your Banner flying'—and we will part no more."

5 ° A Good-Natured Debunking

Nicholas Utechin

Conan Doyle, His Life and Art
by Hesketh Pearson

Two years after the appearance of *Conan Doyle, His Life and Art* (London: Methuen & Co., 1943) an incensed Adrian Conan Doyle attacked it publicly. "In its portrayal of my father and his opinions, the book is a travesty, and the personal values therein ascribed to him are, in effect, the very antithesis of everything that he represented, believed in and held dear. . . . it is nothing more than a vehicle for a stranger's personal and quite unauthoritative opinions."[1] No biography discussed in this volume has excited so much passion. Hesketh Pearson's view of Sir Arthur Conan Doyle is frankly a problem. The family had held high hopes: for Adrian, and his older brother Denis as well, they were dashed on publication; for Jean (now Dame Jean) Conan Doyle, the book "struck me as being very mediocre as a biography. . . . it was *about* my father, yet the essential person he was seemed to be absent from it."[2] But when a writer of the stature of Graham Greene says: "It is an exciting story admirably told. . . . Mr. Pearson as a biographer has some of the qualities of Dr. Johnson—a plainness, an honesty, a sense of ordinary life going on all the time," then the reader must pause and think twice before giving a verdict. On the other hand, Mr. Greene added a singularly backhanded compliment: "it is one of Mr. Pearson's virtues that he drives us to champion the subject against his biographer."[3]

---

1. *The True Conan Doyle* (London: John Murray, 1945). See chap. 6 for a discussion of this work.

2. Letter from Dame Jean Conan Doyle to Nicholas Utechin, December 2, 1980, extracts of which are published here with her permission.

3. "The Poker Face," in *Collected Essays* (Oxford: Bodley Head, 1969); also excerpted as an introduction to the 1977 reprint of Pearson's biography (London: Macdonald and Janes's; New York: Taplinger).

i

If you stopped ten people in a London street and asked them what they knew of Hesketh Pearson, perhaps two would know the name and one might add that he wrote biographies. He was born in 1887, did not write his first book until he was thirty-four, and died in 1964. He was a man of his time and, for literary purposes, that time was the 1930s and 1940s. George Orwell used the word "hack" when discussing Pearson's book on Oscar Wilde, and when you examine the variety of subjects Pearson chose for biographies, from Tom Paine to Shakespeare, from Shaw to Disraeli, then it is easy to categorize him so. Too easy? And should a man who wrote about popular characters for a popular audience necessarily be castigated?

There is little available to read these days about Pearson: he chose to write his own biography, *Hesketh Pearson by Himself*, and was featured as an integral part of Richard Ingram's *God's Apology—A Chronicle of Three Friends*.[4] His youth was spent near Worcester and in Bedford: nothing out of the ordinary or of especial note here but for his hatred of his early schooling, and parents who seem to have contributed little to his artistic upbringing and are rarely mentioned beyond the earliest pages of his autobiography. On leaving school, it was suggested that he should go into holy orders—there was a tradition of that in the Pearson family—but Hesketh refused. "In those days a fellow who was good for nothing went into commerce. I was good for nothing and I went into commerce," he wrote.[5] At the age of twenty-one he joined his older brother Jack in the latter's Brighton car business with no great enthusiasm, prepared to settle for the sort of job that would provide enough pennies until a proper niche could be found.

Drama was the thing for him, it seemed. There is a story he told about himself that points to both this abiding love of the stage and an awesome self-confidence. In 1909 Pearson wanted to go up to London to see the great Sir Herbert Beerbohm Tree's production of *Hamlet*. Tree (of whom Pearson was later to write a biography) was known to give his interpretation of the Prince some depth and duration onstage, and Pearson knew that he would miss the last train back to Brighton if the play ran at the length the actor-manager insisted on. And so this telegram was sent: "Can you play Hamlet in a business-like manner next Thursday so as to enable me to catch midnight train from Victoria?" This reply

4. London: Andre Deutsch, 1977. The other two friends were Hugh Kingsmill and Malcolm Muggeridge.

5. *Hesketh Pearson by Himself* (London: Heinemann, 1965).

came, an extraordinary gesture on Tree's part: "Cannot alter my conception of the part to fit midnight train but will cut a scene if you run to Victoria." Tree did, and Pearson did.

By the outbreak of war in 1914, Pearson had been an actor for three years. Carburetors and spare tires in Brighton were easily exchanged for small roles in *A Midsummer Night's Dream* and *Julius Caesar*, acting in the Beerbohm Tree company. He had a bad war, earning a Military Cross along the way and returning to England in 1919. Pearson wrote his first book shortly afterward: it was called *Men and Mummers* and made little impact. Of much more moment was his meeting at about this time the writer and critic Hugh Kingsmill, who was to be a lifelong friend and source of inspiration. "There was something of Holmes and Watson in their mutual attraction," wrote Richard Ingrams: "Kingsmill was unworldly, intuitive and essentially mystical in outlook. He was superstitious, interested in dreams, and given to periodic fasting. Pearson was practical and straightforward. . . . He had no interest whatever in theoretical matters."

Nearly ten years were to pass before Pearson found his literary niche: he effectively cornered the market in short, popular biographies. *Doctor Darwin*, a life of Erasmus Darwin, appeared in 1929, and over the years he followed with biographies betraying an unusual range of interests: Gilbert and Sullivan, Sir Walter Scott, Charles Dickens, King Charles II, and others—and, in 1943, Sir Arthur Conan Doyle. "Having expressed myself on two heroes of my manhood, Shakespeare and Shaw, I felt like doing the same for a hero of my youth," Pearson recalled later in his autobiography. Ever since he was fourteen years old he had loved Sherlock Holmes, "who for me was a real figure, not a figment of the fancy." It was Conan Doyle the boyhood hero—the man who wrote those marvelous stories—rather than Conan Doyle the human being that made him embark on the biography. The author himself, whom he met once at a luncheon in London, was "hardly a subject of great moment, nor particularly interesting" to Pearson.

But having decided on the project, he proceeded to research his subject by turning to family archives. He thanks Denis and Adrian Conan Doyle in his acknowledgments for having given him access to their father's private papers[6] and permission to quote from both published and unpublished writings; and he either met or corresponded

6. Hesketh Pearson saw only a part of the family papers. At the time that he was researching his book, Adrian Conan Doyle had just moved out of the Conan Doyles' long-time residence at Crowborough, Sussex, to the family's Bignell Wood holiday house in the New Forest, and there was insufficient time to sort out all the papers for Pearson's inspection.

with a large number of relevant people—A. E. W. Mason, Ronald Knox, W. W. Jacobs, Reginald Pound, and Eille Norwood among them. But there were signs that Pearson foresaw trouble: in thanking the two sons, he wrote that they had helped him "with a courtesy to myself and a loyal enthusiasm for my subject which deserve a more whole-hearted agreement with their views and a more generous allowance for their sentiments than will be apparent in my work." And if Denis and Adrian themselves had read an earlier published remark by Pearson, that "No artist worth his salt is concerned with accuracy in detail if it doesn't suit his purpose. . . . In order to achieve essential truth one often has to sacrifice the essential facts,"[7] then they might have wondered what the final product would look like.

That last quotation really is an extraordinary one from a biographer. It should immediately cast doubt upon the authenticity of any description, the veracity of any statement, and the reliability of any judgment. It automatically devalues the currency of "biography."

ii

"Conan Doyle," writes Pearson in the first chapter, "was Irish by descent, Scottish by birth and English by adoption. Being of a plastic nature, all three nations helped to mould his character, which included the chivalry and enthusiasm of the first, the pride and perseverance of the second, the stubbornness and humour of the third." It is all a little glib, and but nine pages are given to Conan Doyle's early life before his arrival at Edinburgh University. Scant mention is made of the stern Jesuit schooling at Stonyhurst, and not nearly enough of Arthur's mother, "The Ma'am," and her lifelong influence. Pearson seems in too much of a hurry to reach the university years and so to introduce his readers to a character who he has decided played the fundamental role in Conan Doyle's literary career, George Budd.

"Budd is the energy of Holmes, the braggadocio of Gerard, the malignity of Moriarty, the violence of Roylott, the fanaticism of Maracot. . . . The description of Challenger's personality is a description of Budd's," according to Pearson. Budd was both a fellow student and later a professional colleague of Conan Doyle's, and while he puts in a vivid appearance in *The Stark Munro Letters* under the guise of one Cullingworth and played the major part in a rollicking interlude for the youthful Conan Doyle, he does not rate the thirty-odd pages granted him by Pearson. Further, most of the chapter entitled "Doctor Budd" is in conversa-

7. *Ventilations* (Philadelphia: Lippincott, 1930).

tional form, as the traumas of the Conan Doyle/Budd relationship are played out in Bristol and Plymouth. While it all makes jolly novella reading, such an approach has little part to play in a biography, however much it is aimed at the popular audience. And the use of this imagined dialogue fails to accomplish even its first purpose—a literary and artistic device to make the reader better understand the character who purports to speak the words. Pearson here did no more than skim Conan Doyle's own recollections of these years, as described in *The Stark Munro Letters* and in his autobiography; if Pearson believed the Budd episode to be so important, one wonders why there is no more of his own comment.

Inevitably the early pages are a preamble to the major portion of the book: Pearson's view of the literary Conan Doyle and the corpus of his output. With hindsight one can suggest that the dislike for Pearson's biography expressed by members of the Conan Doyle family springs from three founts: the criticism of those very works for which Sir Arthur himself wished to be remembered, the discussion of Conan Doyle as "the man in the street," and the interpretation of Conan Doyle's Spiritualist beliefs. To these latter two points I shall return. It is with the publication of *Micah Clarke*, Conan Doyle's first historical novel in 1889, that Hesketh Pearson fires off the critical salvo, amplified in later discussions of the historical fiction. Pearson quotes Micah Clarke himself—"I am fairly tied to the chariot-wheels of history now"—a line that provides the biographer with a neat starting point for his theme: "Doyle's trouble whenever he set out to reproduce a period. To the end of his life it never occurred to him that the accumulation of detail, however accurate or picturesque, does not vivify an age, but nullifies it." This is a perfectly valid critical approach to Conan Doyle's often painstaking immersion in historical detail, which he usually conveys to the reader; and it is a theme to which Pearson returns again and again:

The Doings of Raffles Haw (1892): "The feeblest [tale] he ever wrote. . . . one suspects that Doyle chose the theme [transmuting other metals to gold] in order to display his knowledge of chemistry."

The Refugees (1893): "Of course Doyle's book suffers from his unshakeable conviction that in order to recreate [*sic*] a period one has to introduce a number of prominent people who lived in it, and so the romance halts while all the leading figures of the time parade before us."

Rodney Stone (1896): "as usual the historical personages are not an integral part of the story. . . . [He] provides us with a sort of *Who's Who* in the sporting and social world of the Regency."

And so on.

It may be that this criticism did not stem from Pearson alone. His friend Hugh Kingsmill had said much the same thing some years earlier, as reported in their joint book *Skye High*, published (by Oxford University Press) in 1938. As they retraced the journey of Dr. Johnson and James Boswell to the Hebrides, Pearson and Kingsmill indulged in literary conversation and anecdote, including this fragment from Kingsmill: "The trouble with the book [*The White Company*] is that Conan Doyle thought he could make the Middle Ages real to the reader by a panorama of characteristically medieval customs. None of the persons in the book can stir a step without bumping into material out of Conan Doyle's notebooks." Pearson himself is not entirely unkind to the historical novels of Conan Doyle; he is happy about the writer's heroic treatment of action scenes and makes the fair comment that Conan Doyle's work in this area is a good reflection of writing for a popular audience that in the stuffy and business-oriented Victorian age wanted to turn back to chivalrous and gallant times.

That audience also came to love Sherlock Holmes, as Pearson himself did. In rather superior fashion he claims that "any coal-heaver, docker, charwoman, or publican would recognize what was meant on hearing someone described as . . . Sherlock Holmes. . . . he is a tracker, a hunter-down, a combination of bloodhound, pointer and bull-dog, who runs people down to earth as the foxhound does a fox; in fact a sleuth. He is the modern Galahad, no longer in quest of the Holy Grail, but hot on the scent of the bloody trail, a figure from folklore with the lineaments of real life." And then this accurate and perceptive comment: "The curious thing about him is that, while not a four-square creation like all the greatest characters in literature, it is impossible not to believe in his existence. Wholly lacking the mystery and suggestiveness of a great portrait, he is as vivid as a snapshot."

Given his regard for the Holmes stories, Pearson is impressively restrained in his discussion of them. A brief nod is given in the direction of Poe's creation, the Chevalier Dupin, as a major influence; and there is, quite correctly (remembering that this was the first proper biography of Sir Arthur Conan Doyle to be written), the telling of the now-classic story of Dr. Joseph Bell diagnosing a man to be a recently discharged noncommissioned officer from a Highland regiment that had been stationed in Barbados. Interesting mention is made of further literary origins for the Great Detective—episodes in Voltaire's *Zadig* and Dumas' *Louise de la Vallière*. Nevertheless, "Doyle was the first writer to give vitality and personality to a detective," Pearson concludes, "and will probably be the last writer to produce short stories that are as thrilling and entertaining as the chief characters are vivid."

Reference to Joseph Bell leads to mention of Pearson's view of the originals whom Conan Doyle used for the characters of Holmes and Watson. The reader is not asked to accept Conan Doyle as Sherlock Holmes (as others, with an eye to the Edalji and Slater cases, have tried to put across), but Pearson is tempted to make something of the "Conan Doyle is Watson" angle: it is "unnecessary for us to look further for a model. He frequently and unconsciously pictured himself in the character." Here there was controversy, with Adrian Conan Doyle publicly attacking the idea after the biography was published. The son would have preferred an identification with Sherlock Holmes for his father: the quotations adduced by Pearson from the Holmesian canon to support the Watson theory are, however, impressive.

When Pearson moves on to discuss the Brigadier Gerard stories, he sums up in one brief paragraph what it is that makes them eternally popular. "Every scene is superbly executed, every character is brilliantly etched, and every episode is heightened by a humour that ranges from satire to burlesque. . . . The odd thing is that the absurdity of the leading character never lessens the excitement of the narrative: the humour gives reality to the romance. Doyle never wrote anything else as good as these tales, which welled so spontaneously out of him that their gaiety and enthusiasm infect the reader." And, returning to the familiar theme, Pearson comments approvingly on the naturalism of the Brigadier Gerard stories as compared with the weightier historical novels. (The Professor Challenger stories he regards less enthusiastically, stating that they stem from "a pronounced streak of morbidity in [Conan Doyle's] nature, due to an excess of fancy and an undeveloped imagination.")

Much of the rest of the biography is taken up with the writer's concept of Conan Doyle as "the man in the street" and his view of that all-dominating interest in Spiritualism in the final decades of Conan Doyle's life. It is the former that was perhaps the most important cause of Adrian Conan Doyle's outburst, and years later Dame Jean Conan Doyle had no hesitation in writing that "I think HP overdid his 'average man' angle on my father, who had a great respect for the British 'man in the street' and his innate decency, and shared many of his views, but was in fact a very *rare* person."[8] Pearson took this as one of his basic themes, perhaps prompted to do so by his friend Hugh Kingsmill (Ingrams suggests this). Conan Doyle, Pearson writes, "could not help giving the man in the street what he wanted because he himself was the man in the street; indeed, so exactly did he represent the normal man that one might call him Everyman in the street. But the normal man is not the healthy innocent our newspapers would like us to think him. He is a mixture of strange desires, domestic sentiment, cruelty, kindness, and morbidity," etc.

It is an interesting thesis, and once adopted by Pearson as a key to

8. Letter from Dame Jean Conan Doyle to Nicholas Utechin, December 2, 1980.

the life he was describing, one that he had to cling to. Rarely does a fiction writer of any quality deal in emotions and thoughts of which he has no experience: an unknown place, an unknown time, perhaps—surely not unknown feelings. Of course Conan Doyle put much of himself and his attitudes into his books: and in the bluff, honest comradeship of Watson, Gerard's search for glory, and Sir Nigel Loring's unbending spirit, we undoubtedly have an amalgam of the aims and desires of Conan Doyle's readers. But Conan Doyle was a craftsman: he constructed a good story and earned money by it, and it is simply too facile to suggest that he was Everyman. Surely this is belied by his extraordinary variety of interests, breadth of view, and, above all, record of actual achievement.

Pearson begins his final chapter, entitled "The Last Phase," with another of those sentences that make one question his whole justification for being a biographer: "The biographer is concerned with this world, not the next, so there is no need for me to deal with Doyle's conversion to spiritualism except in so far as it was the inescapable outcome of his nature; for a man's beliefs are important to his biographer only as a revelation of himself." To gloss in such a way is amazing cowardice; even today, for many people, Conan Doyle's crusade on behalf of Spiritualism clouds their entire view of him, and Conan Doyle's motives cry out to be explored. Pearson naturally manufactures a way out for himself: he essays a tortuous argument that Conan Doyle's move to Spiritualism was a logical result of his "ordinariness." Conan Doyle was a materialist—he enjoyed the things of this life—he could not believe that they would not continue with him into the next—Spiritualism thus came naturally: that is Pearson's drift. And then this hypothesis: "it could easily be shown that the most materialistic people are those who are so much in love with themselves, their power, their pleasure or their comfort in this world that they believe devoutly in a continuation of these blessings elsewhere; whereas the spiritual people are those who, having gladly sacrificed the material advantages of this life for its immaterial beauties, are not interested in the persistence of personality and face extinction without a qualm. It is usually the earthbound egotist who longs to be immortal." Surely there is more of Hesketh Pearson here than Arthur Conan Doyle?

iii

Ultimately, *Conan Doyle, His Life and Art* remains an unsatisfactory biography. It is too quirky to give the reader the satisfied feeling that he knows the man whose life has been described. As indicated, there are examples of dangerous incompetence of approach in the book, and this must give rise to some worry in the reader's mind about the credibility of some of Pearson's judgments. His handling of the literary side is certainly more confident than his approach to the more narrowly biographical problems; and one must not for a moment belittle the fact that it was Pearson who decided to fill the vacuum that existed until 1943, that there was no proper biography of Conan Doyle in existence. It has to be said that the biographer in this instance is not altogether complimentary to his subject—the attack on him in the closing pages dealing with Spiritualism is almost offensive—and one can quite see the import of Graham Greene's comment, that in the last analysis one champions Conan Doyle against Pearson. Conan Doyle obviously deserved more than the less than two hundred pages here given to him; he has had worthier biographies—notably the John Dickson Carr classic—and he has suffered at some less impressive hands. Pearson's book is readable and gives some of the facts. But in the end it is hollow.

6 ∘ The Family's Counterattack

James Bliss Austin

The True Conan Doyle
by Adrian Conan Doyle [1]

Adrian Conan Doyle, Sir Arthur's third son, who was born in 1910, was by his own admission a high-spirited and mischievous child. His education was spotty because he traveled a great deal with his family in the 1920s; yet this had its compensations, because his almost daily contact with his father led to an unusually close relationship between them. After Lady Conan Doyle died in 1940, Adrian joined his brother Denis as a co-executor of their father's estate, and Adrian took this responsibility more seriously than might have been expected. He considered himself the guardian of his father's literary reputation and maintained stoutly that it was his father, not Dr. Joseph Bell, who had been the model for Sherlock Holmes. He was very critical of the views and activities of Sherlockian enthusiasts, especially the Baker Street Irregulars whose dogma that his father had been merely a literary agent for Dr. Watson was anathema to him.

That Adrian could be difficult, even disagreeable, was undeniable. The bombastic style that he used on many occasions is well illustrated by the following excerpt from a letter that I received from him at the time that the manuscript of *The Valley of Fear* was broken up to be sold as separate chapters: "What a foul and hideous act of vandalism to have broken up that MS. The dealers responsible for the breaking up should be shunned by every litterateur and, if I can discover their names, I shall see that their money-grabbing vandalism receives the publicity it deserves."

Yet in my own limited contacts with Adrian he was always pleasant. He never failed to answer a sincere question about his father's work, and

1. London: John Murray, 1945; and New York: Coward-McCann, 1946.

he offered many helpful suggestions. Judging from the evident sincerity of the acknowledgments that John Dickson Carr and Pierre Nordon wrote for their biographies of Sir Arthur Conan Doyle, they clearly enjoyed the same kind of cooperation. Hesketh Pearson, who also wrote a biography of Sir Arthur, likewise acknowledged, if somewhat grudgingly, the help he had received from Denis and Adrian in the preparation of his book, though he warned that his evaluations might differ from theirs. But in a letter dated January 29, 1942, Adrian wrote to Pearson that "I know that you will write this book as you yourself see the facts, unswayed by any but your own powers of perception and reason, and I neither expect nor desire anything more fair than that."[2]

But Hesketh Pearson's forebodings were all too well founded, for when *Conan Doyle, His Life and Art* was published in 1943, the Conan Doyle brothers took great umbrage; and Adrian, now thirty-three years old, wrote a rebuttal that was published in 1945 as *The True Conan Doyle*. In it he came directly to the point:

> During the past year, I have been distressed by the number of letters that have reached me from both acquaintances and strangers in protest against an alleged "biography" of my father by a Mr. Hesketh Pearson. As the majority of my correspondents were, naturally, under the impression that the manuscript was submitted to me before publication, I must assure them that this was not the case. In its portrayal of my father and his opinions, the book is a travesty, and the personal values therein ascribed to him are, in effect, the very antithesis of everything he represented, believed in and held dear. Therefore, I will content myself with the statement that, firstly, Mr. Pearson did not even know my father; secondly, that his manuscript was submitted to no member of the family, and thirdly, that it is nothing more than a vehicle for a stranger's personal and quite unauthoritative opinions, and is but another example of the practice that Mr. Isaac Foot has aptly termed "Belittling famous men and disparaging the fathers that begat us." As for the literary aspect, Sir Arthur's seventy-odd books should manage to survive the drone of Mr. Pearson's wearisomely condescending criticism.

Although Adrian contemptuously dismissed Pearson's criticisms, he himself made no attempt at serious criticism of his father's works. In fact, he makes almost no mention of any specific work of Sir Arthur's. Perhaps he took it for granted that Conan Doyle's place as a writer had already been

2. Cited by Jon L. Lellenberg in "Nova 57 Minor: The Waxing and Waning of the Sixty-First Adventure of Sherlock Holmes," *Baker Street Miscellanea*, no. 43 (Autumn 1985).

established beyond question. Pearson was also taken to task for writing about Conan Doyle when he did not know him—to which one might reply that neither did John Dickson Carr nor Pierre Nordon, Adrian's favorite biographers of his father. And carrying this idea to its illogical conclusion, no one should write a biography unless he knew the subject personally.

Yet it cannot be denied that personal knowledge does impart a special flavor, as Adrian's essay demonstrates. Having put Pearson in his place, Adrian gave a brief description of Sir Arthur's ancestry and family background. This account, though a useful supplement to his father's autobiography, *Memories and Adventures*, contains little that is not found elsewhere. Adrian also wrote that it was his intention to devote most of his essay to "intimate glimpses of Conan Doyle in that most natural of all settings, the family hearth." It was such glimpses that Adrian found lacking in Pearson's book, so he adopted an essentially impressionistic approach based on personal recollections, making virtually no use of the family archives.

In Adrian's account of Sir Arthur's childhood, one is struck by the absence of any mention of his father, Charles Doyle. There were several possible explanations for this omission, but it did suggest that Charles Doyle contributed little to the molding of his son's character and that it was his mother who was his mentor in his formative years. Certainly she was a major influence in his later life. She was a remarkable and indomitable lady, an expert in heraldry, obsessed with the traditions of chivalry and, as she had lived in France for some time, possessed of a bias toward things French. Adrian reported that he had it directly from Sir Arthur that his mental surroundings during his childhood were entirely medieval: he lived among the chivalric ways of the fifteenth century, in the bosom of a family to whom pride of lineage was of vastly greater importance than their comparative poverty. Adrian also noted that the boyhood and rearing of young Sir Nigel in Conan Doyle's book of that name was a good approximation to his father's own upbringing.

In another intimate glimpse, Adrian revealed that there was a division in his father's character that was more marked in private than in his public life, as illustrated by the following: "There was a breadth of mind in the man who could convey to his son's consciousness that in case of sexual illness he could rely absolutely on the parental comprehension and assistance. *Au contraire*, there was a narrow-mindedness in the man who revolted violently to the mildest risque observation. In a different measure the same may be said about his reaction to the most harmless liberty taken by a well-meaning stranger. Indeed, there were few things that could stir Conan Doyle more swiftly to a roar of Celtic rage than the clap on the back or the uninvited use of his Christian name." Adrian's brief coverage of Sir Arthur's involvement in public life contains little that is not found elsewhere. He did, however, observe that though his father was a patriot, he was an internationalist rather than a nationalist.

Toward the end of the essay, Adrian brought up the matter that had troubled him so greatly. The Pearson biography carried on its title page a quotation from Sir Arthur: "I am the man in the street." And there was a chapter headed "The Man in the Street." Just what Pearson was trying to do in using this phrase is unclear, but whatever it may have been, it was unwise because Conan Doyle, though possessing enormous empathy for the man in the street, could certainly not be classed as one. No "man in the street" could have done what he did for Edalji or Slater. No "man in the street" could have done the things he did in the Boer War and World War I. Above all, no "man in the street" could have created Sherlock Holmes.

But Adrian quickly set the record straight by relating the origin of the phrase, as given in his father's book *The Wanderings of a Spiritualist*. The occasion was a luncheon given in Sir Arthur's honor by the British Empire League in Australia, and what Conan Doyle wrote was: "I pulled the leg of my audience with some success, for I wound up by saying very solemnly that I was something greater than Governments and the Master of Cabinet Ministers. By the time I had finished my tremendous claims I am convinced that they expected some extravagant occult pretension, whereas I actually wound up with the words 'For I am the man in the street.' There was a great deal of amusement caused." As Adrian pointed out, his father had carefully recorded as a deliberate joke the only occasion in his life when he was known to have used the phrase. And he added, quite understandably, that it was inexcusable for a stranger to quote as a serious self-evaluation a remark that was plainly no more than a humorous pleasantry.

When *The True Conan Doyle* was published, it was not well received. The reviews ranged from cool to caustic, and my own opinion of it was not very high, so I was not surprised when it soon began to appear on the remainder tables. (My copy of the American edition has "2 for 1.00" written on the dust jacket.) But on reading it again forty years later, in an atmosphere free of the recriminations of 1946, I realize that it was not entirely devoid of merit, since some of the intimate glimpses were certainly worth having on the record. But I thought then, and I still believe, that as a response to Pearson's treatment of Sir Arthur, it was ineffective except, possibly, for the issue of "the man in the street," which is the only significant biographical question that Adrian addressed—though this he did only to refute Pearson by quoting from one of his father's books.

Those familiar with Conan Doyle's autobiography, *Memories and Adventures*, and with the subsequent biographies by Carr and Nordon, will find that Adrian's contributes little that is new about Sir Arthur. Indeed, in many ways he revealed more about himself than about his father. And one can detect early signs of some of the eccentricities that he displayed in later life.

In summary, *The True Conan Doyle* is a book that one can read once with some pleasure and profit, but it is hardly a candidate for a shelf of reference volumes. Rather it is an interesting and somewhat elusive item for the collector.

ii
Sir Arthur Conan Doyle Centenary,
1859–1959

The True Conan Doyle was not, however, Adrian's only contribution to our knowledge of his father's life. In 1959, the hundredth anniversary of his father's birth, he edited a commemorative volume with the title *Sir Arthur Conan Doyle Centenary, 1859–1959* (London: John Murray, 1959; New York: Doubleday, n.d.). In a brief preface Adrian gave a checklist of his father's accomplishments: "To those who really knew the life of this strangely gifted man, the creation of Holmes is far overshadowed by that long list of lesser known but nobler accomplishments by which he served his country. Let me name but a few that spring to mind." Most of these eighteen items were self-explanatory, but there were several, including his warning about Koch's consumption cure and the reply to Bernhardi, a name that Adrian misspelled, that will cause some readers to seek further details either from *Memories and Adventures* or from the Carr and Nordon biographies. In a moment of rare objectivity, Adrian appended to his list the admission that his father had two faults. One was that his modesty was such that he would go to almost any length to give credit to another when it was due solely to himself. Adrian deemed this a fault because he thought it was unfair to posterity. The other was that his father's sense of chivalry went so far as to reach puritanism.

Following Adrian's brief statement, there is a biographical essay of seventeen pages by Pierre Nordon (which is discussed elsewhere in this volume). At its end there is the following note, obviously added by Adrian: "With the exception of Mr. John Dickson Carr, Sir Arthur's Biographer, the author of this article alone had access to the immense Conan Doyle Archives." This is demonstrably false, since Hesketh Pearson reported looking through Conan Doyle's papers.

The rest of the volume has no formal text but contains a wealth of fascinating items assembled by Adrian: photographs, reproductions of paintings, drawings and newspaper clippings, along with quotations from the great and near great. The first item is a special delight—a family tree displaying the lineage of both of Sir Arthur's parents. Regrettably, it does not show how he and his sister Annette acquired the name Conan Doyle, whereas his brother Innes and his other sisters remained simply Doyle. Moreover, it has one serious error in that the name of Sir Arthur's second wife, and Adrian's mother, is given as Jane, instead of Jean, Leckie. There are many pages of illustrations related to Sir Arthur's grandfather, John Doyle, and to his distinguished uncles, James, Henry, and Richard, and this time Adrian included Conan Doyle's own artist father, Charles Doyle.

The rest of the book is a kind of photograph album-cum-scrapbook covering virtually all of Sir Arthur's life. There are sections related to his experiences in the Boer War and World War I, and to the histories he wrote of them. The Edalji and Slater cases are well covered, and there is, of course, a section on Sherlock Holmes. This last contains a photograph of Major Alfred Wood, Sir Arthur's secretary, who was, according to Adrian, the prototype for Dr. Watson. Since Nordon in his article had listed a number of clues to what he termed Conan Doyle's "semi-serious" wish to be identified as Holmes, Adrian adduced illustrations of a number of examples, such as a copy of Sir Arthur's notes on the Cornish language (corresponding to Holmes' study of its possible Chaldean roots in "The Adventure of the Devil's Foot"). Finally, there are many photographs of the first editions of his works that would be of interest to collectors.

Though Adrian, in writing *The True Conan Doyle*, made little use of the family archives, he drew heavily on them for the *Centenary* album, not in a scholarly sense, to be sure, but to provide a pictorial history of his father's family, his life, and his times. It is not a book for concentrated reading but rather a tabloid through which one can browse for one's edification for many pleasant and instructive hours.

7 ° THE IDEAL STORYBOOK HERO

Howard Lachtman

The Life of Sir Arthur Conan Doyle
by John Dickson Carr

Although Sir Arthur Conan Doyle was a storyteller of remark- ably broad interests, he is best remembered today as the creator of Sherlock Holmes. John Dickson Carr, the master of the locked-room murder mystery and of the swashbuckling historical melodrama, is equally well remembered as the creator of Sir Arthur Conan Doyle—not the real Conan Doyle, perhaps, but an ideal one whom many readers have preferred to believe was a storybook character in his own right, a man as heroic as Holmes and as lovable as Watson.

That was the Conan Doyle who emerged from the pages of Carr's *The Life of Sir Arthur Conan Doyle*. The first biography of Conan Doyle that most readers encounter, often in their formative years as a result of reading the Sherlock Holmes stories and wanting to know something about their creator, it has been read far more widely than any other biography of Conan Doyle.[1] Over the years since its first publication it has had the strongest influence in creating a portrait of a man whom Robert Louis Stevenson called "Doyle of the white plume."

That happened partly because Adrian Conan Doyle demanded (and got) a monument to his father in exchange for allowing Carr the privi- lege of using the family archives, and partly because the awe-inspiring figure of the valiant Victorian knight, at war with the forces of injustice, best suited Carr's own taste in biographical portraiture. It is doubtful that Carr would have presented a less flattering biography even without Adrian's direction; and though the benefit of using the archives may have

1. Published simultaneously in England and America (London: John Murray, 1949, New York: Harper and Brothers, 1949, widely available in paperback as well in both countries; it was last reissued in 1975 (by Vintage Books, in the United States) during the Sherlock Holmes boom of that decade. It has also been translated into Swedish, Spanish, and French.

been outweighed by Adrian's fixed conception of his father, Carr's biography went on to win a wide audience and popular success.

Primarily this has been due not so much to Carr's merits as a biographer but rather to his skills as a storyteller. Whatever the flaws of Carr's biography, narrative ability is not one of them. The panorama of Conan Doyle's career as young physician, author, sportsman, patriot, and militant crusader for unpopular causes unfolds with a dazzling dexterity. The life reads so briskly, colorfully, and knowingly, and is rounded off with so simple and moving an elegaic epilogue, that readers who go on in search of a better biography are frequently disappointed. After three and a half decades it remains the standard work in the field.

Standard, one might add, but far from acceptable to some critics, who have complained that a sense of proportion and a quality of realism are missing from Carr's portrait. "But what are the shades in the picture," as Hesketh Pearson asked of Carr's book, "the faults and short-comings that would help us accept the virtues and save us from the despair of witnessing perfection in another man? Alas, they are but virtues in disguise."[2]

i

"It would be a miracle if a professional biographer's opinion were an echo of a son's opinion," Pearson had complained to a hotly critical Adrian Conan Doyle, when the latter decided that Pearson (who had not submitted his manuscript in advance) had done his father a biographical injustice.[3] Pearson's work had sent an initially well disposed and cooperative Adrian into a complete turnabout of mood. Convinced that he had been betrayed by a professional biographer whom he had trusted, Adrian repudiated Pearson's biography with cries of "fake" and "travesty" and penned a rebuttal in *The True Conan Doyle*. Soon afterward, Adrian read with rage advertisements placed in the London press by John Dickson Carr, soliciting material in anticipation of a biography about which Carr had not consulted the Conan Doyle family. A success-

2. Hesketh Pearson reviewing the Carr biography in the *Listener*, quoted in Michael Holroyd, "Hesketh Pearson: Biography with Warts," *Confrontation* (Fall 1977/Winter 1978), p. 24.

3. Letter from Hesketh Pearson to Adrian Conan Doyle, March 6, 1944. The letter was actually drafted by George Bernard Shaw, a friend and previous biographical subject of Pearson's. Rejecting Pearson's view, Adrian wrote in *The True Conan Doyle*: "Before putting a few facts on record, I would address myself to any reader who may suffer from the delusion that a son's outlook on his parent is naturally biased. It has been my experience in life that the very opposite is more often true."

ful mystery novelist in his early forties, Carr had decided to try his hand at a life of Arthur Conan Doyle, one of his two favorite authors (the other being G. K. Chesterton, on whom Carr had modeled his principal detective character, Dr. Gideon Fell).

At first Adrian invoked the ghastly specter of British law to chase away the newest biographical interloper. And then something changed his mind. We know not what it was, possibly only a personal meeting with Carr and an agreement on both sides to have a close working relationship with a favorable royalty to the estate. But it is likely that Adrian recognized a kindred spirit in John Dickson Carr, who was deeply conservative and fascinated by romantic notions of the past. "Carr," wrote one of his editors after his death, "probably never should have lived in the 20th century. All his instincts were for a less scientific world, a less mechanized one, a more romantic one. . . . he would have been happier in the 18th century, with sword play and sudden personal dramas, with costumes and carriages, and beaus and belles, with long talks over mugs of wine near the fireplace, and if any crimes had been committed, they were fashionably done, with eclat, and solved by witty, elegant experts, not plodding patrolmen."[4] The same was true of Adrian Conan Doyle, who much preferred his own romanticized notions of the past to the realities of the present: courtly, impetuous, quick to wrath, exaggeratedly proud of his lineage, intensely touchy about his father's reputation, prone to litigation as a poor substitute for duels—expelled once from Hyde Park for medieval jousting without a permit—Adrian spent his last fifteen years in a fourteenth-century Swiss chateau, a setting greatly to his taste despite its lack of some twentieth-century amenities.

But whatever the cause of their collaboration, Adrian was soon happy again, convinced that Carr, the American expatriate whom British readers accepted and whom many American readers mistook for a true Briton, was the very man for the task of convincing the world that the Irish-descended, Edinburgh-born, Jesuit-educated Arthur Conan Doyle was the very model of a modern major Englishman.[5]

4. Joan Kahn, introduction to *The Three Coffins* by John Dickson Carr (New York: Harper and Row, 1979), p. vi.

5. Adrian Conan Doyle and John Dickson Carr would soon come to another understanding—this time about perpetuating the exploits of Arthur Conan Doyle's famous detective, though their second common venture was destined to be a far more ephemeral literary enterprise than the biography in which both men sensed the prospect of glory. For Carr, it was the beginning of an incredibly productive Sherlockian phase that would see him co-author Sherlock Holmes short stories with Adrian (*The Exploits of Sherlock Holmes*, Random House, 1954), write several Sherlock Holmes parodies of his own and a novel filled with Holmesian clues (*The 9 Wrong Answers*, Harper, 1952), not to mention articles, essays, and the editing of Sir Arthur's best short fiction (*Great Stories by Conan*

To appreciate the myth by which Adrian lived is to understand the loyalty to it that he required from John Dickson Carr, the "authorized biographer." Adrian approved and appointed Carr for the purpose of fleshing out the idealistic image of Sir Arthur that Adrian had already sketched in his filial tribute, *The True Conan Doyle*, and to give it the widest possible reading audience. To have a novelist of Carr's standing enshrine the myth in a full-scale biography was the best way of confirming its authenticity. Carr, who had taken up residence in England with his English wife two years after Sir Arthur's death, had acquired a sufficiently English point of view and habit of phrase; all he needed was to be coached by Adrian on what it was like to have been a child of a great man. "The years which I spent under my father's roof have left something far more vital than a mere memory," as Adrian remarked elsewhere: "They have left a glow that will last until the end of my days. The whole essence of the man was noble and strong and selfless. Was not this man something larger than the creator of Sherlock Holmes? I spent my young manhood with him, face to face with his virtues and his faults, and thus learned the true meaning of three words—an English gentleman." [6]

An English gentleman. Those three words sum up Adrian's wish to emulate his father and the wish of American expatriate biographer John Dickson Carr to be accepted by his readers as an Englishman presenting an English point of view about an English hero. By grasping this central fact of Adrian's life and Carr's biography, we come a long way toward understanding why *The Life of Sir Arthur Conan Doyle* had to be on the grand scale, and why it was that the biographer reserved his greatest thanks for Adrian, "who for two years assisted me in a task which I could not have accomplished without his help." We do not know the details of their working relationship, since neither man left a memoir of it, but there seems no reason to doubt that Adrian read the working manuscript, discussed it with Carr, and possibly even corrected it before he allowed Carr to send it off to the publisher.

Certainly, without Adrian's "help," he would not have had access to the family archives. How important a resource that was, Carr indicates in one of his book's most valuable features, its eleven-page appen-

---

Doyle, John Murray, 1959). No wonder Carr later admitted that the high point of his life was the experience of working with the Conan Doyle family and having the opportunity to explore volumes of Sir Arthur's personal material. (See Larry D. French, "The Baker Street-Carrian Connection: The Influence of Sherlock Holmes on John Dickson Carr," *Baker Street Journal*, March 1979, 6–10.) Valuable in itself, the Conan Doyle biography project also seems to have invigorated Carr's career.

6. Adrian Conan Doyle, introduction to *Sir Arthur Conan Doyle Centenary, 1859–1959* (London: John Murray, 1959).

dix describing the Conan Doyle "Biographical Archives": an immense treasure-trove containing genealogical materials and correspondence among the author's forebears, his letters to his mother and hers to him, correspondence with his brother and sisters, "more than fifty notebooks and common-place books," some sixty scrapbooks covering his literary, athletic, public, and political activities, voluminous memorabilia and correspondence relating to those activities, nearly thirty-five "envelopes" and letter boxes of miscellaneous correspondence and mementos, and much more. Obviously the Conan Doyle archives are of tremendous value to scholars of the author's life, career, and works; merely listing them lent Carr's biography a powerful sense of credibility that critics can find difficult to refute.

The price of this assistance was a life of Sir Arthur as formulated and approved by Adrian. But not only did Carr echo the opinion of his subject's son, despite Hesketh Pearson's caveat, he gave it an articulate and entertaining new voice. The biography flowed readily from Carr's conservatism and romanticism and was written as much out of his own personal conviction as from the necessity of complying with Adrian's demands. Carr's fundamental sympathy with Adrian's idealized Sir Arthur may have stemmed in part also from a recognition that the son's tribute was also a son's way of coming to terms with his own imperfections (Carr himself had a Victorian father in whose eyes the mystery-writing son fell rather short of expectations). And in portraying Arthur Conan Doyle— who was *not* English, neither in blood nor birthplace nor upbringing nor personality—as "an English gentleman," both Adrian and Carr may have hoped to acquire that distinction for themselves as well, in the eyes of others.

ii

"In theory, at least," Carr wrote in his *Life*, "the biographer should be as relentless as Gradgrind." Carr's biography was a hit on both sides of the Atlantic, but its success was not due to the dogged devotion to facts that Adrian forever claimed for it.[7] Casual rather than methodical in his

7. Prior to its publication, for example, in an August 7, 1948, letter to the *Saturday Review of Literature*, Adrian Conan Doyle wrote: "the first genuine biography of my father, written by Mr. John Dickson Carr, is to be published at the end of this year simultaneously throughout the whole world. For the first time the real facts . . . will be given to the public based upon Dickson Carr's minute investigations among my father's private papers, none of which had ever previously been examined. This great biography, containing nothing but substantiated facts, will, I believe, be the standard reference work on my father for all time to come."

research, relentless in his romanticism, and eager to honor "the man who was Sherlock Holmes," Carr was the kind of biographer who could not help but equip his Gradgrind with a swordstick, a velvet cape, and a charger. The result was a conspicuously theatrical biography that attempted to stage-manage the entire Conan Doyle clan into the cast of an adventurous romance. Carr was fully aware of the risks he ran with this approach, and at the outset he was cautious enough to try and protect himself against critical charges of dramatizing and exaggerating. "This is a story of adventure, sometimes even melodrama," he conceded in the foreword to *The Life of Sir Arthur Conan Doyle*: "To paint in dull colours, to check the gallop, would be to misrepresent the man himself. But do not let readers imagine that this is a novelized biography. The facts can't be helped. Things happened like that."

But in his desire to avoid being labeled a member of the Irving Stone School of Biography, Carr chose to ignore a fundamental fact of the genre to which he had come with a novelist's zeal. Biography is not life, after all, but rather an approximation, an imitation of life. Biography, we might say, makes its own happenings, fashions its own illusions of people and events, and creates its own perspective of a vanished age. And this is certainly what Carr did in practice. But by erasing the distinction between art and life, Carr was able (in theory) to present his role as that of a reliable reporter of something already accomplished, a witness to Conan Doyle's career rather than the inventor of it: "We deal in the main with a man's life between 1869 and 1919. I have had little to do other than to edit and to arrange," Carr explains, seemingly unaware that the "editing and arranging" of a man's life is itself the biographer's central and consuming task and challenge.

And Carr's biography *does* read very much like a novel. To a great extent, Carr chose to tell Sir Arthur Conan Doyle's life through the device of conversations, between Conan Doyle and his relatives, his associates, his friends, and his adversaries. It is an intimate and, in Carr's hands, a vivid way of presenting his subject's personality; and the notion of Conan Doyle speaking ringingly across the years in his own voice, via "letters, notebooks, diaries, authenticated press-cuttings," and the like, seems a welcome step closer to the actual man. One good example of Carr's method and the dramatic effect created by it is an important conversation he reproduces between the young agnostic physician and his intensely Roman Catholic uncles, the artists Richard Doyle and James Doyle. In early 1882 they had invited Arthur to visit them at their deceased father's London home, to discuss his alarming rejection of their offer to use their Catholic connections to see him well started in practice somewhere:

In the drawing-room at Cambridge Terrace, where the bust of John Doyle stood against one wall, he met Uncle Dick: gaunt-featured now, with a tinge in his face which any medical eye could diagnose. And Uncle James, with his heavy hair and heavy beard. . . . in these cold, polite, tight-lipped men it was difficult to recognize the Uncle Dick and Uncle James of his boyhood; and he raged against it.

"If I practised as a Catholic doctor," he said, "I should be taking money for professing to believe something in which I didn't believe. You could count me the worst scoundrel on earth if I did that! You wouldn't do it yourselves; now would you?"

Uncle Dick corrected him sharply.

"But, my dear boy. We were speaking of the Catholic Church."

"Yes. I know."

"And that is an entirely different thing."

"Uncle Dick, how is is different?"

"Because what we believe is true." The cold simplicity of that remark raised between them a barrier at which no fist could batter. "If only you would have faith—"

"Yes," he burst out, "that's what people keep telling me. They talk about having faith, as though it could be done by an act of the will. They might as well tell me to have black hair instead of brown. Reason is the highest gift we've got; we *must* use it."

"And what does reason tell you?" asked another voice.

"Uncle James, that the evils of religion, a dozen religions slaughtering each other, have all come from accepting things that can't be proved. It tells me this Christianity of yours contains a number of fine and noble things mixed up with a lot of arrant rubbish. It tells me . . ."

Once before . . . he had said to the Ma'am that he could never talk freely unless he was excited. And he was excited now. More of this he poured out, much more. Then, catching sight of their faces, he assumed the same air of bursting politeness and said no more.

Presumably Carr re-created this conversation from diaries, letters, etc., that he found in the Conan Doyle archives. But some critics have paused to wonder if Carr is being more than a little ingenuous in arguing that such a "voice" guarantees the reliability of the biographer. Even if the biographer is nothing more than an editor, he still has to deal with choice: to select some events and materials, and discard others, in order to shape the preconceived pattern of the life he has in mind. And there are moments throughout the book when it is difficult to tell whether Carr is simply putting into people's mouths ideas or hints he has gleaned from elsewhere in the family archives. This has been a complaint of those who distrust this device and prefer each scrap of dialogue and each debatable statement to have a plain and referable source. But Carr gives us history with the labels off, like a butterfly collector who invites us to admire the specimen and accept his classification without inquiring about the genus.

Considered as a work of biography, the *Life* suffers from Carr's obvious idolization of his subject, though it is not quite the unmitigated hagiography that some of its critics have accused it of being. "Conan Doyle was no plaster saint," Carr reminds us at one point: "He was violent, he was stubborn, he was often wrong-headed, he did not easily forgive injury." But there is a damaging lack of psychological penetration, aggravated by Carr's naive assumption that a man's letters and private jottings can suffice to reveal his inner personality. And there are several chronological lacunae, entire years (such as 1908 and 1910) that seem to have dropped out of the book—not to mention the whole of the decade of the 1920s, the years of the Spiritualist crusade, being cut and compressed into the last twelve pages.

In Carr's defense, some of these omissions may have been due to editorial pruning, but not so the deliberate suppressions about problems in the Doyle household. Charles Doyle's alcoholism is swept under the rug, even though Carr does not mind drawing playfully on a piece of evidence that suggests the young Arthur was sometimes too over-indulgent in his own personal habits. He quotes an altogether wonderful letter in which Conan Doyle confessed to his sister Lottie: "I went to a ball the other night and by some mischance got as drunk as an owl. I have a dim recollection that I proposed to half the women in the room—married and single. I got one letter next day signed, 'Ruby,' and saying the writer had said 'yes' when she meant 'no'; but who the deuce she was or what she had said 'yes' about I can't conceive."

One would like to know a good deal more than Carr tells us about young Arthur Conan Doyle's self-confessed habit of falling in love with every young girl he met, including his early off-and-on-again fiancée Elmore Welden. ("We have been flirting hard for a week," he reported at one point in this relationship, "so that things are about ripe.") These and other gems plucked from Conan Doyle's correspondence suggest Carr's eye for telling detail, and his knack for setting down the story should not be underestimated. By comparison with Carr's dashing style and heartfelt attachment to his subject, Pierre Nordon's biography seems dense and ponderous, Charles Higham's slick and disconnected, and Hesketh Pearson's overly mannered and missing the big note.

iii

It was important to Adrian Conan Doyle that Carr's biography recognize his father as the original of Sherlock Holmes. Carr dutifully plays down Joseph Bell and makes a case for Conan Doyle as Sherlock Holmes, but he cuts short a promising line of inquiry with a neat dodge reminiscent of Holmes' own teasing way with baffled inspectors from the official force: "There are seven other identifications, but the Sherlockian will have to find them for himself." End of inquiry. Carr ignores some choice clues to authorial self-portraiture in *The Case-Book of Sherlock Holmes*,[8] mention of which is so cursory as to constitute another glaring omission from the abbreviated chapter on the 1920s.

Some persons missing from Carr's gallery are the inevitable victims of the book's chronological fissures. The absence of 1908, for example, deprives us of revisiting the London Olympic Games of that year. Conan Doyle was on the field as a special press correspondent and, according to some accounts, lent an inappropriate helping hand to Dorando Pietri, the exhausted Italian leader of the Marathon, turning him about in the proper direction and enabling the barely conscious athlete to hold up long enough to cross the finish line. Pietri was disqualified for failing to finish on his own, and according to these accounts, a guilt-stricken Conan Doyle set about raising a fund to compensate an athlete who he felt had been victimized by his own sporting blunder.

And there are a variety of biographical teasers that one wishes Carr had pursued for the sake of his story. While he mentions Bryan Charles Waller several times, he makes it difficult to tell exactly what Waller's contribution was to the young Arthur Conan Doyle and the fatherless Doyle family. Carr says that Waller "for some years was profoundly to influence" Conan Doyle's life, and we are able to gather that Waller's influence affected his choice of profession, reading matter, and adoption of agnosticism; but nevertheless Carr skims very lightly over the role Waller played in the lives of Arthur Conan Doyle and his family. On a different note, what was the "slight" that Lord Kitchener made one evening at dinner at Conan Doyle's home? Why did Lady Conan Doyle feel compelled to write to the hero of the Sudan and South Africa and "instruct him in the manners of a gentleman"? Can we believe that Conan Doyle would have "pretended not to notice" and allowed her to do it, thereby ruining a valuable contact in the area of army reform, about which Conan Doyle cared so much? As Sir Arthur must surely have known, Kitchener never forgot or forgave anyone who rebuked him.

8. See chap. 5, "The Clues of the Casebook," in my book *Sherlock Slept Here* (Santa Barbara: Capra Press, 1985), pp. 110–39, for a discussion of these clues.

The Joan Paynter disappearance mystery, one of Conan Doyle's real-life investigations, with its imitation of the Sherlock Holmes story "A Case of Identity," is another small vexation to a reader in search of information. The case Carr describes is an intriguing one, given its Sherlockian parallel, but Carr reports himself unable to discover how the detective Sir Arthur arrived at the solution and saved the young nurse from a fate worse than unworthy affections. "The biographer, who risks abuse for telling so incomplete a story, can only report that there appears to be no sign of a clue anywhere." But the disappointed reader will only conclude from this that Carr is being too much an obtuse Watson in the presence of an authentic Holmes.

Nor does Carr play fair by withholding the identity of the young woman with whom Dr. Watson had a San Francisco fling in Conan Doyle's uncompleted 1889–90 playscript *Angels of Darkness*, a Holmesless drama based on elements from *A Study in Scarlet*. (It was Lucy Ferrier, in *A Study in Scarlet* the deceased victim of the villainous Mormons who long afterward are being mysteriously murdered in London.) Instead of revealing the mysterious heroine's identity and speculating on the possibilities inherent in the playwright's mind, Carr does the biographically unthinkable by retreating under the cover of Victorian discretion. "To give her name, a well-known one, would be to betray the author as well as the character. At best it would impeach Watson in matters other than matrimonial; at worst it would upset the whole saga, and pose a problem which the keenest deductive wits of the Baker Street Irregulars could not unravel." The biographer doth protest too much, we might respond, remembering with satisfaction that it was the custom of certain Baker Street Irregulars to drink a toast "to the unravelling of the wits of John Dickson Carr" (whom they never made a member), "and may he discover a mystery which even he will be unable to solve." Perhaps a justice-minded Providence sent Carr the Paynter case as an appropriate form of revenge.

As for Conan Doyle's psychic activities, treated with respect earlier in the text, Carr's discussion of the Spiritualist crusade is so condensed in the final chapter that we have no clear idea why the public flocked to hear Conan Doyle and why critics denounced him in that last, hectic decade of his life. By now, one should expect the famous "Cottingley fairy photographs" hoax to be missing from Carr's biography, and it is, but the absence also of Houdini seems strange, given Carr's well-known authorial interest in magic and the occult. Perhaps Adrian decreed that the master magician had no place in an authorized biography of his father, given the self-styled ghostbuster's well-publicized antagonism to Sir Arthur's psychic beliefs and his ungratefulness to Lady Conan Doyle's "automatic writing" attempt in 1922 to make contact with Houdini's deceased mother. Whatever the reason, Houdini does a disappearing act here. Similarly, one misses more substantial accounts of Conan Doyle's worldwide travels on behalf of Spiritualism in the 1920s, with space at least approximating the half-dozen pages Carr devotes to Conan Doyle's 1894 literary tour of America. Interviews with Conan Doyle on the well-documented tours of his last decade give us some of our best views of the old lion in action and deserve more than a biographer's hasty summation.

iv

For the biography to accomplish what both Adrian and Carr wished, it could not make the mistake of Hesketh Pearson and call Conan Doyle "the man in the street." Sir Arthur would have to be kept off the streets and whisked up to the castle, as a champion of the realm and the defender of the downtrodden.

But Carr's biographical thesis contains a central defect: the vaunted "chivalric code" of Sir Arthur Conan Doyle is a storybook invention that does not suffice to explain the complex inner character of the man. The figure of the white-plumed paladin, groomed for knightly service with heraldry lessons at his mother's knee, sounds like one of those "cues" from Adrian that Carr was expected to make part and parcel of history. But one sometimes has the impression of a restless Conan Doyle outgrowing creeds as often as he outwore his clothes. Even Carr, in a remarkable moment of candor, was forced to admit that there was a part of Conan Doyle that escaped easy definition and frustrated a biographer's comprehension: "In this man there was something a little larger than life, some quality beyond chivalry, some flash that escapes analysis." Especially, we might add, when that analysis is constrained within the clanking confines of a suit of medieval armor.

Perhaps the most fruitful place for Carr to have gone in search of the real Arthur Conan Doyle would have been his complicated relationship with his mother, Mary Foley Doyle, "The Ma'am" of countless doting but often argumentative letters from her son. Carr had access to their voluminous correspondence and used some of it in his book, but his reports of mother-son clashes over the death of Sherlock Holmes and the Boer War make us regret the comparative disappearance of "The Ma'am" in the later chapters of the biography. In 1897, when Conan Doyle built his new Hindhead house, it featured stained-glass windows to display all the family arms; the "accidental" omission of the Foley arms takes on a possibly greater significance than Carr suspects, if we interpret Conan Doyle's "absent-mindedness" as a sign of latent rebellion against maternal domination. "Pray forgive me, Ma'am," he wrote on the eve of his departure for South Africa, going there against her wishes, for like many other Britons she was opposed to the Boer War, "if I have ever seemed petulant or argumentative—it is all nerves, of which I possess more than most people know." One would like to know a great deal more about those nerves, and why Mary Foley Doyle seems to have inspired both the confidence and combativeness of her son.

If the analysis of certain key relationships in Conan Doyle's life is one of Carr's weaknesses, one of his strengths is his lively knack of summing up his favorite Conan Doyle stories and novels for the common reader. These enthusiastic appraisals often make readers want to look up and read the stories for themselves. Carr is at his happiest when saluting Conan Doyle's characters and settings, the tribute of one professional storyteller to another. But even here, Carr's choices can be surprisingly narrow. As important an autobiographical work as *The Stark Munro Letters* is not given the attention it deserves. Carr also refrains from dealing with some of Conan Doyle's most experimental (and revealing) fiction. Works like *The Parasite* (1894), with its dark subcurrent of obsession, and "When the World Screamed" (1929), with its comic play on the Earth Mother archetype, might have even as much to tell us about Conan Doyle's state of mind as *Micah Clarke* or *Sir Nigel*. And although Carr discusses *A Duet* at some length, he misses the serious side of the whimsical love debate at the heart of the novel.

In addition, he makes nothing of the fact that Conan Doyle presented a bound copy of the manuscript not to his wife but to his platonic lady friend, Jean Leckie. Missing from Carr's discussion is any inkling that *A Duet* was the author's way of relieving some of the acute tension he must have felt over the vexing problem of being in love with a woman who was not his wife and of being loyal to a wife whose illness made marital relations impossible. Carr was the first biographer to reveal this ironic "romantic triangle," and he handled it delicately and tastefully, but with only an occasional intimation of the powerful feelings of the parties involved. "I fight the devil, and I win," Conan Doyle boasted about his refusal to surrender to his natural feelings for the lovely and love-struck Jean Leckie—a refusal that presumably delighted Heaven, but must have had marked effects on him; it certainly played havoc with a family circle that promptly divided and took sides on the issue. The story of Arthur Conan Doyle and Jean Leckie is as interesting for what Carr does not reveal as for what he does. And like so much else in *The Life of Sir Arthur Conan Doyle*, Carr's account leaves us wanting to know much more than we are permitted to learn.

As Carr's *Life* is essentially a chronological account of events and adventures, he tends to treat Conan Doyle's stories and novels as events in the author's life rather than as creative works calling for criticism and for explication to assess their autobiographical content. Despite Carr's abundant enthusiasm for Sherlock Holmes, Brigadier Gerard, and Professor Challenger, there is no balanced, comprehensive view of Conan Doyle's achievement as a writer, including a sense of Conan Doyle's literary faults. Writing the biography at the point in his own career when he had begun to turn from classical detective stories to historical fantasies, Carr naturally tended to overvalue Conan Doyle's historical fictions, agreeing with their author that the critics, in regarding them as at best rousing adventure tales, missed the main points about personal character, devotion to duty and cause, and the nature of chivalry and feudal obligations that Conan Doyle strove to convey through them: "The popularity of his other work defeated him before he began." As a professional mystery writer and author of historical romances himself, Carr may not have been the best or most credible person to pronounce on Arthur Conan Doyle's place in literature in any event, a point that seems never to have occurred to Adrian.

v

"Let us remember," Adrian declared in paying tribute later to John Dickson Carr's life of his father, "that Carr alone had the entree to Conan Doyle's gigantic collection of biographical papers and to his surviving associates and that every statement contained therein is drawn from the solid facts and not from any chosen conception of the author."[9]

But there *was* a "chosen conception" in this case, and it belonged to Adrian himself. As a champion of the view that Sir Arthur was not only Sherlock Holmes but England itself, Adrian had already selected the theme of the biographical portrait that he wished John Dickson Carr to bring to life with all the vivid colors of his novelist's palette. It was a theme whose lack had led Adrian to denigrate Hesketh Pearson's biography as much as he would overrate Carr's. Pearson's less than idolizing study had not honored what Adrian held as "the first great truth: that Holmes was to a large extent Conan Doyle himself." Accepting that great truth, one could go on and embrace an entire series of other great truths, enough to remove any doubts as to Sir Arthur's being a great man. And in that definition, Adrian could perhaps take measure of himself and explain why greatness had eluded him, for no son could possibly be expected to compete with such a father.

Whether from personal conviction or innate sympathy with Adrian, Carr made Sir Arthur the hero of mystery as well as of history. Stirring

9. Adrian Conan Doyle, introduction to *A Treasury of Sherlock Holmes* (New York: Hanover House, 1955), p. x.

and satisfying as it is when we read it in our youths, *The Life of Sir Arthur Conan Doyle* tantalizes its more mature readers with its untold tales, missing sequences, compressed decades, and untapped possibilities. But perhaps it is vain for us to blame Carr's research or methodology, let alone the father-glorifying obsession of Adrian Conan Doyle; a fuller, more informed life study was as far beyond Carr's capacity as it was alien to his theory of biography. He was no Gradgrind in search of elusive facts and veiled truths, but a storyteller always prepared to sacrifice complexity for the sake of plot and narrative speed.

The way Carr went about it recalls Thoreau's promise in *Walden*: "If one advances confidently in the direction of his dreams, and endeavors to live the life which he has imagined, he will meet with a success unexpected in common hours." Carr met that success, but neither he nor his silent collaborator Adrian realized that the life they created was also a mirror of their own lives, a dramatization of their own dreams as well as a limning of their own limitations. Like Alice's looking-glass, biography is a two-way mirror, capable of revealing an image on both sides of the pane. Thinking himself invisible from scrutiny, the biographer actually reveals himself in a variety of clues: his choice of a subject, his selection of an appropriate style, his use of verbal coloring to heighten and highlight historical fact, and the general design or structural composition he employs to frame the assorted episodes of a lifetime. John Dickson Carr stamped his own personality on the biography as boldly and legibly as the signature a painter uses to identify his picture. In its romanticized attitude toward the past, its pawky humor, its insistence on Conan Doyle's noble and prophetic qualities, its brisk, colorful line, its deliberate mutings and omissions, *The Life of Sir Arthur Conan Doyle* provides as much a revelation of Carr's mind and mood as it does the career of his subject.

For after all, John Dickson Carr had more in common with Arthur Conan Doyle, another mystery writer for whom modernity was a curse and ordeal, than is generally suspected. For both men, it was a case of *en garde* against the ravages of the twentieth century. The old master deserted it for the otherworldly solaces of Spiritualism; the younger fled it by writing a series of time-traveling historical fantasies; and both met in the pages of a biography whose author must have caught fleeting glimpses of himself in the youthful derring-do and mature disillusionment of his subject.

8 ° SCHOLARSHIP TRANSLATED INTO POPULAR BIOGRAPHY

Donald A. Redmond

Sir Arthur Conan Doyle, l'homme et l'oeuvre
by Pierre Nordon
Conan Doyle
by Pierre Nordon
(Translated by Frances Partridge)

The most important single book about Sir Arthur Conan Doyle, the only extensive, impartial literary appreciation, is less known to readers of Conan Doyle's works than it should be, partly because it appeared before the Sherlock Holmes boom of the 1970s. The remarkable thing is that it is a product of Continental criticism of English literature rather than British or American criticism. Pierre Nordon's *Sir Arthur Conan Doyle* was a doctoral dissertation at the Sorbonne, and the French edition (Paris: Didier, 1964) was followed two years later by an English translation (London: John Murray, 1966), but it had not been Nordon's first Doylean study. The biographical essay that formed the opening and major text of *Sir Arthur Conan Doyle Centenary, 1859–1959* (edited by Adrian Conan Doyle) was by Nordon, then an M.A. and already undertaking research for his doctoral project. He had been in correspondence with Adrian at least from the beginning of 1957, and a small-print note following his essay in the *Centenary* volume says: "With the exception of Mr. John Dickson Carr, Sir Arthur's Biographer, the author of this article alone has had access to the immense Conan Doyle Archives."[1]

The academic requirements for a dissertation at the Sorbonne, together with Nordon's access to the Conan Doyle archives, ensure that this is an authoritative and thorough study. The original French edition, re-

1. Actually, Hesketh Pearson had also had access to Conan Doyle's papers, but Adrian Conan Doyle's immense dislike for Pearson's 1943 *Conan Doyle, His Life and Art* led him to deny the fact.

plete with footnotes including extensive quotations in English and frequent citations of unpublished material from Conan Doyle's notebooks or correspondence, bristles with academic documentation. The English-language editions (the American (New York: Rinehart and Winston, 1967) being a photo-offset reproduction of the British text—are quite another matter. Many footnote quotations have been subsumed into the text for smoother reading; the remaining footnotes are merely citations of sources. The English-language version has been edited to produce a more generally readable trade book; something—we shall see what in due course—has been left out.

i

The structure of the English and French versions is the same. Part I, "The Man," is ten chapters; part II, "The Writer," is twelve. Nordon's emphasis or plan is indicated by the chapters: one on ancestry; the second on Conan Doyle's first forty years; three covering Conan Doyle as patriot (1899–1918); three on the Casement, Edalji, and Slater cases, under the heading "The Lover of Justice"; one on Spiritualism; and the last chapter in part I sums up "The Personality of Conan Doyle." The heading of chapter 9, "The Prophet: In the Cause of Spiritualism," is a little misleading, for though it does indeed deal with Spiritualism, it surveys the breadth of Conan Doyle's religious and philosophical views, the development of which Nordon traces from Conan Doyle's school days to his active advocacy of the Spiritualist message after 1916. The biographical chapters in part I, while concentrating on certain periods in Conan Doyle's life, are intended to illustrate facets of his character as background for the understanding of Conan Doyle as a writer. Conan Doyle's nonfiction, the war histories, the didactic monographs (ranging from *The Crime of the Congo* to *The Case of Oscar Slater*), and his Spiritualistic works are discussed in part I; the fiction in part II.

In part II, five chapters deal with Sherlock Holmes. The next four chapters are on the historical, chivalric, and domestic fiction and the Professor Challenger science fiction. The final chapter addresses "The Writer and His Role." The four chapters covering Conan Doyle's non-Holmes fiction together comprise only fifty pages, as against eighty on Holmes.

The first paragraph of Nordon's biographical essay in the *Centenary* volume is worth quoting; it well expresses Nordon's approach to Conan Doyle criticism. The note as a whole is a little too laudatory but serves as an excellent prolegomenon to Nordon's later and longer book:

Because he has remained in the background of our childhood, aloof, mysterious, fascinating, Conan Doyle is still a somewhat illustrious stranger to most of us. But he will remain a stranger even to the more inquisitive and adult critic, although for different reasons. That formidable figure of modern fiction, Sherlock Holmes, bestrides the world of Conan Doyle's works like a colossus. Without his ponderous presence, it would be a great deal easier to assign a definite place to his creator on the literary scene, the importance of Conan Doyle and his contribution to the development of English prose might be assessed more distinctly. . . . But fairness is always desirable in the face of some ambiguities, some myths, and some ignorant references, especially when entertained by some men, who, pretending to guide our judgment, will for some obscure reason best known to themselves, misrepresent or diminish, either in their work or in their person, the most admirable figures of a literary heritage.[2]

It would seem that the outlined structure of Nordon's book would hardly suffice for his aim, "to assign a definite place to his creator on the literary scene," and that the treatment might be as casual and highlight-touching as those of the briefest popular biographies of Conan Doyle. But the difference is substantial. Nordon had the cooperation of Adrian Conan Doyle in his project and chose not to duplicate the discursive treatment of John Dickson Carr's book, already endorsed by Adrian as *the* biography of his father. Carr carries his reader along in adventuresome reconstruction. For the Sorbonne, a much more analytic and critical treatment would be required. Hence the chapter structure takes milestones from Conan Doyle's life, using them as examples and drawing from them, and from aspects of his whole life, conclusions about the personality of the man and the writer.

Nordon aims to show, in fine, the effects of heritage, of maternal training and maternal personality, of independence and the discovery of his writing ability, of dogmatic family and scholastic religious prejudice, in producing a multi-faceted, fearless, upright, conscientious craftsman, withal Victorian in rearing and outlook, a gentleman of the old school; and the effects on him of the impact of domestic strain, of wars and losses, of public and private injustices, of the final flowering of a philosophy or religion in which he could believe; and the reflection of all these things in an incredibly varied output of written work. To accomplish this analysis is almost more than should be expected of a single work.

2. An obvious allusion to Hesketh Pearson.

This was the shortcoming of Conan Doyle biography from the beginning. In his own *Memories and Adventures*, Nordon points out, Conan Doyle "hesitates to draw the reader into purely autobiographical regions. . . . he is not concerned with exposing his own personality." Nordon remarks on Conan Doyle's "reluctance to occupy the center of his own stage" in either the autobiography or the cryptoautobiographical *Stark Munro Letters*, for which Conan Doyle long held special regard. Nordon perceptively states: "surely we cannot fail to see a similarity between his character and the armour of imperturbability in which the hyper-sensitive Sherlock Holmes occasionally allows us to see a chink." Other biographers saw, or related, only those facets of Conan Doyle that interested them. Lamond slighted everything except Spiritualism; Pearson was brief and scornful; Carr like Conan Doyle himself stressed action and adventure; and so it has gone on. Nordon has tried to find the man beneath the adventure, the beliefs beneath the causes and rallies, and consequently the explanation for his writings. Some biographers, indeed, hardly mentioned Conan Doyle's writings other than Sherlock Holmes.

The accomplishments of Nordon's study are many. His approach and critical method have already been suggested, but a quick skimming of highlights from the work will illustrate these further. The opening chapter on Conan Doyle's ancestry stresses "the social and religious traditions he inherited" and shows Conan Doyle's autobiographical drawing upon them. For instance, the Loring family (in *The White Company* and *Sir Nigel*) parallels Conan Doyle's heritage: "Conan Doyle could neither relegate these traditions completely to the past, nor integrate them wholly in the present; but we cannot understand him if we ignore them. They explain his vocation as an artist and the impulse that urged him to other activities beyond literature."

In the three chapters covering Conan Doyle as patriot, Nordon's estimate of Conan Doyle as a military historian is higher than that of Julian Symons, in his later biography, who considers him unreliable because of his closeness to the generals. Nordon emphasizes Conan Doyle's defense of the justice of the British cause in the Boer War, and the Allied cause in World War I, his denunciation of inadequate preparations, and especially his clear vision of future military tactics. "It was the book's historical accuracy which impressed an attentive reader," he says, about Conan Doyle's history of the Great War (*The British Campaign in France and Flanders*).

Nordon's clear discussion of Conan Doyle's unsuccessful 1900 Edinburgh election campaign, including reference to Conan Doyle's letters, shows marked superiority in method and detached clarity over other accounts. Carr, who had access to much of the same material, used his fictional-conversational style: it was much more effective as narrative but much less analytical and dispassionate and consequently, from the critical viewpoint, much less convincing—better reading perhaps as overall biography but much less adequate as a study of Conan Doyle the writer, Conan Doyle the man driven by a sense of public rectitude and duty, and consequently of Conan Doyle's permanent impact. Nordon's discussion of Conan Doyle and divorce law reform—based on his own perceptive study of Conan Doyle's long struggle in duty to his sick wife and chivalric idealization of the woman who was to become his second wife—becomes very important in understanding some of the Sherlock Holmes stories. His discussion of Conan Doyle's attitude toward women, the suffragettes in particular, occupies two full pages, as against a total of ten sentences scattered in Carr's biography and lacking any detail or analysis.

Conan Doyle put his own feelings into the mouth of Sherlock Holmes: "It is always a joy to meet an American." Nordon emphasizes Conan Doyle's liking for Americans; he was "always careful to keep the American public informed, and eager that they should understand his motives." The picture of Conan Doyle that the biography builds (and perhaps the public picture that Conan Doyle himself built in his actions as well as his autobiography) is of a man who would have been thoroughly at home as frontiersman, explorer, or comrade of Walt Whitman's robust view of American life. "As for the Americans, they saw him as an Englishman after their own hearts, and adopted not only his books . . . but also his personality, his love of sport and fair play."

A paragraph of prolegomenon to Nordon's study of Conan Doyle's religious attitudes and Spiritualism illustrates Nordon's method. "To account for Sir Arthur Conan Doyle's conversion we must first reject every over-simple *a priori* argument." The analysis that Nordon undertakes of Conan Doyle's thought processes, philosophical struggles, and extensive reading and digestion, is lacking in other accounts of Conan Doyle's life. Carr's sketchy mention of *The Stark Munro Letters* ("a book which in all but a few incidents is autobiographical") is in contrast to Nordon's pointed discussion of its significance in regard to Conan Doyle's Spiritualism: "The author's primary aim was to externalize his religious doubts, the better to exorcise them." This may be exaggerated; Conan Doyle's primary aim in producing the *Letters* at that stage was undoubtedly monetary; to read philosophy into every line and action may be as much overcontrol as to gloss over the implications and concentrate on action, as do Carr, Conan Doyle himself, and other biographies.

Nordon does not pretend to "defend" Conan Doyle's Spiritualism (in contrast to the Lamond biography, which is certainly an apologia) but examines Conan Doyle's reasoning, motives, and belief. Nor does he accuse him, either, of credulity, as others have: "But, above all, the circumstances of his conversion are so significant that we see in him one of his most secret characteristics, which set him apart from his age. This element of revolt in him was opposed both to the open, active side of his nature and to his confidence in man's steady progress. But there was a Carlylean element of deep seriousness in Conan Doyle's personality, which caused him to testify with increasing vehemence to what he had himself witnessed." Nordon well expresses Conan Doyle's underlying stature—his sense of human dignity and his outrage at offenses against it. In commenting on "his refusal to go with his century," on the same page, there is a much more positive appreciation of Conan Doyle than saying, as some have, that he was an outdated Victorian. Nordon makes clear, however, that Conan Doyle's own affirmations of proof for Spiritualism were limited in their thoroughness and based too much on argument *ex cathedra*. "He is caught in an irreducible fallacy . . . he constantly uses affirmation instead of demonstration," observes Nordon.

The discussion of "The Personality of Conan Doyle" is especially important in distilling conclusions from part I. To endeavor to extract what Nordon calls "the most obvious elements of his character" is nearly as frustrating as Watson's attempt in *A Study in Scarlet* to list Sherlock Holmes' limits, but here is an attempt:

- indecision, as seen in *The Stark Munro Letters*
- deliberate masking of his own personality
- pride in his physical energy and his diversity of activities
- extraordinary memory, method, and persistence; profound serenity
- a "mysterious yet definite feeling of being born to accomplish some important task"
- compensation for a frustrated childhood by emphasis on toughness
- strict sense and rules of honor, received from his mother
- "love and respect for the past, sense of the marvellous, the courtly piety of his chivalry, discreet tenderness"
- the long testing of his knightly nature through his first wife's illness, extreme reaction to her death, lassitude that gave way to euphoria after his second marriage
- constant effort to give the phlegmatic appearance of even temperament
- tremendous sense of humor; a habit of self-parody
- serene gaity coming from optimism and confidence in human progress
- a certain rigidity of temperament and occasional vehemence in expressing his opinion

- moral discipline but not to the extent of encroachment on liberty of opinion and conscience
- patriotism, imperialism, nineteenth-century views, paternalism
- human, concrete nationalism; inherited good citizenship
- a disdain toward money for money's sake
- animistic view of human nature; puritanism from allegiance to the masculine and social model of the "gentleman"; enlightened conservatism
- "a solidarity with his own class of which he was probably barely aware"
- indifference to material objects and surroundings
- ambition that was both realistic and disciplined by a sense of duty; public spirit; desire for action
- beneath curiosity, insistence on certainty, finding its ideals in the past

Answers become obvious, from these things, to some of the allegations about Conan Doyle-as-man-in-the-street or Conan Doyle-as-Watson. Conan Doyle was of proud lineage and firm in his outlook with the views of his class, yet he possessed a rare ability to communicate (both in person and through his writings) with persons of every class and calling. He was far too complex to resemble the solid, simple John H. Watson, yet something of himself appears in Watson as much as in Holmes.

Part II commences by analyzing the Sherlock Holmes phenomenon, first as myth, one chapter being a brief mention of the Sherlockian movement, then a discussion of "The Character of Sherlock Holmes." The third chapter on Holmes, "The Origin and Structure of the Cycle," is a dispassionate and critical examination of the nature and development of the tales: "Is it not in the person of Sherlock Holmes, amongst all his other creations, that Conan Doyle reveals himself as the spokesman of his generation?" "Sherlock Holmes and the Reading Public" examines the sociological phenomenon of the Holmes saga, showing that Holmes was a "product of a society which believed almost unanimously in its own values, resources and future." Conan Doyle's style and descriptive ability are well outlined, but the artificial, stylized nature of his picture of Victorian London is stressed: "It is clear that all the inhabitants of this world are keenly aware of where they belong—are 'class-conscious' in fact. . . . it is implicit in the way the characters reveal themselves in the dialogue, or by the choice of their surnames." This sociological picture and Conan Doyle's "solidarity with his own class," noted already, also dispose of the man-in-the-street question regarding Conan Doyle.

The following chapter, "Watson, Holmes and Conan Doyle," examines the source of what one of Msgr. Ronald Knox's fictitious Holmesian authorities might call the Watson-Idea and the Ur-Holmes.[3] Nordon points out Conan Doyle's indebtedness to Boswell, and his deliberate use of Boswell's method: "he had sufficient artistry to make use of it to immortalize his own imaginary characters." Autobiographical traces are remarked: "Because he is like Conan Doyle, because he is Conan Doyle, Sherlock Holmes is much more than a portrait; he is one of the last incarnations of chivalry in the literature of the English language."

Going on to the historical and chivalric novels, between which Nordon distinguishes, he first points out the "datedness" of the historical novel tradition of the mid-nineteenth century (Scott, Macaulay, Thackeray) in which Conan Doyle followed: "This is only another aspect of his neo-Conservatism, and his later development made his inability to adapt himself to his age even more obvious." Nordon stresses Conan Doyle's personal knowledge of material in his chivalric novels and again shows autobiographical traces: for example, Dame Ermyntrude in *Sir Nigel* as a portrait of Mary Doyle; episodes in Nigel's life from the history of the Doyles. "Conan Doyle has created a world of dreams rather than an historical one, and transferred something of his own spiritual make-up to the character of his hero. The heroes of both the novels of chivalry are autobiographical. . . . The character of Nigel Loring definitely portrays his inner self, and this novel allows us to see more plainly than before to what extent Conan Doyle was at variance with his own century." Contrary to Conan Doyle's own hopes for his historical fiction as his "best work," Nordon is more realistic: "*Uncle Bernac* and *The Refugees* are not merely the weakest of Conan Doyle's historical writings, but they represent the reef on which his historical fiction foundered."

Nordon's opinion of Conan Doyle's science fiction, on the other hand, is a high one: "*The Lost World* alone, and the stories which followed it, would have been enough to assure Conan Doyle's literary reputation."

ii

The English-language editions present problems, partly of editing, partly of translation. Little over three-quarters as long as the original, the translation omits not only extensive footnotes but also four appendices of background material from the Conan Doyle archives. Textual

3. Ronald A. Knox, "Studies in the Literature of Sherlock Holmes," his 1912 Oxford University student paper that satirized the biblical scholarship of the day by applying the same sort of exegetical analysis to the Sherlock Holmes stories. The first great milestone in the "Higher Criticism" of Sherlockiana, the paper was collected in Knox's *Essays in Satire* (London: Sheed and Ward, 1928) and has been reprinted a number of times since then in England and America.

deletions have been made, many of which in fact remove useful, even essential, facts from the background of Nordon's argument and at times lead to non sequiturs or misapprehensions. Only a few sample omissions can be cited here (the translation of the French text by this writer in each case). From pages 49 and 50 of the French text, a long passage of background to Conan Doyle's view of the South African situation is omitted, including a quotation from the *Windsor Magazine* and the following by Nordon:

> Here we must always be careful not to represent or depict our author as an ardent imperialist throwing himself headlong into the melee. Imperialist he indeed is, in a certain measure and in the specific guise of an Englishman in 1899. But this is not to say that he felt the war justified for humanitarian considerations. Even though it is true that later, notably in the light of his 1902 monograph [*The War in South Africa—Its Cause and Conduct*], he could appear in the eyes of overexcited opinion to be one of the spokesmen of imperial politics, his viewpoint on the war is always devoid of the least *Weltanschauung*.

From pages 56 and 57 are omitted Conan Doyle's ideas on military affairs, regretting the British lack of a Napoleon with complete power to order reforms in the Army. From pages 198 and 199, where Nordon discusses Conan Doyle's stressful situation during his first wife's long illness, the English text strangely omits two important paragraphs discussing Mary Doyle's role in her married son's closeness to Jean Leckie. The omission of the second paragraph of a quotation from Conan Doyle's tract on divorce law reform (not, as far as I can remember, adequately discussed by any other biographer), the paragraph being critical of religion, much weakens the force of the quotation as given in the French text (pp. 79–80). The English translation misses a main point of emphasis from the French text of pages 256 and 257 where Nordon acknowledges Conan Doyle's debt in *The Sign of the Four* to Wilkie Collins and Robert Louis Stevenson, quoting from "The Rajah's Diamond" and going on:

> Conan Doyle's originality lies elsewhere. It is in the arrangement of elements specifically Holmesian which we shall study further, in the creation above all, beginning with borrowed or transposed data, of an atmosphere of dramatic tension.

The English text picks up at this point in the sentence, but renders only:

133

Conan Doyle's chief concern is to create an atmosphere of dramatic tension subtly calculated to make the reader thrill with horror or suspense, as even Stevenson could not do without recourse to the supernatural (*Dr. Jekyll and Mr. Hyde*). He leads us to the frontiers of the supernatural but does not cross them.

The English text then omits the rest of an important paragraph:

The Sign of Four seems, not without audacity, to address a public which had read "Murders in the Rue Morgue" and was waiting to discover an identical situation. The invention of the pygmy, already mentioned, is actually a happy one, for it contrives a surprise for the reader while delaying the solution of the enigma. The episode of the barrel was inspired by an 1888 incident, recalling the misfortunes of the bloodhounds when Scotland Yard strove to capture the celebrated Jack the Ripper. These reminiscences combine to make a more individualized or personalized inspiration.

Nordon has occasional difficulties of his own; the French text speaks of the Reverend Mr. Edalji as of "Parsee origin, that is to say Hindu," and seems not to have found a French equivalent of "raps," the Spiritualist expression, while the Royal Society of London is curiously given as "la Société Dialectique de Londres." The French usage is "spiritisme" where English uses "Spiritualism," but a complete reversal of sense thereby occurs on page 141 of the English translation, from page 151 of the French original. It is of course difficult for a nonnative speaker of French to assess the style of Nordon's *Conan Doyle* in its original language, but Nordon does have a fine turn of phrase in either French or English. One of the best is in his *Centenary* volume essay: "Conan Doyle, like Holmes, was a Knight Eloquent of Justice."

The difference between the French and English texts can be accounted for by the desire to produce a book of wider appeal and more general readability. Adrian Conan Doyle was intensely interested in the translation and publishing project, insisting on the integrity as far as possible of the French text translated. The published translation was a compromise in which author, translator, publisher, and the son of the biographer's subject were all evidently involved.[4] One is tempted to suggest that Adrian Conan Doyle, in giving in to certain omissions, perhaps, was as always endeavoring to have his father seen in the best light. But his assistance in the development of the original was important and is documented by Nordon; and undoubtedly his influence was equally

4. Personal communication from Dr. Nordon is gratefully acknowledged.

present in the preparation of the English version. For the scholar of Sir Arthur Conan Doyle, recourse to the French original is obligatory because of its greater fullness. Nonetheless, the translation is a strong and useful work of criticism.

iii

The Nordon book, which could be classed as literary criticism rather than biography—for the biography is incidental to the criticism—is the only full-scale study of Conan Doyle without axe-grinding of some kind. John Dickson Carr's biography remains the fullest treatment of Conan Doyle's life, but at times his reconstructed-dialogue method becomes a little contrived. Conan Doyle's letters can well speak for him—why then disguise them as conversation in unattributed quotations, some of which are not even exact? The weakness of the English translation of Nordon's work is precisely that a large part of the firsthand statements, whether in letters or other sources, have been omitted, for reasons of understandable exigency. But the arguments (they must be called that) in treatments such as those of Hesketh Pearson and Adrian Conan Doyle himself are neither disinterested enough or extensive enough to provide the reader with evidence sufficient to allow him to judge for himself and to support the argument and conclusions of the writer. Pierre Nordon has managed to do these things, as a thorough academic study should. It is possible that not everyone will agree with his conclusions. Pearson probably would not; the wonder is that Adrian Conan Doyle did; Sir Arthur's spirit is probably roaring with mighty laughter at the whole thing.

9 ° FOUR MINIATURE PORTRAITS

Edward S. Lauterbach

❧ The year 1964 saw not only the English-language publication of Pierre Nordon's massive *Conan Doyle* but also a slim biography by Michael and Mollie Hardwick, *The Man Who Was Sherlock Holmes*. This was followed in 1965 by two biographies for younger readers, *The Real Sherlock Holmes* by Mary Hoehling and *The Man Who Hated Sherlock Holmes* by James Playsted Wood. Finally, in 1972, Ivor Brown published *Conan Doyle: A Biography of the Creator of Sherlock Holmes*. All of these biographies focused on the similarities and differences between Sherlock Holmes and his creator. And since all are brief, all are necessarily selective in the facts and details they offer about Sir Arthur Conan Doyle's life and work.

i
The Man Who Was Sherlock Holmes

As well as many other books on a wide variety of subjects, Michael and Mollie Hardwick have written a number of Sherlockian items: among them are *The Sherlock Holmes Companion* (John Murray, 1962), the novelization of Billy Wilder's motion picture *The Private Life of Sherlock Holmes* (1970), and dramatizations of Holmes material for radio, television, and the stage. Most recently, Michael Hardwick has written several successful Sherlock Holmes novels by himself, beginning with *Prisoner of the Devil* (Proteus Books, 1980).

The Hardwicks' biography is the shortest of those considered in this chapter and really little more than an extended pamphlet. Years after it was published, Michael Hardwick stated that he was "a commercial writer," and that he and his wife often wrote very quickly.[1] Possibly due

1. "An Interview with Michael Hardwick," *Baker Street Miscellanea*, no. 25 (Spring 1981): 11–13, conducted October 12, 1980, by Jon L. Lellenberg, editor of this volume. I wish to thank also J. Randolph Cox, librarian at St. Olaf College,

to the rapidity of their writing as well as the brevity of the book, the overall impression given by *The Man Who Was Sherlock Holmes* (London: John Murray, 1964; New York: Doubleday, 1964) is that of journalism rather than scholarship, an appreciative sketch of Sir Arthur Conan Doyle. There is no bibliography, no indication of any use of Conan Doyle family papers, and no acknowledgment of the family's cooperation, though Michael Hardwick did indicate later that he and his wife had worked closely with Adrian Conan Doyle.[2] The lack of documentation makes it impossible, for the most part, to know whether statements by Conan Doyle are taken from letters, journals, diaries, or published autobiographical writings. One can seldom tell whether quotations from Adrian Conan Doyle are from his book *The True Conan Doyle* or from personal conversations. As a piece of journalism, perhaps *The Man Who Was Sherlock Holmes* needs no sources and footnotes, but it would carry more authority had it been buttressed with a slightly more scholarly approach.

The Hardwicks' treatment is generally chronological, but as the text is so short, the facts of Conan Doyle's life are greatly compressed. The most detailed sections concern his efforts to prove the innocence of George Edalji and of Oscar Slater, and they contain the Hardwicks' main argument for Conan Doyle's use of the methods of Sherlock Holmes. However, the narrative is sometimes so compressed that the style becomes almost hop-skip-jump: on one single page, for instance, Conan Doyle shows a lack of interest in the deductive method of Dr. Joseph Bell; his first published story, "The Mystery of Sasassa Valley," is mentioned; his father dies; he makes his trip to the Arctic as a ship's surgeon; he receives his medical degree; he makes his trip to West Africa, again as a ship's surgeon; he returns to England; and he is invited to visit his aunt—all recorded on one page at a nearly breathless pace.

The dust jacket of the American edition of *The Man Who Was Sherlock Holmes* states that the purpose of the book is to give "a dual profile" of Conan Doyle and Sherlock Holmes, and in their foreword the Hardwicks say that "the idea of this book is show that the brilliance of Holmes is the reflected light of his creator's many-sided character." We know this identification of Sir Arthur Conan Doyle with Sherlock Holmes pleased the former's son Adrian. In his memoir of his father, Adrian emphasized the Sherlockian qualities,[3] and somewhat later, on an "Invi-

---

Northfield, Minn., and Bliss Austin, another contributor to this volume, for some of the information used in this chapter.

2. Ibid, pp. 12–13.

3. Adrian Conan Doyle, *The True Conan Doyle* (New York: Coward-McCann, 1946), pp. 16, 18–19. See chap. 6 for Bliss Austin's discussion of Adrian's book.

tation to Learning" radio program, when Lyman Bryson suggested "your father was Sherlock Holmes, especially in the acuteness of his mind" and "in a real sense, your father was Dr. Watson with Sherlock Holmes' brain," Adrian agreed: "Well, let me say that my father was a combination of the two: the Holmes mind—you put it so well, Mr. Bryson—and the Watson physique."[4] Michael Hardwick has admitted that "it was Adrian's idea that we write *The Man Who Was Sherlock Holmes*,"[5] and it is not surprising that they support Adrian's concept of his father.

The Hardwicks quote Dr. Bell, from whom Conan Doyle derived so much of Holmes's deductive method. Bell wrote his former student: "You are yourself Sherlock Holmes!" and on this statement the Hardwicks build their argument. They cite the fact that Conan Doyle himself wondered whether he had the qualities that he had depicted in Holmes and go on to describe parallel after parallel. Though this comparison was not startlingly new, the Hardwicks accumulate a great deal of evidence for it. For example, if Holmes had art in his blood, there were well-known artists in the Conan Doyle family. Though Holmes seems to scorn women, his attitude toward the feminine sex was always gentle, generous, and chivalrous like that of Conan Doyle himself. As a capstone for their argument, the Hardwicks point out that when Sherlock Holmes came to the aid of his country on the eve of World War I, in "His Last Bow," Conan Doyle, with fervid patriotism, gave Holmes a *nom de guerre*—Altamont, his father's middle name—that clearly identified the detective-hero with himself. (The Hardwicks, however, also point out where the lives and characteristics of Conan Doyle and Sherlock Holmes differ, finding, for example, no similarities in the childhood and early education of the two.)

The more Conan Doyle wrote about Sherlock Holmes, the more he seemed to develop his own detective gifts. Often in the stories, Holmes echoes the methods or ideas of his creator. In order to emphasize this aspect of their study, the Hardwicks juxtapose canonical passages with their narrative of Conan Doyle's life, especially in the two chapters concerning George Edalji and Oscar Slater. In each case, Conan Doyle proceeded step by step to collect evidence, analyze it like Sherlock Holmes, and arrive at solutions that, they say, proved each man innocent.

The Hardwicks have some interesting thoughts about the death of Holmes in "The Final Problem." It was remarkable, they say, because Conan Doyle left the actual corpse out of the story, thus opening the

4. Adrian Conan Doyle, Gilbert Highet, and Lyman Bryson, "Conan Doyle: Adventures of Sherlock Holmes" (as broadcast July 27, 1952), in *Invitation to Learning*, 2 (Fall 1952): 251–57, esp. p. 256.

5. "Interview with Michael Hardwick," p. 13.

door for Holmes' later resurrection. Perhaps this omission was instinctive, or perhaps Conan Doyle felt the presence of a "second finger" guiding his hand as he wrote what was supposed to be the last Sherlock Holmes adventure. The Hardwicks speculate on Conan Doyle's reasons for reviving the Great Detective. It was certainly not need of money, they conclude (but money certainly had much to do with it, we know): "More likely the reasons are that . . . Conan Doyle wished to show that Holmes could be brought back and his . . . absence explained without difficulty; and that the reluctance remained deep down [in Conan Doyle]—though it had never been acknowledged as such—to banish for ever one who was, after all, a great part of himself."

The final point the Hardwicks make is that Conan Doyle never used Sherlock Holmes as a mouthpiece for his political or religious views. Had he attempted to support his own belief in Spiritualism with Holmes he might have done irreparable harm to the image of his detective. This showed remarkable restraint on his part, since as the Hardwicks show, so much of Sherlock Holmes was derived from the multi-faceted personality of Sir Arthur Conan Doyle.

ii
The Real Sherlock Holmes:
Arthur Conan Doyle
The Man Who Hated Sherlock Holmes:
A Life of Sir Arthur Conan Doyle

Mary Hoehling's *The Real Sherlock Holmes* (New York: Julian Messner, 1965) and James Playsted Wood's *The Man Who Hated Sherlock Holmes* (New York: Pantheon Books, 1965) were both intended for readers twelve to sixteen years old—the principal age group encountering the Sherlock Holmes stories for the first time. This was Hoehling's first book on Conan Doyle or Sherlock Holmes, though she had written other juvenile biographies, as had Wood in addition to other books. *The Real Sherlock Holmes* contains no indication that Hoehling made use of any Conan Doyle family papers; however, in her acknowledgments she does thank Conan Doyle's children for their "help and encouragement." Wood's *The Man Who Hated Sherlock Holmes* does not refer to Conan Doyle family papers or to working with the family.

Though errors in a book may be due to poor editing and proofreading, it is unfortunate that these two juvenile biographies are marred by so many small inaccuracies. Hoehling changes the title of the Sherlock Holmes story "His Last Bow" to "His Last Blow," refers to *Blackwood's*

Magazine as *Blackwood* magazine, and lists "The Disintegration Machine" and "When the World Screamed," two Professor Challenger stories, as "The Disintegrator Machine" and "The Day the World Screamed." Wood seems to have trouble with proper names and numbers. He misspells Innes [Doyle], [James] Payn, and [Ward,] Lock and credits Conan Doyle with writing seventy-two Sherlock Holmes stories, when—as anyone can easily ascertain from any complete edition—there are but fifty-six short stories and four novels. These may seem to be small matters, but since young minds lack knowledge and experience, the writers of juvenile biography should take great care to be accurate and precise.

Though both give the main facts of Conan Doyle's life in chronological order, it is interesting to see Hoehling and Wood, writing for the same audience, describe some of the same events in greater or lesser detail. Such selectivity and emphasis is, of course, the prerogative of any biographer, and the amount of space given to specific incidents can vary even in full-scale biographies such as those by Carr, Nordon, and Higham. Hoehling describes how Conan Doyle, on a train journey, met Louisa Hawkins and her family when he gave emergency medical treatment to Louisa's brother: little did the young doctor know at the time that Louisa would be his first wife. Wood makes no mention of such a meeting. Hoehling's vivid description of Conan Doyle's struggle to subdue Jack Hawkins is dramatic and sensational: "One flailing heel crashed through the carriage window before [Conan Doyle] managed to climb astride the lad's knees and get a firm grip on his wrists." However, other Conan Doyle biographers indicate that he was simply called in to consult on Jack Hawkins' symptoms of cerebral meningitis.[6] Though Hoehling's description of Conan Doyle's meeting with his first wife may make thrilling reading, her tendency to romanticize leads her into inaccuracies about Conan Doyle's life.

Wood offers more details than Hoehling about Conan Doyle's early life as a young doctor beginning in practice at Southsea, but Hoehling describes more fully Conan Doyle's efforts in the Boer War and the problems he faced at his Bloemfontein field hospital there under siege. And she gives a somewhat romanticized account of Conan Doyle's courtship of Jean Leckie, his second wife, whereas Wood merely draws upon Conan Doyle's brief mention in his autobiography to write: "In a quiet ceremony in London, September 18, 1907, Sir Arthur Conan Doyle married Jean Leckie, a young and beautiful woman whom he had known well for over a decade and who was a close friend of his mother and

6. For example, see Carr's *Life of Sir Arthur Conan Doyle*, pp. 41–42; Nordon's *Conan Doyle*, p. 32; and Higham's *Adventures of Conan Doyle*, pp. 65–66.

sister." Hoehling finds the roots for Conan Doyle's belief in Spiritualism in his grief over the early death of his elder sister Annette: "Could so much goodness and beauty have vanished into the alien earth, leaving no trace?" Wood describes Conan Doyle's lifelong interest in Spiritualism more fully as he moved from skepticism to belief.

Hoehling devotes most of her attention to biography, with only a minimum of material on Conan Doyle's non-Sherlockian fiction. By contrast, Wood's real strength is the enthusiasm he brings to discussing Conan Doyle's literary work, the non-Sherlockian fiction as well as the Holmes stories, skillfully conveying the mood of Conan Doyle's works: *Micah Clarke* "is painstaking in its profuse detail, realistic and even brutal in some episodes"; *The White Company*'s "pages roll with broad humor, flame with ardor, ring with exaltation as the steel-helmeted archers of England and her mounted knights seek out her massed enemies." Wood is pleased with Conan Doyle's Brigadier Gerard stories, and emphasizes the amount of research Conan Doyle gave to his historical fiction. With great zest for the Professor Challenger stories, Wood writes: "*The Lost World* is a dazzling book. It is a rollicking book. It is even, somehow, a convincing book." Wood's discussions of Conan Doyle's fiction are, of the four short biographical studies, the most likely to encourage a reader to seek out and read Conan Doyle's works.

The title of Hoehling's book, *The Real Sherlock Holmes: Arthur Conan Doyle*, indicates her emphasis on Conan Doyle's Holmesian qualities. This theme is stressed through chapter titles such as "Sir Sherlock" and "Wedding Bells for Sherlock Holmes." Hoehling, like the Hardwicks, also emphasizes the Holmesian qualities in Conan Doyle's investigations of the alleged crimes of George Edalji ("a crime whose sinister nature intrigued the mind of Sherlock Holmes [i.e., Conan Doyle]") and Oscar Slater ("with Holmesian logic, Conan Doyle built up his case that the murderer must have been known to his victim"). Hoehling traces the creation of Sherlock Holmes from Conan Doyle's own experiences, showing the influence of Dr. Joseph Bell. But, as she points out, Conan Doyle became more and more reluctant to write about the detective, coming to feel that Holmes was taking time away from his serious fiction. He was embittered when what he considered his finer works, such as *The White Company* and *The Refugees*, received only halfhearted praise, while the Sherlock Holmes stories were lauded to the skies. By emphasizing the identity of Conan Doyle with that of Sherlock Holmes, and by juxtaposing this identification with the growing dislike Conan Doyle felt for that particular creation of his, Hoehling shows the tremendous irony in Conan Doyle's life.

In *The Man Who Hated Sherlock Holmes*, Wood also traces the creation and development of the Holmes stories, pointing out that at first Conan

Doyle did not realize what he had created in Sherlock Holmes, and that later he came to hate him. Wood feels that Conan Doyle "was Sherlock Holmes, of course . . . but the coldly deductive detective represented only a small part of his full and many-faceted nature." With his eye-catching title and by alluding to Conan Doyle's dislike of Holmes throughout his biography, Wood probably exaggerates Conan Doyle's hatred of Holmes. Since Conan Doyle dreamed of writing "literary" novels, undoubtedly his pride was hurt when Holmes proved so popular and his "serious" fiction, by comparison, received much less attention. Yet Holmes was the source of Conan Doyle's fame and fortune, and his attitude toward Holmes must have been equivocal.

Wood feels that Conan Doyle, as a doctor, had "a cumulative knowledge and wisdom that few other men can have." His early experiences in medical practice had enabled him to observe human nature firsthand, and the Holmes stories are filled with details based on these observations. Conan Doyle's readers found in his creations "the warm and living reality of the place, the time, and two remarkable men." Wood's final estimate is that "by his own standards, Conan Doyle must be counted among the great fiction writers in English. He had imagination, and he made his imagination contagious. He had the power to make men and women forget their own lives and surroundings and live where and when his stories took place and with his characters." If Conan Doyle disliked Holmes, it was probably because originally he had tried to make Holmes into a cold, rational machine. Though Wood stresses Conan Doyle's dislike of Holmes, he softens his estimate at the end of his biography. Inevitably Conan Doyle's own personality slowly appeared in the character of Sherlock Holmes as the years passed. Wood feels that the transfer of Conan Doyle's qualities to his fictional character infused Holmes with life. Conan Doyle's "own warmth of heart, humor, and high principles of conduct crept in, and Sherlock Holmes became as real as his maker."

Actually, Hoehling's *Real Sherlock Holmes* and Wood's *Man Who Hated Sherlock Holmes* often complement each other. With her romanticized approach, Hoehling presents a vivid portrait of Conan Doyle; and Wood conveys his own delight in Conan Doyle's fiction. However, both the Hoehling and Wood biographies should be read with caution. Like many other writers of fictionalized biography, Hoehling invents imaginary thoughts and conversations, even imaginary events, for Conan Doyle, and both biographies contain errors and inaccuracies. A young reader would be more wisely directed to John Dickson Carr's *Life of Sir Arthur Conan Doyle*, which can be read as easily as Hoehling or Wood.

iii
Conan Doyle:
A Biography of the Creator
of Sherlock Holmes

Ivor Brown is a prolific writer. Among his publications are studies of Shakespeare and Dickens, several collections of essays, and a number of books on drama. He has also written an occasional article on Sherlockian matters. *Conan Doyle: A Biography of the Creator of Sherlock Holmes* (London: Hamish Hamilton, 1972) contains no indication of any use of Conan Doyle family papers. Therefore, except for brief references in the text to Hesketh Pearson, Vincent Starrett, and Adrian Conan Doyle, there is little to suggest the sources Brown used for this study.[7] These are certainly diverse sources, and had Adrian Conan Doyle not died two years before the publication of Brown's biography, he would surely have reacted harshly to finding himself in Hesketh Pearson's company—and also to Pearson's influence.

Brown's estimate of the importance of Sherlock Holmes in Conan Doyle's life is reflected in the subtitle of his biography. To further point up this emphasis, Brown, instead of starting out with the early years of Conan Doyle's life, devotes most of his first two chapters to Holmes and his enduring popularity. After that Brown moves back to Conan Doyle's childhood, and the rest of his book follows the chronology of his life. Like the other biographers discussed in this examination, Brown is selective. He emphasizes Conan Doyle's relationship with George Budd, the half-charlatan doctor and seeming friend who later served as a model for Professor Challenger. Brown also emphasizes Conan Doyle's efforts to write plays, his movement away from historical novels toward science fiction during his later years, and his religious beliefs and final acceptance of Spiritualism.

Sherlock Holmes is discussed at some length throughout the book, though Brown, like Wood, has some trouble counting the exact number of Holmes stories. Brown makes it clear that Conan Doyle disliked his fictional detective and describes Holmes as Conan Doyle's enemy. After the publication of *Micah Clarke*, Conan Doyle felt that Holmes was be-

---

7. Vincent Starrett was an American journalist, bookman, and novelist who was one of the earliest Baker Street Irregulars; his book *The Private Life of Sherlock Holmes*, first published in 1933, is a classic of its kind. While Adrian did not approve of the Baker Street Irregulars, who tended to refer to his father (when they referred to him at all) as Watson's Literary Agent, he was on friendly terms with Starrett most of his life.

neath his "literary" endeavors. However, Brown believes that by *The Hound of the Baskervilles*, Conan Doyle had somewhat gotten over his resentment of Holmes, and that eventually Holmes was no longer a plague on Conan Doyle's life.

Brown differs from the Hardwicks, Hoehling, and Wood in asserting that Sherlock Holmes was definitely *not* a projection of Conan Doyle's personality. "To claim that Doyle discovered Holmes inside himself," says Brown, "is going rather far." Brown feels that a better case can be made for seeing Watson as a self-portrait of Conan Doyle: Watson was an educated man, a man of action who could participate in as well as narrate the adventures of Holmes; both were doctors, both had great physical courage and loyalty, and both were authors.

Brown sees Conan Doyle's interest in justice and social reform as stemming from his humanitarian instincts, supported by his "independent Christianity." Conan Doyle "was unsparing in his dedication to the good behavior of a conscientious and consistently helpful man. He was . . . an excellent citizen . . . incessantly busy with the promotion and execution of much-needed reform." In summing up Conan Doyle's patient work on the Edalji and Slater cases, Brown makes an interesting comparison between him and his creation: "Holmes rarely took a long time to get a guilty man into prison. His creator [in contrast] was ready to work at length as well as with inflexible determination to get two innocent men out of it." Yet, in his estimate of Holmes, Brown emphasizes that Holmes too is touched by Conan Doyle's humanity. "Unbelievable in his brilliance of detection we may often find him, but he is never an inhuman piece of showman's apparatus."

The popularity of the Sherlock Holmes stories, Brown believes, was partly due to Conan Doyle's shrewdness in estimating that the reading public wanted a continuing character in a series of short stories. Brown also points out that Conan Doyle was able to compress a whole novel into a short story with none of the padding so often used to attenuate Victorian novels of crime and mystery. He had the ability to tell a good story and to capture the reader's imagination. The strength of these stories is derived as much from Conan Doyle's simple, direct style of writing as from the public's fascination with the eccentricities of Sherlock Holmes. Brown is correct in noting the difficulties of literary critics who attempt to analyze the Sherlock Holmes stories while ignoring the great finesse with which Conan Doyle tells them.

At the end of his study, in his discussion of *The Lost World*, Brown stresses that something of the boy remained in Conan Doyle throughout his adult life. Brown quotes his well-known quatrain about "the boy who's half a man, or the man who's half a boy" and calls Sir Arthur

Conan Doyle "the man-boy novelist" who loved chivalry, romance, adventure and mystery, qualities that infused the best of his fiction—qualities that, combined with a clear writing style, have made the Sherlock Holmes stories so appealing to readers ever since they were first published. Conan Doyle "wanted to please and he did please. When he created his master-detective he became for a while, to his own chagrin, irresistible. He should not have been ashamed of Baker Street; it was the home of his best invention. But at that time he had not realized his own man-boyishness."

10 ∘ A SEARCH FOR EMOTIONAL PEACE

Peter E. Blau and Jon L. Lellenberg

The Adventures of Conan Doyle
by Charles Higham[1]

❧ "It's a fine book, but he mixes too much fantasy with his facts" was one critic's description of William S. Baring-Gould's tongue-in-cheek biography of *Sherlock Holmes of Baker Street*. The description is also appropriate for Charles Higham's "Life of the Creator of Sherlock Holmes," which is well written but at the same time flawed by error, exaggeration, and unsupported surmise.

Indeed, the flaws in Higham's book earned it the distinction of being the first of the many biographies of Sir Arthur Conan Doyle to receive a formal rebuttal from the author's daughter, Dame Jean Conan Doyle. In a November 27, 1976, letter to the *Times* of London, Dame Jean lamented "the surprising number of inaccuracies which appear in this entertaining, if somewhat fanciful, book."

But despite its flaws, Higham's biography cannot be quickly or easily dismissed. As one of only two biographies of Conan Doyle to have been published in a paperback edition in the United States (the other being Carr's *The Life of Sir Arthur Conan Doyle*), the book received wide circulation and is still frequently consulted and cited by authors of articles in both general and scholarly media. Fortunately, there is much to praise about Higham's book. As a "historical biography," dealing with the events in Conan Doyle's life and career, the presentation is generally well done and sympathetic. Higham sees Arthur Conan Doyle as more than simply a product of his era and environment—he sees him as a man whose unusual personal experiences and emotional trials impinged upon a natural storytelling talent to produce a writer of remarkable imagination and narrative ability. Conan Doyle, according to Higham, was influenced

1. New York: W. W. Norton, 1976; and London: Hamish Hamilton, 1976.

by others, especially Edgar Allan Poe, but he broke new ground, and his accomplishments in certain genres were extraordinary and lasting.

i

Higham's account opens in 1886 with a vivid description of Portsmouth and of Conan Doyle's home and of Conan Doyle himself, writing what Higham justly calls one of the most famous introductions of one person to another in fiction: "Dr. Watson, Mr. Sherlock Holmes."

Then there is a shift, to 1859 and Edinburgh. The city where Conan Doyle was born is presented with a strong sense of time and place, and as Higham's biography continues he displays a fine series of well-constructed portrayals of the world in which Conan Doyle lived. Higham is the first of Conan Doyle's biographers to have attempted such a description, and those pictures of Conan Doyle's world are welcome indeed. In this respect, Higham's book is the verbal equivalent of an album of photographs, an appealing concept, and an important one to the modern reader who can easily lose that sense of time and place when the biographer concentrates only on events. (The Boer War, for example, is for Americans a long-ago and hazy conflict between other peoples in a remote and unfamiliar place. Higham makes clear the stakes as the Britons and Boers perceived them, and he gives a vivid idea of the appalling conditions Conan Doyle faced there as a volunteer doctor in 1900.)

And the events in Conan Doyle's life have not been neglected by Higham.[2] He has relied heavily on earlier biographies, but he has also consulted unpublished sources such as the collection of Conan Doyle's correspondence at the Metropolitan Toronto Library.[3] And he was the first of Conan Doyle's biographers to learn of, or at least to disclose, the alcoholism and institutionalization of Arthur Conan Doyle's father and to speculate about the implications of this tragic family secret on his personality and development as a writer.

2. Nor events following his death. The book contains a ten-page epilogue, sensationally entitled "Seances, Mystery, and Murder," that deals with the Conan Doyle family's Spiritualist contacts with the deceased author in the 1930s and the disposition of his literary estate over 1955–75. It should perhaps not be taken entirely at face value. "Not for the first time," according to Dame Jean Conan Doyle ("The Higham Biography: A Familial Observation," *Baker Street Miscellanea*, no. 10 [June 1977]), "Mr. Higham has attempted to condense an extremely complicated subject, of which he knows only a small part, into a few paragraphs. The result is a misleading impression, and he is less than fair to my late brother Adrian."

3. See Cameron Hollyer, "'My Dear Smith . . . ': Some Letters of Arthur Conan Doyle to His *Strand* Editor," *Baker Street Miscellanea*, no. 44 (Winter 1985), for a detailed review of this correspondence.

The factual aspects of Higham's presentation are, by and large, accurate. His errors have two causes: his reliance on other sources and his failure to check his stories with those who could have corrected his mistakes. But it is likely that both author and publisher were under some pressure to benefit from the Sherlock Holmes boom of the 1970s. By 1976 the boom was well under way, initiated by the Royal Shakespeare Company's revival in 1973 of the William Gillette melodrama *Sherlock Holmes* and propelled by Nicholas Meyer's best-selling novel, *The Seven-Per-Cent Solution*. The dust jacket of Higham's book carried a last-minute sticker quoting Meyer calling it "the most complete, as well as the most completely fascinating" of the Conan Doyle biographies.

Higham is certainly not the first of Conan Doyle's biographers to have encountered such problems, which are all too common in the "secondary" biographies whose authors did not obtain access to the family archives or seek out members of Conan Doyle's family. But Higham did acknowledge the assistance of Conan Doyle's daughters Mary and Jean, describing the latter as having been "extremely cooperative in supplying information about her father's life." That statement is unfortunately misleading, and Dame Jean pointed out in her London *Times* letter that "our help was limited to answering a few questions." In later comments, Dame Jean expressed concern that Higham's acknowledgment of their help might lead readers to conclude that information in the book came from or was checked by "the Doyle children,"[4] and mention of their assistance was deleted at her request when the paperback edition (Pocket Books, 1978) was published.

Consultation with Dame Jean would have enabled Higham to avoid one of his most egregious errors: his statement that at the 1955 reburial of Sir Arthur and Lady Conan Doyle "the coffins were taken taken to their new resting place in a laundry van, and buried very late at night." His account was corrected, at Dame Jean's suggestion, in the paperback edition: "the coffins were taken in a hearse to their new resting-place where a service was held in bright sunshine on a morning in July in the presence of members of the family and friends." Higham's first version was, to be sure, a more colorful story, and his search for the colorful led to other errors, perhaps less important but still giving cause for concern. He names many of Conan Doyle's "close friends," for example, in a list that includes Kings Edward VII and George V, but there is no evidence for a "close friendship" between Conan Doyle and the two monarchs, let alone politicians such as Joseph Balfour, Winston Churchill, and Austin Chamberlain.

4. Dame Jean Conan Doyle, "The Higham Biography: A Familial Observation."

This search for color and celebrities stems, perhaps, from Higham's earlier work. His speciality is the "Hollywood biography"; his subjects include Orson Welles, Katharine Hepburn, Marlene Dietrich, Ava Gardner, Charles Laughton, Errol Flynn, Bette Davis, and Merle Oberon. Of these, *Charles Laughton: An Intimate Biography* (Doubleday, 1976) and *Errol Flynn: The Untold Story* (Doubleday, 1978) received the most attention. Higham revealed Laughton's homosexuality, and accused Flynn of being not only bisexual but also a Nazi sympathizer who was of significant aid to the Germans during World War II. The book triggered a lawsuit by Flynn's daughters. Their lawyer, Melvin Belli, hoped the case would allow a frontal attack on the long-held principle that the dead cannot be libeled, but the attempt failed when the California Supreme Court refused to review a lower court's ruling that there was no legal basis for the suit.

There are, to be sure, no revelations of this sort in Higham's biography of Arthur Conan Doyle, and many if not most of the "historical" errors are likely due to Higham's enthusiasm, which led to uncritical reliance on reporting by others (including paid researchers of his own), just as his exaggerations can be ascribed to a desire to make the book as interesting as its subject—aiming at a broad audience that might reasonably be expected to take an interest in the creator of Sherlock Holmes at a time of renewed public excitement about the literary character.

But as a "literary biography," dealing with the relationships between a subject's life and work, *The Adventures of Conan Doyle* is weak indeed. This weakness is, presumably, also a result of Higham's lack of expertise in writing about the lives of men and women who were writers. If one is to write about the relationship between events in an author's life and details in his work, one must possess considerable knowledge in both areas. Higham lacked that knowledge, forcing him to rely on the research of others and on a search for coincidence. Higham did both, and not well.

The search for coincidence is always intriguing, but those who engage in it seldom admit that coincidence is what they have found. It is the parallel that is the true quarry in this hunt. Now it is quite true that the geometrical definition of parallel lines requires that there be no intersection of those lines, but the parallels of literature are pleasantly exempt from that rigorous demand. Certainly there are connections to be made between Conan Doyle's work and events in his life, but at the same time one should remember that coincidence has a long arm. The farther one must reach in the attempt to make a connection, the more likely it is that it is coincidence that has been grasped.

Higham researched the papers and magazines that Conan Doyle

read (or could have read), and as the biography develops there is growing emphasis given to drawing parallels between Conan Doyle's fiction and its possible sources. By way of example, Higham discovered the anonymous story "My Detective Experiences" in the April 4, 1886, issue of *Chambers's Journal*, a magazine Higham describes as one of Conan Doyle's favorite publications. We are given two quotations, one about "an herculean individual in the garb of a navvy, with large sandy whiskers and red hair," and the other about "a somewhat diminutive individual, attired as a clergyman . . . his 'get-up' to the last detail was faultless, even to the gold eye glasses." Higham then suggests that "it cannot be mere coincidence that in *A Scandal in Bohemia* Conan Doyle disguises Holmes as a humble groom and a clergyman, that the King of Bohemia is described as resembling a 'Hercules,' that Conan Doyle later wrote a story entitled *The Golden Pince-Nez*, or that his next tale was *The Red-Headed League*."

How easy it is: find something that Conan Doyle could have read, describe the magazine as one of his favorite publications, search for similarities in his work, and then blithely suggest that those similarities "cannot be mere coincidence." But let us pause for a moment to reflect. Leaving aside the question of whether *Chambers's Journal* was indeed one of Conan Doyle's favorite publications (and there is no evidence for this), note that "My Detective Experiences" was published in 1886. "A Scandal in Bohemia" was published in July 1891, "The Golden Pince-Nez" in July 1904, and "The Red-Headed League" in August 1891.

And consider how far the long arm of coincidence has been stretched. Starting with an examination of the spring 1886 issues of *Chambers's Journal* (not unreasonable research, since *A Study in Scarlet* was written at that time), one finds a story about detection that contains a reference to a herculean individual, a navvy, red hair, a clergyman, and gold eyeglasses. Then, finding no parallels in *A Study in Scarlet* or *The Sign of the Four*, one turns to "A Scandal in Bohemia," published five years after "My Detective Experiences," to discover a Hercules, Holmes disguised as a groom (not a navvy, but let that pass) and Holmes disguised as a clergyman. And "The Red-Headed League," the next story published, does indeed involve red hair, and in the title of the story. Now, is there another story in the table of contents of the canon where a parallel can be found in the title? Yes, "The Golden Pince-Nez"—published only eighteen years after "My Detective Experiences" and thirteen years after "A Scandal in Bohemia."

Can this be "mere coincidence"? Indeed, yes.

There *is* such a thing as coincidence, after all. Higham has joined others in noting similarities in the names of friends and acquaintances and associates of Conan Doyle to the names of characters in his work, but this is essentially a sterile pastime, and the few new discoveries unveiled by Higham are so remotely connected as to be more humorous than scholarly. "H. G. Wells is subtly referred to in the 'Artesian Wells' of *The Three Garridebs*," according to Higham, and Wells is (of course) one of Conan Doyle's "favorite authors." Even more startling is Higham's discovery of a stonemason named Slater in "The Adventure of Black Peter." "This is very odd," Higham declares, "for later Conan Doyle was to be involved in the defense of an Oscar Slater, whose punishment for a crime he had not committed was to break stones at Peterhead jail."

There is also a demonstrable absence of serious research in the field of Sherlockian scholarship. This is not just a matter of obvious but minor error, such as calling the story "The Mazarin Stone" unique for being told in the third person, but rather of serious neglect. Higham cites most of the cornerstone books of the Sherlockian "Higher Criticism" in his "Selective Bibliography," but there is scant evidence that he read them carefully, and there is no mention whatsoever of the *Baker Street Journal*, the *Sherlock Holmes Journal*, or William S. Baring-Gould's *Annotated Sherlock Holmes*, the principal sources of information available at that time. It is difficult to imagine anyone attempting a serious discussion of the Sherlock Holmes stories while ignoring the wealth of information available in *The Annotated Sherlock Holmes*, but it is obvious that Higham did just that. And this led, in some cases, to astounding mistakes that severely reduce the value of Higham's literary criticism and his assessments of the relationship between Conan Doyle's life and literary output.

By way of example, the book's dust jacket proclaims that Higham "has discovered the source of the famous 'dancing men' code which so intrigued Holmes." And he does note the similarity between the cipher in "The Dancing Men" and the earlier "Language of the Restless Imps" published in *St. Nicholas* in May 1874. But Higham is not the first to notice that similarity, which was discussed in the *Bookman* as early as April 1910. Baring-Gould's annotations on "The Dancing Men" mention not only "The Language of the Restless Imps" but also other even earlier possible sources for the cipher. Most important perhaps was Conan Doyle's 1903 visit to Hill House, at Happisburgh in Norfolk, where he discovered young G. J. Cubitt's name and address written in an autograph book in "dancing men" letters. "The Dancing Men"—published in December 1903—is set in Norfolk, and Holmes's client is named Cubitt. Higham needed only consult *The Annotated Sherlock Holmes* to find a much more likely source for the cipher than a twenty-nine-year-old children's magazine. There are many other examples, and another essay at least as long as this one would be required to discuss them all.

ii

As a literary critic, Higham is uneven in his treatment of Conan Doyle's works. Sherlock Holmes gets considerable attention, as the author's most celebrated work, but Conan Doyle's many novels do not; they are mentioned in passing, if mentioned at all. Conan Doyle's sporadic career as a dramatist receives more detailed attention than they do. On the whole, Higham gives Conan Doyle good marks as a writer. Some of the novels he condemns: Higham feels that *The Refugees* "combined the worst of French historical fiction with a lame imitation of Mayne Reid," that *The Great Shadow* was not much better, that *Uncle Bernac* was "an artistic failure, reflecting his mood of depression and impatience at the time." Higham has praise, on the other hand, for the autobiographical *Stark Munro Letters* ("one of his most attractive and good-natured works"), the domestic novels *Beyond the City* and *A Duet*, the historical novels *Micah Clarke*, *The White Company*, and *Sir Nigel*, and tales of adventure like the Brigadier Gerard stories ("impish humor and strong sense of irony") and *The Tragedy of the Korosko* ("handsome and lively . . . He matched the best colonial adventure writing in this small epic of courage and survival"). But even for these, Higham has only brief and desultory comments.

What does interest Higham as much as Sherlock Holmes are Conan Doyle's horror stories. "He was at his best in the horror story," Higham proclaims, and he regards the horror stories, along with (in fact more than) the Sherlock Holmes stories, as expressions of the state of Conan Doyle's psyche throughout his life. Higham sees Conan Doyle's lifelong interest in the preternatural arising from his family's artistic fascination with it, and deepening in reaction to the problems of his early home life, his loneliness and religious doubts at school, his discovery of Poe, and his break with his family's church while in medical school.[5] Higham pictures Conan Doyle in his mature years swaying anxiously between gloomy pessimism about the purposelessness of nature and Victorian optimism about progress and empire, plagued by emotional distress over first his father's institutionalization and then his wife's protracted illness and eventual death, complicated by his ten-year unsatisfied love for Jean Leckie.

Higham claims that nightmares supplied Conan Doyle with elements of his horror stories, and in those stories he sees "Conan Doyle's equation of sexuality and death." This judgment, whatever its accuracy

5. "His experience of London [while visiting his Doyle relatives there in 1874] had changed him from being an average, bluff young Victorian into a youth who was privately haunted; Poe added a few ghosts to his mental landscape," says Higham.

(arguments can and have been made for it), suggests that Higham's views were influenced by Samuel Rosenberg's *Naked Is the Best Disguise*. Rosenberg's book, published two years before Higham's, does appear in Higham's bibliography; like Rosenberg, Higham perceives frequent syndromic sexual themes or veiled allusions in Conan Doyle's work, particularly in his short story "The Leather Funnel."

Higham sees Conan Doyle's horror stories as catharsis for the author's psychological turmoil over personal tragedies and religious quandaries. *The Parasite* (1894), for example, is a tale of malignant feminine mesmerism, described by Higham as "a strikingly personal revelation of neurotic sexual obsession, reminiscent of Poe but nevertheless expressive of Conan Doyle's mysterious and highly individual character as an artist." Higham considers the book to be Conan Doyle's reaction to sexual frustration caused by Louisa's illness, saying that its "equating of crime and sex is representative of the author's guilt feelings." But Higham evidently considers this catharsis a healthy literary and psychological outlet for Conan Doyle: it gave us the horror stories Higham admires so much, and it assured their author's emotional survival. "After cleansing himself with this curious self-revelation, Conan Doyle turned yet again to the writing of historical romances" (the Brigadier Gerard stories, which Higham also admires) is the way that Higham puts it.

Higham sees these impulses expressing themselves in the Sherlock Holmes stories, but not so strongly, and he allows of other, more external influences. He appraises the early Holmes stories straightforwardly, explaining the public's immense dismay over the death of Sherlock Holmes in "The Final Problem" in these appealing terms:

> People felt that a representative of pure disinterested goodness in a wicked world had been swallowed up at the Reichenbach Falls; that an embodiment of reason had been killed by an embodiment of madness. The symbolism was, many felt, all too clear: the sturdy, reasonable security of the Victorian age was crumbling rapidly before the forces of moral and intellectual disorder. . . . On a more mundane level, there was the sheer displeasure of being deprived of new and exotic Sherlockian adventures amidst the unexotic purlieus of London suburbs and quiet country towns. . . . The people of an increasingly scientific age yearned for fantasy, for magic, and for wild adventure; and now they were, it seemed, to be deprived of the most delectable fantasies yet obtainable.

In *The Return of Sherlock Holmes*, written in the early years of the twentieth century, Higham sees rather less of Conan Doyle's personal psychology than might be expected, for these were the years of Conan Doyle's unsatisfying relationships with his dying wife and with Jean Leckie. Instead, Higham emphasizes other factors: concern on Conan Doyle's part about the international balance of power; the author's "familiarity" with English nobility and royalty (an overstated familiarity, according to his daughter); Conan Doyle's own rich storehouse of past experiences (e.g., the whaling background in "The Adventure of Black Peter").

And Higham has considerable praise for *The Case-Book of Sherlock Holmes*, which Conan Doyle wrote near the end of his career. "Dismissed critically at the time," he says, "the tales are in many ways among the most interesting of his entire *oeuvre*." He concedes their "valetudinarian portrait" of Holmes and Watson, but he argues that this was "no doubt the falling off after 1923–1924 in Conan Doyle's health and energy, which was drained by his touring on behalf of the spiritualist cause. . . . But the imagination was as fresh and fertile as ever."

Indeed, "Conan Doyle's imagination flourished as powerfully as ever in the twenties," Higham says, arriving at that judgment as a result of a strong liking also for the author's science fiction, beginning with 1912's *Lost World*. Higham calls that first of Conan Doyle's Professor Challenger tales "perhaps his finest work in fiction . . . a masterpiece of imaginative fiction, reminiscent of Jules Verne but not suffering from the comparison," and says that its sequel, *The Poison Belt*, "in sheer imaginative force very nearly equalled the first." Conan Doyle continued to write pioneering science fiction in the 1920s, and Higham has high praise for it all, including the spiritualist Challenger novel *The Land of Mist* (1926), the "freudian" Challenger story "When the World Screamed" (1928), and the author's last novel, a tale of Atlantis, *The Maracot Deep* (1929).

Probably not many critics would agree with Higham, even those most generous to Conan Doyle. In truth, "imaginative force" seems by far the most important criterion in Higham's literary criticism, but that quality does not really go far enough to compensate completely for the loose plotting and construction of *The Land of Mist* and *The Maracot Deep* (leaving aside the polemical use of fiction to promulgate Spiritualism). Since it is the Sherlock Holmes stories, the horror stories, and the science fiction stories that most excite Higham's interest and earn his praise, the question (unaddressed by Higham) of whether Conan Doyle's place as a writer is in literature or in popular culture depends on one's assessment of these genres. Higham clearly regards Conan Doyle as a good and, more, an important writer.

But Higham places highest value on those very genres that most academic criticism dismisses as subliterature. Higham seems unaware of this. His enthusiasm for the "imaginative force" of the Sherlock Holmes, the horror, and the science fiction stories (perhaps exactly those genres most amenable to the Hollywood movie craft with which Higham is familiar) blinds him to flaws in some of Conan Doyle's later work. That leads him to embrace a half-truth, that it was Spiritualism that caused the literary critics to turn against Conan Doyle's later work: "He had, sadly, become a laughingstock in Bloomsbury, and the excellence of his later work in fiction was largely overlooked."

iii

Higham is not a Spiritualist, as John Lamond, Conan Doyle's first biographer, was, but he is second only to Lamond among Conan Doyle's biographers in dealing with Spiritualism sympathetically. Higham traces Conan Doyle's interest in Spiritualism to his early years, asserting that he was influenced in part by his father's fascination for the supernatural. He sees Conan Doyle's growing interest in Spiritualism, as the years passed, not only in reaction to the religious void in his life. Yes, he had abandoned Roman Catholicism without finding the scientific materialism of Edinburgh medical training a satisfactory substitute; but the personal problems in his life also played an important part, Higham contends: for example, "it is significant that at this time [1894], following his father's death and his wife's death sentence, and given the fact that the husband of a tubercular woman was then condemned to sexual abstinence, Conan Doyle reverted to an interest in other worlds." Higham notes that he was impressed by the interest in Spiritualism shown by some leading scientific figures, especially the physicist William Crookes: "The Watson in him, rather than the Holmes, responded to Crookes's experience," Higham says, contending that Conan Doyle did not understand that scientists can be unscientific in matters affecting them emotionally.

Then in 1897 Jean Leckie came along. Higham does not develop his argument, but he considers this relationship ("one of the most extraordinary in the history of literature") to be of tremendous importance. But it "had to survive great suffering. From the very first moment, he told her that he would not divorce his wife. He would never hurt the sweet, simple, and devoted Louise, and emphatically would never betray her sexually. . . . The effect on his health, the sheer pressure on a man in his prime, with normal desires, was crushing. He began to head towards a nervous breakdown." Conan Doyle's deepening interest in Spiritualism, Higham says, along with his great love for sports, was a way of working off the strains of his triangular romantic relationship. The Sherlock Holmes in Conan Doyle was also involved in the author's interest in Spiritualism, according to Higham, and it in turn influenced the development of the Holmes canon. "The idea of the survival of the personality excited Conan Doyle as much as cocaine excited Holmes," he remarks, rather facilely: "It seems charmingly appropriate that Conan Doyle should have brought Holmes back from the dead in this period [circa 1903] of hope and reverie."

In covering Conan Doyle's continuing investigation of Spiritualism, Higham does not regard it as an unhealthy fixation on Conan Doyle's part, as others have; he draws a balanced contrast between the "dark seances" and sunny sports that existed side by side in Conan Doyle's busy life. He also makes an unusual assessment of the effect of World War I on Conan Doyle's views. Conan Doyle did not simply leap at Spiritualism in reaction to the war's terrible carnage, Higham says: "Behind every line [of Conan Doyle's war history] can be sensed an agonized yearning. It is clear in these pages, more than in any other of his works, that he longed for service more than for anything else. Those who believe that an excess of pacifist feeling about the mass deaths at the front later drove him into spiritualism have entirely failed to understand the man."

But who has charged Sir Arthur Conan Doyle with an "excess of pacifist feeling"? Higham is simply off-target here. For all his attention to Spiritualism, he provides only limited insight into Conan Doyle's personal views, and his explanations are superficial: "As a lapsed Catholic, and a Celt to his fingertips, with a lifelong interest in ghosts, goblins and fairies, Conan Doyle found it relatively simple to embrace and propagate a faith that had an intense moral and emotional appeal," and so on. Most of Higham's biography from that point on deals with the Spiritualist crusade, drawing on *Memories and Adventures* and Conan Doyle's accounts of his speaking tours in the 1920s. But Higham's narrative provides little new information or insight, and his account of Conan Doyle's relations with Houdini gives no hint of the bad faith, trickery, and exploitation with which the magician has been charged in his dealings with the author (though not by Conan Doyle himself). Higham does provide a useful description of a well-rounded Arthur Conan Doyle during the Spiritualist period of the 1920s, contradicting the picture of an obsessed, spook-ridden *naif* that anti-Spiritualists often given the public:

> Conan Doyle's life in these years, despite all of his problems, continued to be well balanced between work and play, between hours at his desk and enthusiastic bouts of golf or long walks across the Sussex Weald, between attending countless committee meetings and enjoying the happiness and consolation of his family. He remained utterly devoid of pretense, mentally youthful, enjoying good eyesight and hearing, and refusing to tolerate insincere and calculating people. He was passionately absorbed in all aspects of politics, reli-

gion, science, painting, and literature, and despite grave misgivings about the future of the world, and his fascination with the future life, he remained very much a practical man, never foolish about what he believed to be a pursuit of the eternal verities. Oliver Lodge, the scientist and great friend of Conan Doyle's, was to say of him after his death that he "lacked the wisdom of the serpent," and this was true now and then in his encounters with blasphemous false mediums; but one can only marvel at his sense of wonder, the purity and almost childlike inquisitiveness of his approach to experience, characteristic also of his fellow Irishman William Butler Yeats, who similarly loved stories about ghosts and fairies.

Conan Doyle, Higham concludes, was "ahead of his time. He ventured into realms which are only now being fully explored. His misfortune lay in the character of the mediums whom he investigated."

iv

Was Conan Doyle a simple or a complex man, then? Was he Holmes or was he Watson? Higham never confronts these questions directly, and never refers to the "man-in-the-street" debate of so much Conan Doyle biography; in fact, Hesketh Pearson's *Conan Doyle, His Life and Art*, surprisingly, is not even listed in Higham's bibliography. Higham plumps for complexity from the outset, however, by posing in his preface the question of whether Conan Doyle was Sherlock Holmes.

Yes, Conan Doyle *was* Holmes, Higham says—and he was Watson, too. Both characters were facets of the author's personality, he argues, referring more than once in his book to "the complex maze of the mind of Conan Doyle-Holmes-Watson." Outside influences were certainly present in the development of Conan Doyle's literary interests and style, but Sherlock Holmes was in the main Conan Doyle's self-creation. Higham acknowledges Joe Bell as "yet another of the images on which Sherlock Holmes would be based," but dismisses him after barely one and a half pages of discussion. In finding both Holmes and Watson in Conan Doyle—"at once sportsman and mystic-logician"—Higham sees the two personalities as in opposition. He does not develop this idea fully but illuminates his concept of it in his exposition of Conan Doyle's life and literature. Conan Doyle's fiction was inspired by both sides of his personality, he says: the Watson in him moved him to write things like the Regency prizefighting novel *Rodney Stone*, the Holmes in him found expression in the Sherlock Holmes stories, the horror stories, and the science fiction stories. The Holmes in Conan Doyle led him to investigate psychic phenomena, the Watson in him made him more credulous and trusting than he should have been.

Unfortunately, Higham goes wrong often enough to weaken the credibility of his judgments about Arthur Conan Doyle. There are many instances of easily avoidable error in Higham's book, and it is a pity that he was not more careful in his research and in his analysis. Many of his opinions are vulnerable to charges of shaky evidence, flawed reasoning, and inadequate critical acumen.

Readers already familiar with Conan Doyle's life and work encounter mistakes early on in the book, and are thus warned not to take too much on faith. But readers for whom *The Adventures of Conan Doyle* is the first, or the only, biography of Sir Arthur are in some danger. Dame Jean Conan Doyle has described the book as "a 'good read' about my father, even though at times a fanciful one," and she is quite correct. Higham's biography is thoroughly readable, like John Dickson Carr's to which Higham owes a considerable debt, and it is to be hoped that it helped the general public to gain some understanding of Sir Arthur and his work. But for the serious student of Conan Doyle, its many problems limit its usefulness and make its conclusions about his life and work at best tentative ones requiring further testing.

11 ° **A SNIDE DEBUNKING**

David R. Anderson

Conan Doyle: A Biographical Solution
by **Ronald Pearsall**

Ronald Joseph Pearsall, born in 1927 in Birmingham, in England's West Midlands, and educated at King Edward's Grammar School, pursued a career as an artist and musician from 1952 to 1961 before taking up writing. Since then he has published over twenty books, most of them about aspects of Victorian and Edwardian culture. They include, prior to his biography of Conan Doyle, *The Worm in the Bud: The World of Victorian Sexuality* (1969), *Edwardian Life and Leisure* (1973), *Victorian Popular Music* (1974), *Edwardian Popular Music* (1975), *Collapse of Stout Party: Victorian Wit and Humour* (1975), *Night's Black Angels: The Forms and Faces of Victorian Cruelty* (1975), and *Public Purity, Private Shame: Victorian Sexual Hypocrisy Exposed* (1976). He had also written *The Table Rappers* (1972), a book about Spiritualism, and he belongs to the Society for Psychical Research.

Pearsall's bibliography establishes his credentials—their nature and limits—as a biographer of Sir Arthur Conan Doyle. Neither a biographer nor a literary critic by trade, he is a student of Conan Doyle's era, in particular the "unofficial" aspects of its culture: popular art, forms of wit, Spiritualism, cruelty, and especially sexuality. Thus, he is equipped (in some ways, at any rate) to set the life of Arthur Conan Doyle in the larger matrix of his times, to measure the man and his works against the ideas, events, and attitudes that helped to create and to sustain his achievement.[1]

1. Although Pearsall's book does contain a five-page bibliography, in part a listing and in part a narrative discussion of sources, it does not document facts, a common feature of popular biographies. Thus, the reader may know in general what sources the writer consulted, but it is impossible to determine at any given point in the book whether the information presented derives from the author's own published or unpublished research or from one of the sources listed in the bibliography. (The bibliography seems to suggest that the author consulted the Conan Doyle family archives, which actually were no longer available to scholars by that time.)

Such an approach to Conan Doyle should be a healthy one. The extraordinary appeal of Sherlock Holmes as a character has actually impeded scholarship about his creator, both because of the widely adopted fiction that Holmes truly existed, and thus could be the subject of biographical study in his own right (Pearsall's bibliography lists twenty-one Sherlock Holmes biographies, chronologies, and other works of Sherlockian "Higher Criticism"), and because of the rather uncritical attitude—typified by John Dickson Carr's biography—that many admirers of the Sherlock Holmes stories adopt toward Conan Doyle. On the other hand, there is the danger that the historian of culture, in transferring his attention to a single figure, will fall short as a biographer: that he will tend to oversimplify the character and personality of the individual, in order to "place" him in a preconceived milieu.

Pearsall's subtitle suggests that his biography seeks to identify the problems posed by the life of Conan Doyle and then solve them. In fact, however, the book does not take that approach, despite exhibiting instead both the virtues and weaknesses that might have been expected of it. Pearsall writes well about Conan Doyle's relationship to the people and events of Victorian and Edwardian England, but his treatment of Arthur Conan Doyle as an individual is simplistic and often condescending, sometimes to the point of snideness. This biography does not offer any new information or many new insights into Arthur Conan Doyle the man or the writer; its snideness makes its account of Conan Doyle's life as unobjective as the biographies that idealize Conan Doyle; but it does paint a valuable background against which a more definitive portrait of Conan Doyle may one day be placed.

i

Perhaps the central problem posed by Conan Doyle's life and works has been that of the extent to which his character was simple or complex. On the one hand, it seems unlikely that the naive, straightforward man in the street portrayed by some of Conan Doyle's biographers could have written works of such lasting interest and value, or that he would have engaged in such incongruous activities as defending Britain's conduct in the Boer War and pleading for mercy for the convicted traitor and notorious homosexual Sir Roger Casement. On the other hand, Conan Doyle did exhibit a shocking gullibility in believing in photographs of fairies, and in many other ways—his love of sports, his admiration for Kipling and Teddy Roosevelt, his contempt for conscientious objectors and women's suffrage—he can appear to be the typical bullyboy.

In *Conan Doyle: A Biographical Solution* (London: Weidenfeld and Nicolson, 1977), Pearsall portrays him as the Victorian man in the street. In doing so, he follows the example of Hesketh Pearson, who described Conan Doyle as "'the average man' made articulate," as "a big boy of a man," as a simple man who "believed his nature to be inextricably complex," who "felt as the average man feels."[2] In Pearsall this point of view finds similar expression. Conan Doyle is an "innocent" in contrast to the "knowing" Oscar Wilde, and on his first trip to America he is "an innocent abroad"; his motivations in wanting to fight in the Boer War were "not complicated"; he was "too honest and straightforward for the intricacies of party politics"; he "shared the tastes of the man in the street," and he "often voiced the opinion of the man in the street."[3]

The notion that Conan Doyle shared the attitudes of the man in the street serves as the basis for Pearsall's assessment not only of his subject's intellect but also of his psychology, aesthetics, and morals. For example, Pearsall comments that

> Doyle was both proud of being a writer and ashamed of it. He had the ordinary man's aversion to artiness, and was at pains to dissociate himself from aestheticism. . . . He liked to have about him plain men who spoke their minds, and who would not overawe him with long words. This possibly arose from a sense of inferiority, and his life-long interest in sport from a need to compensate.

In commenting on Conan Doyle's well-known efforts to correct the injustices done to George Edalji and Oscar Slater, Pearsall draws this distinction:

2. I quote from Hesketh Pearson's *Conan Doyle, His Life and Art* (1943). It was, of course, Pearson's remarks about "the man in the street" that angered Conan Doyle's sons and produced Adrian Conan Doyle's rebuttal *The True Conan Doyle*. In fairness to Pearson, it should be noted that his conception of the man in the street is not as simplistic as it may seem: "But the normal man is not the healthy innocent our newspapers would like us to think him. He is a mixture of strange desires, domestic sentiment, cruelty, kindness, and morbidity; and Doyle expressed his less pleasant characteristics as unerringly as his more presentable ones."

3. Adrian Conan Doyle argued that the best parallel to his father was not the man in the street but Sherlock Holmes, whose gifts Arthur Conan Doyle himself displayed in everyday life. Pearsall addresses that point of view in this way: "There is little doubt that Holmes possessed characteristics that Doyle had. . . . Holmes also had characteristics that Doyle would have liked to have had. Holmes was almost always right. Doyle often *thought* he was right, when he was merely being a conventional middle-class Victorian, just, in fact, like Dr. Watson. There is a good deal of Doyle in Dr. Watson." It seems unlikely that this analysis would have satisfied Adrian Conan Doyle any more than Pearson's had done.

It was not general altruism on behalf of the underdog; Doyle's social conscience, in so far as the poor, the unemployed and the aged were concerned, was no more active than that of his bloated pleasure-loving contemporaries. . . . Doyle's interest was in the victims of injustice, casualties arising from the clumsy machinery of the law.

Conan Doyle's aesthetics merit Pearsall's scorn, again because he shared them with the man in the street:

He epitomized middle-class prejudice in his attitude towards anything out of the ordinary in the arts. . . . [Of a passage in Conan Doyle's journal]: There speaks the voice of Victorian reaction, the assembled chorus of fuddy-duddydom which deplored all artistic manifestations that were unfamiliar and novel. . . . Doyle's attack on the Post-Impressionists as mad was symptomatic of the choleric-colonel approach to art. . . . He was among the mob in deploring them, indignant that such proof of arrant decadence should disgrace the walls of a gallery. And he was the voice of the mob; the public trusted him.

Dismissing Conan Doyle's collection of horror tales, *Tales of Twilight and the Unseen*, Pearsall again falls back on his man-in-the-street postulate:

Doyle shared the tastes of the man in the street. . . . The interest in sadism could result from suppressed sexuality, and it must be remembered that between the illness of his first wife and his remarriage, Doyle lived a tense unsatisfied life, celibate because his code of conduct demanded it. If strange fantasies lurked and sidled out through the medium of fiction it was not remarkable; it would have been odd had his conflicts not been apparent in some way.

The general notion that Conan Doyle reflected the attitudes of the man in the street, and these passages in particular, illustrate the weakness of Pearsall's handling of Arthur Conan Doyle's biography. He is more interested in the extent to which Conan Doyle's views on the important topics of his day reflect those of the typical Victorian and Edwardian (if, indeed, it is even possible to speak with any accuracy of a "typical" Victorian or "typical" Edwardian) than in seeming to understand the complexity of Conan Doyle's own character.

Where Pearsall does admit some complexity in his subject, it tends to be psychosexual and highly speculative. Pearsall's attempt to account for Conan Doyle's antipathy to "literary" types serves as an example. He suggests that Conan Doyle suffered from a sense of inferiority, though he neither specifies the precise nature of that inferiority nor offers evidence for it, and on this shaky foundation offers the further possibility that his interest in sports served to compensate for that sense of inferiority. His argument underplays Conan Doyle's great pride in the artistic accomplishments of his family, his intense admiration of many past and contemporary writers, and his relationships with writers like George Meredith, James Payn, and James Barrie. Pearsall's argument also draws upon generalizations about Victorian life. Pearsall believes that many Victorians "had emerged from public schools which were devoted to sport and where anything savouring of the artistic was treated with contempt," and he creates an image of the "typical Victorian hearty" that matches his image of Conan Doyle. These are the ways in which this book sacrifices character and personality to culture.

Pearsall's argument that Conan Doyle's defense of Edalji and Slater stemmed not from "general altruism on behalf of the underdog" but, rather, from an "interest in the victims of injustice" shows the same process at work. Pearsall denies Conan Doyle a social conscience primarily because he believes that Conan Doyle's "bloated pleasure-loving contemporaries" had little social conscience, and that Conan Doyle is to be considered a typical Victorian. In fact, however, Pearsall goes on to chronicle Conan Doyle's championing of the natives of the Belgian Congo, who were being cruelly mistreated by Europeans, and his efforts to reform England's divorce laws, where, as Pearsall states, "Doyle worked hard to change the law when it seemed to work against the underprivileged." After denying him a social conscience, Pearsall explains away Conan Doyle's defense of the underdog by reference to his culture—"he epitomized old-fashioned virtues" of Englishmen—without confronting and accounting for the apparent contradiction.

Pearsall often underplays evidence that appears to contradict the man-in-the-street thesis. He attributes Conan Doyle's interest in horror stories to the fact that "he shared the tastes of the man in the street," though, as we have seen, he also suggests that Conan Doyle's interest in horror stories may have had inner psychological causes in repressed sexuality. (But the period of repressed sexuality to which Pearsall refers lasted approximately ten years, the mid-1890s until 1907, whereas Conan Doyle was already publishing horror stories in the early 1880s and writing them still in the 1920s.) However, Pearsall points out that whereas "this tendency was deplored by Doyle's contemporaries," Conan Doyle "did not bother to apologize for [his horror stories]." Of his horrific medical story "The Curse of Eve," Pearsall says: "Another writer would have realized the repulsiveness of the theme and hastily destroyed the manuscript, but not Doyle." Thus, we have a man who shares the tastes of the man in the street, but who—unlike the "typical" Victorian—does not deny them, and a writer who is singular in not rejecting a story of a particularly horrific theme. Arthur Conan Doyle here seems atypical rather than typical—but Pearsall remains silent on Conan Doyle's claims to individuality and complexity, preferring to see him as a representative of a certain kind of Victorian world view.

Pearsall does not ignore all the instances in Conan Doyle's life when he exhibited a kind of complexity of thought or character that contradicts the man-in-the-street thesis, though he does, as we have seen, tend to play down the significance of those moments. Perhaps the most representative example of his treatment of a character that was in many ways unique occurs in the concluding paragraph of his biography:

> Conan Doyle . . . has been roundly dismissed as a Victorian philistine even by those who love his Sherlock Holmes saga, and he was impetuous, wrong-headed, and held views that were later taken up by patrons of the public bar and which today, to say the least of it, are hardly respectable. So did most of his contemporaries. But he did have the courage of his convictions, a strong sense of honour, and the stern awareness of where his duty lay no matter how inconvenient it was. He did not ditch his first wife when he fell in love with Jean Leckie, he helped to support a body of relatives even when they were not worth propping up with funds, and when he was in the midst of enteric fever in the Boer War he did not decamp back home to safety and a welcoming fire as many of his colleagues did. He saw glamour in war, but so did many others, he saw the light in spiritualism, but this is better than seeing nothing but annihilation as H. G. Wells came to do. He also anticipated retribution on those who did not respond to his call. But so did many missionaries of the past. Doyle's Jesuit upbringing, decry it as he did, had its effect after all.

In this final summary of Arthur Conan Doyle's character, Pearsall acknowledges the admirable facets of his subject's character: the courage of his convictions, his sense of honor and family loyalty, his physical courage. He does not, however, grant him individuality: his opinions were those of the patrons of the public bar, his attitude toward war that of his contemporaries, his missionary zeal that of the Jesuits. Pearsall never suggests that while some Victorians may have glamorized war and some may have believed in Spiritualism, few, perhaps, did both. Taken singly, Conan Doyle's beliefs and attitudes may not have been remarkable; taken together, they very possibly were.

ii

At the same time that Pearsall's concentration on the Victorian and Edwardian milieu tends to undermine his biography, it enriches our awareness of the context in which Conan Doyle lived and wrote. It is possible to read the important earlier biographies of Arthur Conan Doyle and not come across names like Aubrey Beardsley, Max Beerbohm, Arnold Bennet, Thomas Carlyle, Havelock Ellis, John Galsworthy, Thomas Hardy, Aldous Huxley, John Ruskin, A. C. Swinburne, and Richard Wagner. Pearsall does not write at length about any of these figures, but they serve as guideposts in an account of Conan Doyle's life to remind us of which figures and which issues formed the intellectual culture of his day.

Pearsall offers more than allusions to high culture. He also offers useful thumbnail sketches of Victorian medical education and practice, the institution of the circulating library, Victorian detection, Victorian police reform, and the Victorian taste for the occult. His most valuable chapters, however, are those devoted to "Detectives and Detection" and "The Rivals of Sherlock Holmes." They discuss the context out of which emerged the Sherlock Holmes stories, and the other detective writers of Conan Doyle's day, respectively.

Pearsall's capsule history of the detective story traces a line from the Bible through Voltaire, Godwin, Vidocq, Poe, Gaboriau, Dickens, Collins, and Le Fanu. Unlike Pearson, whose biography's similar history included only Voltaire, Dumas, Dickens, Collins, and Poe and argued that Conan Doyle did not owe much of a debt to any of those writers,[4] Pearsall takes Conan Doyle's debt to the tradition seriously, particularly his debt to Poe. "Doyle's debt to Poe is incalculable, and he admitted it," he argues, pointing out the similarities between Poe's "Murders in the Rue Morgue" and Conan Doyle's *Sign of the Four* (in one the murderer is an orangutang, in the other a pygmy) and "The Speckled Band" ("a window is replaced by a ventilator, and an ourang-outang is replaced by a snake"), and between Poe's "Gold Bug" and Conan Doyle's "Dancing Men" (both hinge on deciphering a code). More than that, Pearsall suggests that Conan Doyle owed another kind of debt to Poe: "Doyle took many of his themes from Poe. His most powerful and striking Sherlock Holmes tales are those where there is an element of the awful and a hint of the supernatural, for instance the spectral creature in *The Hound of the*

4. Pearson had observed: "But all this is beside the point, which is that Doyle was the first writer to give vitality and personality to a detective, and will probably be the last writer to produce short stories that are as thrilling and entertaining as the chief characters are vivid."

Baskervilles. . . . At no time did he ever pretend that the macabre side of Poe's talent had no influence on him."

Pearsall's chapter on "The Rivals of Sherlock Holmes" surveys the competitors Holmes encountered in 1903 when he reemerged in "The Empty House" from his watery grave. They were, he suggests, a sorry lot: "To describe the stories as invariably clumsy would be to over-generalize, but a brisk trot through them gives the impression of haste and disinterest, and sheer incompetence." Pearsall notes the presence on the scene of Bennet's Cecil Thorold, Clifford Ashdown's Romney Pringle, R. Austin Freeman's Dr. Thorndyke, and Baroness Orczy's Old Man in the Corner, as well as the creations of lesser writers as Max Pemberton, Arthur Morrison, Guy Boothby, Mrs. L. T. Meade and Robert Eustace, Jacques Futrelle, and Sexton Blake. (As Pearsall notes, "Clifford Ashdown" was a pseudonym of R. Austin Freeman.) These, again, are names that, for the most part, one seeks in vain in the earlier biographies of Arthur Conan Doyle, and their presence here helps the reader to "place" Conan Doyle the writer more accurately. Taken together with Pearsall's history of detective fiction, and with his continuing reference to the figures from Victorian and Edwardian high culture named earlier, the reader sees that Conan Doyle must occupy a kind of middle position as a writer—below Hardy, Shaw, Dickens, even below Swinburne, but far above the Max Pembertons, the Baroness Orczys, and the Arthur Morrisons of his day.

iii

Pearsall's biography belongs to the "life and works" type—that is, he interprets both Conan Doyle's life and his writings.[5] This is, of course, a difficult task in the case of Conan Doyle because he was such a prolific writer. In a book of this length, Pearsall can touch only briefly upon most of Conan Doyle's Sherlockian and non-Sherlockian works. On the whole, he regards the quality of the Holmes stories as very high, especially in comparison to other detective writing of the day, although he does express reservations about most of the stories. However, Pearsall does not devote enough space to literary criticism to produce satisfying judgments. Readers may turn to this book for his rather severe capsule

5. While Pearsall's bibliography includes the Conan Doyle biographies by John Lamond, Hesketh Pearson, Adrian Conan Doyle, John Dickson Carr, and Michael and Mollie Hardwick, it is noteworthy that there is no mention of Pierre Nordon's important biography *Conan Doyle*, which contained the best literary criticism of Pearsall's subject available at the time of his research and writing.

evaluations of particular Sherlock Holmes stories (e.g., "'The Five Orange Pips' has little to commend it except the title, 'The Engineer's Thumb' is melodramatic rubbish, and 'The Noble Bachelor' might well have featured in the pages of *Girl's Own Paper*") but not for extended analysis of how they work and why they succeed.[6]

Pearsall's basic thesis is that although the Sherlock Holmes stories are flawed in many particulars, they have sufficient energy and life so that the technical errors do not matter. Pearsall applies this reasoning to the issue of the many contradictions in the Holmes saga: "Doyle did not write for learned snail-watchers who would build a hide about each contradiction, and chatter to each other over their latest findings. There may be some uncertainty about Holmes's habits, but there is a commendable zest and certainty in building up the picture of the individual himself." But although this thesis may be useful for clearing the ground of nonissues, it generates, as the passage above demonstrates, rather vague criticism. "Commendable zest and certainty" does not, finally, mean anything specific, and Pearsall does not here help the reader to understand why the Holmes stories have pleased so many for so long.

He does, however, offer elsewhere some general suggestions as to why the Holmes stories please. He admires Conan Doyle's "unerring sense of place," his "way with the vivid phrase," and his "economical and persuasive description." He also argues that Conan Doyle is "at his most masterly" when the clients are stating their cases because he can create character and generate plot in so few words.

Pearsall's most comprehensive explanation for the popularity of Holmes, however, is a historical one: "Doyle had done more than find a formula—he had popped a needle into the vein of the public, introducing an antibiotic against the ills of the *fin de siècle*. He gave the reading public an archetype, a hero figure who was absolutely new and unique." While this thesis is appealing, one wishes it were more complete. As a passing judgment it may work well enough, but as literary-historical criticism, it lacks authority because it lacks development. What, in Pearsall's view, were "the ills of the *fin de siècle*"? Precisely how did the Sherlock Holmes stories serve as an antidote to them? And above all, how would Pearsall explain the continuing popularity of the Holmes saga now that we are in a new century with our own ills?

6. Perhaps it was judgments like these that prompted one of Conan Doyle's later biographers, Owen Dudley Edwards, to write: "Ronald Pearsall's *Conan Doyle* (1977) wants its readers to know its author is more worthy of admiration than its subject, and despite its enthusiasm for this enterprise, fails: it might have included information of value if the author could have forgotten the importance of his opinions long enough to deliver it." (See chap. 13 for a discussion of *The Quest for Sherlock Holmes*, Owen Dudley Edwards' 1983 biography of Conan Doyle.)

iv

Finally, then, Ronald Pearsall's *Conan Doyle: A Biographical Solution* occupies a kind of middle ground among the biographical studies of Arthur Conan Doyle. Pearsall brings to his subject a considerable knowledge of Conan Doyle's times and a sometimes refreshingly critical attitude toward both the man and the work. At the same time, the strictly biographical sections of his book offer little new information, and Pearsall's simplistic view of Conan Doyle as a person prevents him from offering a biographical "solution" after all. His general discussions of the Holmes stories and novels are of interest, but by and large they tend to be too undeveloped to constitute an important contribution to criticism. The most interesting and valuable sections of this book are those that focus not on biography nor on criticism but, instead, on Victorian and Edwardian life and times. It is useful to see Arthur Conan Doyle from the perspective of the history of culture—but the mystery of the man himself remains unsolved.

12 ° VICTORIAN PHILISTINISM RECONSIDERED

Richard Lancelyn Green

Portrait of an Artist—Conan Doyle
by Julian Symons[1]

    Julian Symons was born in London in 1912 and is the author of more than forty books covering a wide range of subjects such as Dickens, Carlyle, Horatio Bottomley, and the General Strike of 1926. He is best known as an authority on crime literature and has written around two dozen novels, including several award winners, and a standard history of the detective story, *Mortal Consequences* (1972). He has been chairman of the Crime Writers' Association, editor of Penguin Crime books, and he succeeded Agatha Christie as president of the Detection Club. His enthusiasm for Sherlock Holmes goes back to his youth. He has written two Sherlockian novels, *A Three-Pipe Problem* (1975) and a sequel (not yet published at the time of this writing), and has contributed introductions to the 1974 Murray/Cape edition of *His Last Bow* and the 1981 Secker & Warburg *Complete Adventures of Sherlock Holmes*.[2]

    If Symons' biography of Sir Arthur Conan Doyle was awaited with some trepidation, it was because he had previously dismissed his subject as a "super-typical Victorian, a bluff Imperialist extrovert," and a "Victorian Philistine."

    Symons' stated intention in the biography was to present Conan Doyle's life "rather differently from the way it is generally seen to-day" and to sum up the author's achievement for a "new generation." In neither of these aims is Symons wholly successful, but then the book is barely more than a hundred pages, containing only some twenty thousand words, as well as many illustrations. The text is divided into six

1. London: Whizzard Press/André Deutsch, 1979.
2. *Mortal Consequences* was published in Great Britain under the title *Bloody Murder* and has recently been reissued in a revised edition. Symons' earlier monograph *The Detective Story in Britain* (Longmans, Green, 1962; rev. ed. 1969,

chapters with headings like "The Crusader" and "A Public Man." If these do nothing else, they reveal by implication the gaps in biographies of Conan Doyle. There is too little about his agnosticism or his private life, no attempt to trace the literary and artistic influences on him or examine the effect his schooling and medical training had on his writings. Symons is content to take on trust Conan Doyle's own self-assessment and thus fails to elucidate the areas that Conan Doyle deliberately concealed. There is a brief mention of his father's alcoholism—based on Michael Baker's introduction to *The Doyle Diary*, which recounted the illnesses and institutionalized fate of Charles Altamont Doyle—but otherwise little about the pressures on Arthur Conan Doyle as a child, the possibly detrimental influence of his mother, or the constricting effort of his sudden rise to fame as the creator of Sherlock Holmes.

Symons had no access to the family archives, though he was able to check some details with the surviving members of the family. As a result his major sources were the previous biographies by Hesketh Pearson, John Dickson Carr, and Pierre Nordon, whose research he relies on and therefore tends to echo. He is less prejudiced than Pearson, less colloquial than Carr, and less pretentious than Nordon. He softens and shortens without achieving a greater focus. He was constrained by the lack of new material and could not therefore examine Conan Doyle's psychology or concern himself with the controversy inaugurated by Pearson's classifying Conan Doyle as "the man in the street." Symons does not suggest a complex personality but recognizes that there are areas of Conan Doyle's life for which a simple explanation is inadequate.

Symons' knowledge of the social background and of the ephemeral world of Sherlockian affairs provides an interesting gloss, but the biography really only serves as a larger canvas on which to draw an already familiar portrait. He places some emphasis on Conan Doyle's attempt to gain leniency for the convicted Irish traitor Roger Casement, for example, suggesting that it reveals an unexpected side to his character—but he does not examine the background to the friendship or the circumstances that led up to the petition. Both should be seen not only in the context of Conan Doyle's interest in the Congo and his friendship with human rights advocate E. D. Morel who introduced him to Casement, who had been the British consul in the Congo, but also as a corollary of his changed attitude toward Ireland.

A theory to which Symons subscribes is that Conan Doyle was both Holmes and Watson, but this is more fully developed elsewhere by other biographers. He suggests that Conan Doyle did possess some of the

---

Writers and Their Work no. 145) also includes some discussion of Sherlock Holmes and Conan Doyle.

qualities of Sherlock Holmes but does not commit himself one way or the other on the question of Joseph Bell's importance as a model. The dichotomy is true to the extent that Conan Doyle used his own characteristics, but that can equally well be found in other literary characters he created. Conan Doyle's most autobiographical works of fiction—*Beyond the City, The Stark Munro Letters, A Duet,* and *The Land of Mist*—are the places to look for unguarded revelations about their author's nature. Symons correctly classifies these novels as "oddities" but fails to draw many conclusions from them.

Symons finished his biography of Arthur Conan Doyle with a greater admiration for the subject than when he started and even contemplated writing a full-length biography, though the current legal complications that make the Conan Doyle archives inaccessible to scholars discouraged him from doing so. His admiration for Conan Doyle's works other than Sherlock Holmes does not appear to have increased to any great extent. He enjoys Brigadier Gerard and Professor Challenger but considers them the work of a good craftsman with a gift for narrative, and he finds the historical novels stilted. These are judgments with which many would agree, but they are also the clichés of Conan Doyle criticism that do not go much beyond the disappointment many people feel when they reread stories that once appealed to them. Conan Doyle's stories will continue to have their readers, but as the defects become more obvious, so they assume new significance as a reflection of Conan Doyle's character.

The book contains 122 illustrations, some in color, which were supplied by the Illustration Research Service and photographed by John Freeman. Symons had no say in their choice or in the captions, which at times strain to make the illustrations appear relevant. He should, though, have corrected the caption that misidentifies "The Brazilian Cat" as a Sherlock Holmes story. The illustrations do include some interesting unpublished material from the collection of Sir Arthur Conan Doyle's nephew, Brigadier John Doyle, and from that of Stanley MacKenzie, one of Great Britain's outstanding collectors of Sherlockiana, but otherwise they are somewhat diverse, being pictures within the text rather than illustrations to it. The relevance of a medieval battle scene, the fall of the Bastille, the inception of Mormonism, and street fighting in the Russian Revolution are not explained. Magazine illustrations are poorly reproduced, and the arrangement of the illustrations is sometimes clumsy. While some of the photographs and documents are of greater interest than the text itself, others are absurd, like the title page of the twelfth impression of *Micah Clarke*, presumably cut down to delete a signature. The lack of discrimination is unfortunate as it diminishes the overall effect.

The book's supplementary material consists of a bibliography, a chronology, a list of illustrations (which gives the sources), and an index. The bibliography is divided into six sections. The first lists the Sherlock Holmes stories, then the novels (without *Beyond the City* and *The Great Shadow*), followed by the short-story collections (with *Tales of Adventure and Medical Life* but without the other five volumes in the same series), the histories, autobiographies and belles-lettres, poems and Spiritualism. Conan Doyle's plays and pamphlets are not listed here, though some are given in a second bibliography within the index. The chronology is too brief to be of much use and is, in places, inaccurate. There are a few mistakes in the text, whether misprints like "The Last Special" or errors of fact: for example, Symons wrongly implies that *The House of Temperley* was performed during the 1890s, when in fact it had to wait until well after the turn of the century. Nor was it a success, or Conan Doyle would not have had an empty theater on his hands and thus the incentive to write a play out of *The Speckled Band*. Symons is also surprisingly inaccurate in his references to the Sherlock Holmes stories. The woman who shot Charles Augustus Milverton was not Lady Eva Bracknell but an unnamed lady who had been the wife of a "great nobleman and statesman"; Prendergast was not used as an aristocratic name—there is Jack Prendergast who was the leader of the convicts taking over the "Gloria Scott" and Major Prendergast who was saved by Holmes in the Tankerville Club Scandal; and the Duke of Holdernesse did not arrange the kidnapping of his innocent younger son, his offense was to conceal it.[3]

In short, Julian Symons wrote a biography addressed more to his own generation than to a new one. It has the feel of a potboiler and is disappointing in that the author could, had he had the time and the facilities, have produced a work of more importance. In particular Symons did not have the wherewithal to study Conan Doyle's life before 1890, or even from his birth to his first marriage. These are the important years, and they deserve very close study if a biography of Arthur Conan Doyle is to contribute seriously to our knowledge and understanding of the subject. But as Symons' book is well written, intelligent, and neatly ordered, it is, for all its faults, arguably the best *short* biography of Arthur Conan Doyle that has yet been written.

3. Further errors within the text are the reference to Arthur's grandfather John Doyle having four sons who possessed artistic merit. This should be five, as Francis ("Frank") Doyle, who died when he was fifteen, produced an impressive booklet of drawings called *Heads of Macbeth* (1840). Conan Doyle's interest in Spiritualism began at least five years before he joined the Society for Psychical Research. Jean Leckie was seventeen, not fourteen, years younger than her husband. *The Great Boer War* was started before Conan Doyle left for South Africa and not after his return to England.

13 ° FORESHADOWED BY HIS YOUTH

Christopher Redmond

The Quest for Sherlock Holmes
by Owen Dudley Edwards

"I am presenting a new story, and a new character," writes Owen Dudley Edwards in introducing his full-length study of a less-than-full-length Arthur Conan Doyle. Like several previous biographers, he uses the name of his subject's best-known creation in the title: *The Quest for Sherlock Holmes* (Edinburgh: Mainstream Publishing, 1983). Yet his book contains only modest amounts about Holmes and no full consideration of Conan Doyle's work. Though its author presents many new facts about the man we thought we knew so well—the second word of the text provides one such hitherto unsuspected fact, Arthur Conan Doyle's astonishing baptismal name of Ignatius—and many new theories and explanations, by no means does he present a complete narrative of Conan Doyle's life. He presents, instead, a certain kind of scholarly biography, which is a very different thing.

i

One might, in assessing the place of this fascinating book, generalize by saying that there are two sorts of biography, and that Conan Doyle, though often considered in both sorts, has so far been treated satisfactorily in neither of them. One sort is factual, chronological: it tells (and always with dates) of journeys, dinners, interviews, weddings, publications. The other is interpretative: it presents a portrait of its man, or appropriate aspects of him, and buttresses the portrait with selected data. Of course most biographical books balance the two, more or less uneasily depending on the skill of the author and the availability of the data. For Sir Arthur Conan Doyle, remarkably, the data are still fragmentary—no published source gives, to take a tiny example, the precise date of his arrival in Canada on his quixotic speaking tour of 1923—and biographers have frequently retreated into making bricks without straw (if not quite, as Sherlock Holmes once reasonably said he could not do, making them without clay). At the same time, they have been pusillanimous in avoiding any real attention to many things in Conan Doyle's life, in particular his curiously idealized perceptions of women, and have failed to provide a portrait of a man complicated and contradictory enough to be fully human.

The sequestering of the "Conan Doyle Estate" papers for more than two decades has no doubt been a factor in this difficulty, but so has the deliberate choice of previous biographers, whose work has concentrated on description and artistic judgment of their subject's writings (rather than the minutiae of his life), when they have not been producing mere hagiography or bland stories of Sir Arthur Conan Doyle the public figure. The recent publication of a definitive Conan Doyle bibliography provides by the way an essential compenium of biographical information,[1] but much remains to be compiled. Still, beyond the raw information, must come the interpretation and synthesis. Unless such efforts as Carr's adulatory *Life* of a generation ago may be counted, or more recently Pearsall's biography's attempt to let "its readers know its author is more worthy of admiration than its subject,"[2] that task has barely begun.

Edwards performs the balancing act between fact and analysis in an altogether new way. Indeed he presents—though it can never stand alone—the most credible biography of his subject yet written, credible most of all because of its scholarly distance from its subject. Edwards is neither making a myth nor deliberately breaking one; he is examining data in a way that is both microscopic and imaginative—and, some might say, heartless. He makes the result manageable by limiting himself in time and in emphasis and by refusing to limit himself in another vital attribute of the biographer: imagination, the ability and willingness to read life into census data, and to make ingenious leaps from the subject's life to his work and back again. There lies his strength, and there lies his weakness.

"There is a certain advantage," Edwards writes in his introduction, "in being cut off from the easy option." He makes it clear that he believes that previous biographers have taken the easy option. They have worked from what seemed to be on the record, either in the Conan Doyle papers (available to Pearson, Carr and Nordon), or in Conan Doyle's published writings and a superficial scan of other material. "It was very clear to

1. Richard Lancelyn Green and John Michael Gibson, *A Bibliography of A. Conan Doyle* (Oxford: Clarendon Press, 1983).
2. Edwards, *The Quest for Sherlock Holmes*, p. 20.

me," Edwards explains, "that if I wished to get anywhere, it would have to be with what I could find myself." And so he turned to the material at hand, to the records of "two areas of his life known to me, Edinburgh and Catholicism," and fashioned a biography out of what he found.

The limitations of the large and dense book that resulted will probably surprise some readers, for Conan Doyle, who lived to the age of seventy-one, is here taken through barely a third of his life—and it is the first third, during which he published no stories, wrote no letters to the *Times*, associated with neither literary giants nor political celebrities, preached no Spiritualist cause, made no triumphal tours, married no wives, saw no battles, and dreamed of no Sherlock Holmes. From his birth in Edinburgh in 1859, with distinguished forebears but in modest circumstances, until his tentative establishment in medical practice in Plymouth in 1882, Arthur Conan Doyle was naturally an interesting child and an interesting young man, but there was little evidence that he would one day be a world-famous writer and speaker. Edwards of course does not hide the existence of Conan Doyle's later life, and indeed devotes much of his attention to explaining it in terms of what came earlier, but he does not narrate it systematically, save through a sketchy overview in the ten-page introduction. (An epilogue of thirty-five pages, a tenth of the book, looks ahead from Conan Doyle's nonage to his earliest years as a published author—before he had given up medicine for writing—but not further.) This book is not meant for those who have never read a conventional life story of its subject (or, given the author's apparent contempt for all of them as partial and superficial, perhaps several such conventional biographies).

Perhaps it would be fairer to say that Edwards' system is different from the system we have seen before, the chronological system of Carr and his followers. It is rather the system of, if not Freud, at least the Freudian historians, the considerable school who trace an adult's public work, like his or her personal life, back to childhood, and who expect to find in that childhood the sources and even the foreshadowings of that later public work. Granted that premise, it is reasonable enough for Edwards to organize his study of Arthur Conan Doyle's life into ten chapters based on the experiences and influences of his first twenty or twenty-five years. Some commentators have wondered whether Edwards might now write a further volume, taking Conan Doyle into later years. Although such a study would be welcome, it could hardly follow the precedent of this one; by the time a man is twenty-three years old, the formative influences on him are history. On the other hand, the value of the present book will be limited if it is not somehow followed by equally probing study of Conan Doyle's middle years, in which the characteristics set out by Edwards naturally continued. The unusual family circumstances that gave Conan Doyle a two-dimensional view of women, to mention one topic to which Edwards gives close attention, continued to be an influence for most of Conan Doyle's life. And though Edwards does have something to say about his subject's early intellectual life, we are still lacking most of the material that would make possible a convincing study of how Conan Doyle came by his Spiritualist beliefs—perhaps a *Quest for Professor Challenger*, the iconoclastic scientist eventually converted to Spiritualism in *The Land of Mist* (something that Conan Doyle never did with Sherlock Holmes).[3]

It goes almost without saying that a biographer who attempts this task in this way thinks that his subject is worth it. The picture of Arthur Conan Doyle as bluff, good-hearted simpleton, the model for Dr. Watson and nothing more, must be thoroughly discredited by now, to the point that Edwards does not even try to contradict it, simply proceeding to shed light on a whole complex man with one small candle after another. He says little about the question of "creativity" and makes no evaluation of Conan Doyle's merits as an artist, simply taking for granted that the work is significant enough to justify attention to its creator. In the accretion of detail it becomes clear how Edwards connects the blood and pain in Conan Doyle's writings with the blood and pain in his early life, the women with the women, the good humor with the good humor. That is why he need not write explicitly about Conan Doyle's middle and later years, although the reader must be aware of further stresses and influences that those years provided: the sexual and ethical complications of Conan Doyle's two marriages, the exposure to literary acclaim at home and to war and savagery in Africa, and so on. For Edwards' freudian purposes it is enough, in broad terms, to portray the mature man as a machine whose life's work grew from his early development.

3. Edwards previously distilled his views on this subject in his introduction to *The Edinburgh Stories of Arthur Conan Doyle* (Edinburgh: Polygon Books, 1981), where he states: "Conan Doyle rejected the crude acceptance of Roman Catholic doctrine, with all of its certainties, which his school training had sought to inculcate, but he also remained doubtful about the equal self-assurance of scientific scepticism as transmitted by the Edinburgh University medical school. His life, both literary and spiritual, constantly reflected a mental conflict between science and the supernatural. Ultimately, Doyle was to find resolution of his long internal conflict in the spiritualistic faith, and to express the victory of spirit over science in the conquest of Professor Challenger, but a finer artistic expression of that resolution is to be found in the passages where the scientific Holmes acknowledges his belief in the spirit." (Those occur mainly in the late, and critically less well regarded, stories of *The Case-Book of Sherlock Holmes*.)

ii

Edwards is Reader in Commonwealth and American History at Conan Doyle's alma mater, Edinburgh University, where he is admirably located for the kind of firsthand research into his subject's early years that North Americans can only dream of—to say nothing of the atmosphere of smoke, Scots intellectualism, medical tradition, and Highland Catholicism that envelopes the city. His published writings deal primarily with the history of Ireland,[4] but among literary scholars he is known for *P. G. Wodehouse: A Critical and Historical Essay*.[5] Comparison of *The Quest for Sherlock Holmes* with that book is perhaps inevitable but would be misleading. For example, the Wodehouse study contains some twenty-one pages of footnotes, an apparatus entirely lacking in the Conan Doyle biography. But the reader will find that since the Wodehouse book is literary comment rather than biography, almost all the footnotes are page references to Wodehouse's own writings. There was no call (as there might be in the Conan Doyle book) to document statements about medical school examinations, travels, letters, and so on. *The Quest for Sherlock Holmes* does, one must immediately add, document its statements, though not in footnote form. In any case, this book is dense with fact (and, as will be seen, dense with speculation that is not yet proven fact); *P. G. Wodehouse* is bright with personal readings.

It has already been suggested that this biography is "scholarly" in a way not characteristic of previous books about Arthur Conan Doyle. Three factors make it so: its lavish supply of detail, drawn from disinterested primary sources such as civic and university records; its specialized point of view, brought out through the selection of certain subjects for close study; and its willingness to tackle the complexity of a man who, after all, was the product of many influences, not all consistent and not all positive. Within the first few sentences, for instance, Edwards forces the reader to confront the alcoholism of Arthur Conan Doyle's father, Charles Altamont Doyle, and he later elaborates both on the evidence for it and on the effect that it apparently had on his son's thoughts and writings. No previous biographer has pointed out so starkly the dark trail that drunkards and their violence leave throughout Conan Doyle's work; none certainly has dared to be so explicit about the unsatisfactory father whose memory remained with the young Arthur, and presumably with his beloved mother, all their lives.

4. His first book was *The Sins of Our Fathers* (Dublin: Gill and Macmillan, 1970), and Edwards is the author of a number of major essays as well as the editor of some volumes.
5. London: Martin Brian O'Keeffe, 1977.

Less original, but still emphasized here in a more candid way than previous writers have apparently felt able to do, is the concept of women that Arthur Conan Doyle's strong-willed mother somehow instilled in him, and that limited him all his life. Edwards has little use for the aristocratic matriarch who has been most biographers' idea of Mary Foley, as they obediently accepted the image Conan Doyle himself created for "The Ma'am." Rather, he speaks thus of her: "She may have become a great lady by force of personality, but she seemed [during Arthur's youth] to have nothing between her and the gutter but a salary of £200 of which more and more vanished on drink. . . . It is this which accounts for her son's triumphant belief in the superiority of women. . . . The little Irish girl in her twenties gave him his first real taste of indomitable courage, resolution, and a love for her children, above all for him, that was ready to rise above the most cruel privation and degradation." Not all readers of Conan Doyle's writings, noting how many weak, victimized women—and evil women—he presents, will agree that the "superiority" of women is made obvious; but certainly the picture of women is unrealistic. It is extraordinarily difficult to think of a woman in Conan Doyle's writings who is a convincing, and not supranormal, human being.[6]

The major factors that Edwards chooses to consider are those one might expect, given that he is discussing his subject's early years: immediate family (especially that inadequate father and perhaps overadequate mother), ethnic heritage, city, religion, and education. A valuable chapter discusses, for example, the Jesuits of Stonyhurst College, the secondary ("public") school where Conan Doyle spent some five years away from home. Scholars thus learn for the first time about the Reverend Cyprian Splaine, who influenced Arthur Conan Doyle as he influenced Gerard Manley Hopkins. Similar close attention is given to the medical professoriat of Edinburgh University. There were other figures at Edin-

6. Again, in his introduction to *The Edinburgh Stories*, Edwards says: "The diabolical women themselves, however, reflect a different aspect of Doyle. He was a believer in 'the new woman' in many respects: the great creative period which produced *The Parasite* also included two very powerful statements for the rights of women in professional life, 'The Doctors of Hoyland' and *Beyond the City*. In our two stories [*The Parasite* and "John Barrington Cowles"] the women are evil, and women in Doyle's fiction are normally forces for good, if at times ambiguous and frustrated in that work. Doyle believed in the superiority of women, very largely because of his overwhelming admiration for his own mother, who kept a struggling family together despite his father's alcoholism and inability to take responsibility. These two stories show a female superiority turned to evil consequences, but the testament to that superiority is still there. Elsewhere in his work the point is as vigorously made in happier contexts. It will be remembered that the first of the Holmes short stories, which were to put him on the road to immortality, was a firm, almost brutal, assertion of his defeat at the hands of a woman."

burgh as important to Conan Doyle's thought and style—to say nothing of his stock of characters—as the legendary Joe Bell himself. The existence of some of them, and the importance of William Rutherford in particular, were not unknown before Edwards wrote, of course. But he also presents more detail about such men as John Hutton Balfour and Robert Christison, and thus a fuller picture of the influences at work in the Edinburgh medical school, than had been available.[7]

While there are many revelations large and small, of which Arthur Conan Doyle's baptismal name of Ignatius is but an example, the most striking new information provided in this biography is the influence on Conan Doyle of two previously little-known figures: Henry Highland Garnet and Bryan Charles Waller. Each earns a chapter in Edwards' work. After identifying Garnet, the black American abolitionist orator, writer, and diplomat whom Conan Doyle met in Liberia in 1881 during his months as apprentice doctor aboard a merchant ship, he discusses the ways in which Garnet permanently broadened Conan Doyle's horizons in the course of a three-day acquaintanceship—including the passionate treatment of slavery in Conan Doyle's second noteworthy story, "J. Habakuk Jephson's Statement," published in the *Cornhill Magazine* in January 1884. Edwards also begins the exercise of tracing black men and wooden-legged men, and the many ambivalences they raise, in Conan Doyle's later work. It will take more scholars than one, and psychologists as well as critics, to finish that considerable job, although some have already taken a few tentative looks at the repeated motifs of crippled legs and scarred faces—which (needless to say) may owe as much to Conan Doyle's surgical training as to any one memorable encounter later.

As for Waller, a medical man six years older than Arthur Conan Doyle, it would be no exaggeration to say that Edwards considers him the most important single figure directing Conan Doyle's life and thought and work. Previous biographers, Nordon in particular, have given Waller credit for instilling in Conan Doyle the practical, brash agnosticism—not unprecedented in doctors by any means—that led him to break with the Roman Catholicism of his family, remained his philosophy for most of his life, and led him at last to Spiritualism. Edwards goes much further, making clear that he believes it was Waller who led Conan Doyle to the practice of medicine itself, Waller (a poet and the descendant of a family of literary folk) who reintroduced him to the world of literature (fatefully including, perhaps, Edgar Allan Poe), Waller whose professional style and personality provided the real model for Sherlock Holmes. (It is no-

7. Ely M. Liebow's study of that place and period, *Dr. Joe Bell: Model for Sherlock Holmes* (Bowling Green University Popular Press, 1982), was being written at the same time as Edwards' life of Arthur Conan Doyle; neither author was able to consult the other's work, and both make considerable contributions.

table that Waller was born in July 1853, within months of the popularly presumed date of Holmes' birth, January 6, 1854, and that young authors traditionally portray heroes who are just slightly older than they are themselves.)

In investigating Waller's hitherto unsuspected role as a major influence on Arthur Conan Doyle, Edwards works, as elsewhere in his book, from fragments of data, such as the census and tax assessment records that indicate Waller moved into the Doyle household in Edinburgh as a boarder but soon was paying the rent on the house. He examines Waller's poems for emotional clues, tries to determine just when Waller supplanted Charles Doyle as the real head of the Doyle household, convincingly pictures Waller co-signing the certificate to have the alcoholic, epileptic artist finally confined to an asylum. He reminds readers that Conan Doyle's revered mother lived for some considerable time on Waller's family estate at Masongill, Yorkshire (until moving in her old age to West Sussex near her daughter Connie, Mrs. E. W. Hornung). It is not hard to believe his theory, though he is able to offer no direct proof of it, that Waller was in love with Arthur's older sister Annette and that she rejected him. Such a rejection, with the embarrassment and family disagreement that would be bound to follow, plausibly explains Conan Doyle's reticence about Waller in his later writings and (says Edwards) in his letters, even the letters he wrote to a mother who must still have been in frequent contact with Waller.[8]

Even if Annette had nothing to do with the case, the reticence is psychologically plausible if Conan Doyle was as profoundly influenced by Waller as Edwards says, and as previous biographers with access to the Conan Doyle papers have hinted but not quite said. Influence brings counterreaction, and if Waller—just enough older than Arthur to be influential—lent him books, introduced him to people and ideas, helped him with his medical studies, and gave him a lifelong philosophical outlook, a certain amount of rebellion was probably inevitable. Cullingworth, the madcap doctor in Conan Doyle's half-autobiographical novel *The Stark Munro Letters*, may owe something to Waller as well as to the better known George Turnavine Budd. (Edwards also associates Budd with Professor Challenger but regrettably does not touch on Conan Doyle's choice of the odd name of a real Dr. Cullingworth to disguise Budd in the earlier novel.)[9]

8. It is not clear how Edwards knows; the bulk of Arthur Conan Doyle's letters to his mother are believed to be among the family papers not currently available to scholars.

9. One continues to wonder why Waller has been so little discussed in previous biographies (and some of what Nordon did write in the original French edition of his book has disappeared in the English translation). The unpublished letter

iii

All these things, and much more, Edwards tells in a generally lively, though formal, style. He has exasperated some critics and readers, however, for two closely linked reasons: an alleged shortage of documentation and the speculative matter he presents. The former complaint may be a disguise for the latter, of course, in the sense that surprising or disconcerting claims might be accepted a little more readily if the incontrovertible proof were baldly presented on the page. Edwards could occasionally have avoided that particular criticism with a few words of explanation. When hard facts are at issue, detailed documentation is certainly sometimes lacking in the Edwards biography, though less seriously than critics have believed. Ten pages of "Sources, Acknowledgments and Procedures" are only a small consolation for the lack of footnotes, since they do not tell the scholar where to find proof of any particular statement or make further study of specific points easy. But there is strictly speaking no need for a footnote when Edwards says in his text that "The Valuation Rolls preserved in the Scottish Record Office, the City Directory and the matriculation rolls of the University, taken together, convey" certain information. File numbers might be welcome, but their absence is an annoyance, not a flaw in the argument.

The more important criticism is that Edwards often leans heavily on probabilities, even guesswork. To be sure, his book would be markedly thinner if the only statements in it were the ones for which he could provide proof. Neither letters nor reminiscences exist, for example, to provide firsthand evidence of a romance and a break between Bryan Charles Waller and Annette Conan Doyle, let alone the reasons for any such break. (Waller did write a sad poem entitled "Annette's Music," but we must be well aware from our studies of Conan Doyle that it is dangerous to presume autobiography in any published literary work.) One reviewer of the book observed that Edwards' study "turns all too often into a relentless ransacking of the life for sources what 'explain' the events of the fiction."[10] Whether the existence of so much speculation is a distinc-

from Adrian Conan Doyle to William S. Baring-Gould, editor of *The Annotated Sherlock Holmes*, dated January 20, 1966, previously mentioned in another chapter of this book, describes Waller's influence as "deep" and states that his "remarkable" letters to Conan Doyle were then at Adrian's Chateau de Lucens in Switzerland. Presumably they are among the papers which are now the hostages of litigation.

10. Richard Deveson, writing in the *New Statesman*, December 31, 1982. Similar phrases could be cited for example from Patricia Craig in the London *Times Literary Supplement*, December 24, 1982, and H. R. F. Keating in the *Spectator*, January 8, 1983. Edwards himself says in the biography that "I have simultaneously been seeking to explain how many of the stories came to be written, and

tion or a blemish depends on the reader—on whether each example of it seems persuasive to the reader, and on how well the reader will tolerate an author who remains appropriately skeptical about Arthur Conan Doyle, even while exercising the imagination, rather than uncritically describing his "steel true and blade straight" (to cite his epitaph). To many readers, in the end, most of Edwards' suggestions will seem persuasive, and his approach both acceptable and successful. At a minimum, one can argue that the speculations are the most convincing offered to date, and of course any reasonable hypothesis is a little better than none when we attempt to understand Arthur Conan Doyle at something like a century's remove.

Further, it is only fair to Edwards to make clear that he does show an understanding of the difference between demonstrated fact and plausible theory. He says, in pointing to incidents in the life of Edinburgh University that seem to be the originals of incidents in Conan Doyle's fiction: "It is very unlikely that Arthur missed all of the Edinburgh meetings, although we know that he was there no more than we do that he attended Hartington's Rectorial." A statement that Arthur Conan Doyle's absence from a major event is "unlikely" hardly amounts to a reckless allegation that he was there, especially when coupled with an explicit disavowal of any hard evidence. This degree of caution is typical throughout the book, and readers who have missed it may not be giving Edwards the fair and close attention his work deserves. They remain, of course, at liberty to disagree with him, to deplore his occasional risky suggestions, and even to question his wisdom in speculating so much, but they cannot really claim that he confuses speculation with fact.

A general frustration, at least for North American readers, is that so many of the sources Edwards used can in practice only be consulted on the spot; one envies his location in Edinburgh for more than just the atmosphere. Much of his material appears to have been made available through the kindness of members of the Conan Doyle family and others to whom scholars on this side of the Atlantic do not find it easy to apply. He apparently did not have access to Conan Doyle's own papers—those remain sequestered under the authority of some court, though after a generation they seem more a chimera than a temporarily unavailable reality, and one awaits with resignation some explanation of who has them and when scholars may get at them. Much material not part of the

---

employing the evidence they give about their author to fill in gaps in what is known of his life." Anthony Burgess (in contrast to the critics mentioned above) wrote enthusiastically in the *Observer*, December 5, 1982, that Edwards had done an excellent job: "This is a long dense book, admirably executed, and the labour that has gone into it finds its justification in the author's conviction that Conan Doyle was a great writer."

estate archive, however, is in the hands of surviving members of the family, especially Sir Arthur's daughter, Dame Jean Conan Doyle, and his nephew, Brigadier John Doyle, and Edwards records his gratitude for their help. (Perhaps out of courtesy to the family, he is circumspect in his phrasing about such unpleasant matters as Charles Doyle's degeneration.)

The "Sources, Acknowledgments and Procedures" mentions a number of other sources, chiefly British and Irish, which apparently have not been consulted before. Edwards observes, for example, that he has gleaned much from Conan Doyle's letters to Roger Casement, now held in the National Library of Ireland—not just much about the Casement treason case of 1916 and about the everyday matters on which Conan Doyle was working at the time, "but in more general terms . . . much about ACD's sense of his Irish and Catholic heritage." (Such abstractions are of course difficult to summarize but must have been in Edwards' mind as background for the specifics he was reporting.) His brief essay on sources does more, in fact, than attempt to compensate for the shortage of documentation elsewhere in the book; it tells the reader a good deal about a scholar's approach to a new subject—which is of course not the approach of an enthusiast already familiar with it—and might well give useful guidance to the next scholar to take up the work. That so rich a trove was waiting for Edwards' investigative eye says something, too, about how little has really yet been done in the way of research into Arthur Conan Doyle's life and work, and how easy it will be to do a great deal more.

Epilogue ∘ **THE QUEST CONTINUES**
Jon L. Lellenberg

Arthur Conan Doyle's outward appearances have led many people to assume—rashly—that he could be easily summed up, even dismissed (in words once used by Julian Symons), as a "supertypical Victorian, a bluff Imperialist extrovert."[1] And the universal, often cultlike, following that Sherlock Holmes attracts has helped ensure that Conan Doyle's life would receive more popular than scholarly attention. Eleven of his thirteen biographers have been amateurs, popularizers, commercial writers, or mystery novelists. Only two have been scholars. And as one worked outside the world of English letters, and the other was a historian indulging a personal inclination toward pet literary subjects, the academic community has not felt obliged, it seems, to take their efforts very seriously.

But those outward appearances, it should be clear by now, were deceiving. We know enough about Arthur Conan Doyle now to glimpse a more interesting person and artist than most people have realized. His own nature as a very private person, hidden behind the attributes that misled Symons and others, has been largely responsible for the misunderstanding. Even as a celebrated author and a public figure, Conan Doyle resented familiarity, and out of a strong sense of discretion about certain deeply personal issues, he chose to tell an impersonal and incomplete version of his life in his autobiography. Sometimes he was more candid in his fiction, and unguarded biographical disclosures can indeed be found in *The Stark Munro Letters*, *Beyond the City*, *A Duet*, and *The Land of Mist*. It is a sad fact that all but the first of these novels have been overlooked by most of his biographers. And in giving attention to the first, Hesketh Pearson exaggerated George Budd's significance and ignored the novel's discussion of the young Conan Doyle's religious quandaries and loss of faith. Conan Doyle biography has not yet fully recovered from the effects of Pearson's blunder.

Biographically, Conan Doyle's fiction is probably of greatest untapped significance on the subject of his religious uprootedness, which

1. Julian Symons, *Mortal Consequences, A History—From the Detective Story to the Crime Novel* (New York: Harper and Row, 1972), p. 64.

to date has been too much neglected by his biographers and critics. Nothing harmed Conan Doyle's reputation as a writer and a public figure more than the supposed simplemindedness of his embrace of Spiritualism and other psychic pursuits.[2] People unfamiliar with him, except as the creator of Sherlock Holmes, did not realize that this was no sudden reversal of course. Conan Doyle had an apparent emotional need to believe in things, and he was a Spiritualist at heart much earlier than he was prepared to admit, even to himself.[3] *The Stark Munro Letters* provides Conan Doyle's frankest commentary about his break with Roman Catholicism, his adoption of an agnosticism allowing for some Causality beyond mere physical phenomena, and his yearning for a new religiosity. *The Land of Mist* treats, in somewhat epic fashion, the finding of one in Spiritualism. But that was not the first time the subject had appeared in Conan Doyle's writings. Spiritualism crops up in stories and novels by him from the early 1880s on, and almost always sympathetically, despite his claims of skepticism prior to 1916—suggesting that a Spiritualist conclusion to his search for religious fulfillment was perhaps preordained. But he was autobiographically taciturn on those subjects, and his Spiritualist convictions have all too frequently been mistaken for an aberration arising from wartime emotional upheaval.

Some other things of great importance in Conan Doyle's life were also mentioned barely or not at all by him: his father's alcoholism and the last fourteen years of his life spent in asylums; the curious role of Bryan Charles Waller in the affairs of the Doyle family and his influence on the young Arthur; the pitfalls of Conan Doyle's early days in practice followed by the traumatic collapse of his expectations and a new attempt to stand more modestly on his own; his family's occasional helping hand at this time and his own later one to members of his family; the strong

2. "Poor Sherlock Holmes—Hopelessly Crazy?" was the title of a not atypical 1922 American magazine article about the publication of Conan Doyle's book *The Coming of the Fairies.* See Michael Baker, *The Doyle Diary* (London: Paddington Press, 1978), p. xix. The starkness of the apparent contrast between the occultist creator and his superrationalist creation is sharply defined in Martin Gardner's essay "The Irrelevance of Conan Doyle," in *Beyond Baker Street,* ed. Michael Harrison (Indianapolis: Bobbs-Merrill, 1976), pp. 123–35.

3. Conan Doyle's earliest letter to the press on the subject, for instance, decades before his "conversion" in 1916, was not at all the letter of a doubter or even an impartial, unbiased inquirer. "Some months ago," he wrote to the Spiritualist paper *Light* on July 2, 1887, "I read [various Spiritualist] writings on the subject. After weighing the evidence, I could no more doubt the existence of the phenomena than I could doubt the existence of lions in Africa, though I have been to that continent and have never chanced to see one." See Arthur Conan Doyle, *Letters to the Press,* ed. John Michael Gibson and Richard Lancelyn Green (London: Secker and Warburg, 1986), pp. 25–27. Conan Doyle's early, nearly forgotten novel *The Mystery of Cloomber* (1889) is almost embarrassingly pro-Spiritualist.

influence his mother continued to exert until nearly the end of his life; his stressful platonic relationships, over ten years, with his dying wife and with Jean Leckie, the new, great love of his life; and the details of the occult experiments and controversies that delivered him eventually to Spiritualism.

Few of Conan Doyle's biographers ever came close to grips with these crucial aspects of his life or with his careful exclusion of them from his own accounts of it. His worshipful fellow Spiritualist John Lamond viewed everything in Conan Doyle's life as a preparation for the author's conversion to Spiritualism, but Lamond's account was unanalytical and uninformed about some important details of that life. Lamond put his finger on one vital point, in viewing Conan Doyle's life as a series of "knightly quests," but he praised that trait without inquiring into what lay behind it. Nor did any serious literary criticism lead him to his conclusion that Conan Doyle occupies a first-rate place in literature.

Hesketh Pearson's iconoclastic desire to play the critic resulted in his cavalier explanation of Arthur Conan Doyle as "the man in the street." That misleading perception lingers today, despite Adrian Conan Doyle's noisy attempts to eradicate it. Thinking of himself as an artist rather than as an historian, Pearson's preferred image of Conan Doyle blithely ignored important aspects of his subject's life. He went wrong from the start by taking Conan Doyle's self-assessment of his early years at face value, and his failure to treat Conan Doyle's Spiritualism responsibly was equally deplorable. Pearson appreciated the fact that Sherlock Holmes is a remarkable creative achievement transcending the printed page of fiction, but Conan Doyle emerged from Pearson's uncomplimentary biography with little credit for it. Pearson's dramatist's instincts also led him to look for memorable characters, and finding one not in Conan Doyle himself but in George Budd, he sought to explain away all of Conan Doyle's creativity through Budd.

Adrian Conan Doyle never passed up an opportunity to attack Hesketh Pearson and his "fakeography" of Adrian's father. Absolutely convinced that his highly idealized view was the only legitimate one, he tried to bring the critics and public around to see his beloved father just as he did: as definitely Sherlock Holmes but much, much more. Adrian's overblown and strident efforts never convinced, because his unblemished view of a very human person was manifestly unrealistic.

Adrian had great hopes, however, of succeeding through John Dickson Carr's biography, and to a great extent he did. Carr's *Life of Sir Arthur Conan Doyle* has been the most influential of the biographies by far, at least among the public at large, creating however sincerely an idealized portrait of the man and his life. Carr may have captured Conan Doyle's personality better than most, but he failed by default to explain the making of that personality. The entire first decade of Conan Doyle's life was given inexcusably short shrift, and his relationships with his mother, with Waller, and with his first wife and Jean Leckie, while acknowledged, did not receive the examination they deserve. Nor did the Spiritualist crusade of Conan Doyle's last eleven years. Carr's "editing and arranging" of Conan Doyle's life was intended instead to propagate the image of a gallant Knight contending with the forces of injustice, and many people now think of Conan Doyle precisely that way, thanks to the luminous narrative power of Carr's biography.

Carr's discussion of Conan Doyle's literary work, though quite enthusiastic, was short on criticism. Carr regarded Conan Doyle as a first-rate writer, but he lacked the credentials and critical approach needed to persuade the more disinterested of his readers that he was not simply reflecting his own literary tastes and qualities in praising Conan Doyle's. This apparently did not occur to Adrian Conan Doyle at the time; Adrian simply felt that his father was a truly great man, had become so because he was a great writer, and therefore his literary works were great works.

But Adrian deserves more credit than he tends to receive for cooperating with Pierre Nordon, the first (and nearly the only) scholar to consider Conan Doyle's literary career seriously. He gave Nordon largely unhampered access to the family archives, and Nordon subjected the evidence he found there, and elsewhere, to an analytical and critical treatment that Conan Doyle has scarcely ever received from others. Unlike Carr, Nordon did not ignore or gloss over touchy issues. Nordon sought to explain how Conan Doyle became the man he had been; how developments throughout his life affected his personality, views, and emergence as a public figure; and how these things were reflected in a wide and diverse literary output. Nordon may not have had all the important facts, but his study surpassed *Memories and Adventures*, and the four biographies prior to his, in focusing attention on aspects of Conan Doyle's life that affected his development as a man and a writer.

Unfortunately for the English-speaking world's understanding of Arthur Conan Doyle, the English translation of Nordon's book was regrettably inferior to the French original as a scholarly work. Its English and American publishers made an editorial decision to produce it as a popular trade book instead of as a scholarly tome. Adrian was at first appalled, but compromises were made by him and Nordon both, and in the end all parties agreed to the version published in England and America.[4] It remains useful, but much of the French edition's extensive

4. Personal communication from the publisher, Mr. John G. Murray, C.B.E., August 6, 1986, to whom I am grateful.

documentation was dropped, and many abridgements were made that lessened the insight or persuasiveness of Nordon's treatment of important issues in Conan Doyle's life. The French edition may not be the last word on the subject of Arthur Conan Doyle, but it is immensely valuable, and serious students will want to consult it rather than the translation.

The next four Conan Doyle biographies to appear were all slight contributions, revolving around the already somewhat stale question of whether or not Conan Doyle was Sherlock Holmes—a sure sign that Nordon's work was, at best, imperfectly absorbed. Their authors argued their cases for or against Conan Doyle as Sherlock Holmes without making any definitive judgments or new insights. Some years later, Julian Symons may have surpassed them at writing a short biography of Conan Doyle, but he too made no important new contribution to the subject, save perhaps for signs of a maturing awareness that Conan Doyle might have been something other than the "Victorian philistine" that Symons had once thought him.

Charles Higham's *Adventures of Conan Doyle* in 1976 was the first ambitious new presentation in two decades. Haphazardly researched, hastily written, and breathlessly journalistic, its widespread readership in recent years has been larger than it deserves; certainly Higham has been more widely read and quoted than Nordon, whose study (even the English translation) is unquestionably the better one. Higham relied too heavily on Carr, and went wrong too often on his own as well, to be taken at face value. His book usefully evokes Conan Doyle's long-vanished world, it raises interesting questions about the derivative nature of Conan Doyle's art, and it was the first to disclose Charles Doyle's fate and to speculate about the effects of that and of Conan Doyle's complicated marital and extramarital relationships on his personality and development as a writer. But Higham knew too little about Conan Doyle to do that well or produce a strong biography, and his weak critical acumen led him to uneven and superficial treatment of Conan Doyle's literary work.

If Higham's biography should be handled with caution, however, Ronald Pearsall's can be ignored altogether with few regrets. Possessing no independent knowledge of Conan Doyle's life, and apparently acquiring none, Pearsall approached his subject as a snide sort of superior cultural historian with an axe to grind against the bourgeois aspects of the Victorian age—misrepresenting Arthur Conan Doyle as a personification of its intellectual, psychological, aesthetic, and moral defects. Pearsall may furnish a cultural context missing in other biographies of Conan Doyle, but the woeful deficiencies of Pearsall's treatment weigh heavily against that as a redeeming factor.

Finally in 1983, more than fifty years after Conan Doyle's death, Owen Dudley Edwards became only the second scholar to write a biography of Conan Doyle's life (the first twenty-three or so years, actually). In taking it for granted that the creator of Sherlock Holmes is worthy of serious study (as Christopher Redmond observed), Edwards was "neither making a myth nor deliberately breaking one"—a welcome and all too rare thing in Conan Doyle biography. More than others, Edwards comprehended the realities of Conan Doyle's early life in the making of his personality and in general did an impressive job of portraying the complexity of a man who "was the product of many influences, not all consistent and not all positive." On many specific points, however, Edwards' diffuse style of discussion, tendency toward surmise, and lack of documentation do tend to blur the distinctions between speculation and fact. He sets interesting, occasionally fascinating hypotheses about Conan Doyle's early life, but it will take someone else further research— in the still-unavailable family archives, especially—to test many of them.

i

All this voluminous biographical effort, unfortunately, has done disappointingly little to provide satisfactory answers to the principal problems of Conan Doyle biography. Was Arthur Conan Doyle a simple or a complex personality? Was he merely "the man in the street," and can his literary success really be explained by resort to that catchphrase? Hesketh Pearson said so, as did, more recently, Ronald Pearsall; but the former had fastened upon a simple key to explain his subject's life, about which he bothered to learn rather little of real importance, and the latter, comparably ill informed, had seized upon his subject as a symbol of values and tastes that he despised.

They were wrong. The "man-in-the-street" explanation—which at a superficial glance may seem to fit Arthur Conan Doyle—falls into tatters upon a more informed consideration of his life. Probably wrong also, however, would be those who tried to claim for Conan Doyle too much in the way of hidden depths. His difficult upbringing and diverse experiences do not necessarily rule out altogether the simplicity of outlook, the boyish character, and the tendency to oversimplify complex subjects that many commentators have remarked in him. He was not really the person he appeared to be, but still he frequently seems to have been complicated without being profound and diverse without being deep. On the other hand, it is too slighting to say, as Hesketh Pearson did, that Conan Doyle "was simple enough to think himself complex"; for if he was not complex, there are, as Julian Symons came to realize, areas of Conan Doyle's life for which a simple explanation is inadequate. And a simple explanation for the creative achievement of Sherlock Holmes is simply impossible.

Pierre Nordon observed that without Sherlock Holmes "it would be a great deal easier to assign a definite place to his creator on the literary scene." No doubt that is so. Conan Doyle himself had critical things to say in *Memories and Adventures* about much of his early fiction and various minor works, nor have his biographers spared the historical novels which he prized most highly. Hesketh Pearson and Pierre Nordon alike were critical of his tales of chivalry, with their perhaps too painstakingly researched efforts at verisimilitude. And while both praised the Challenger and Gerard tales as well as Sherlock Holmes, even as sympathetic a critic as Nordon made no case for Conan Doyle as one of the giants of literature. But there is no getting away from Sherlock Holmes, who undermines every disparaging estimation or scornful dismissal of Conan Doyle's literary stature. Even those who denigrate the literary value of Sherlock Holmes cannot deny the creation's immense success. He overshadows everything else Conan Doyle wrote and helps keep some of his other fiction in print today that might not survive otherwise. Sherlock Holmes demands again and again that we look afresh, and seriously, at his creator.

Did Conan Doyle simply create Sherlock Holmes insensibly out of himself? Or is Joe Bell as the putative model for the character sufficient afflatus to explain the act of creation and Holmes' awesome power to fascinate? Adrian Conan Doyle was guilty of much special pleading about his father, but he was surely more right than wrong in saying that Bell contributed vital characteristics to Sherlock Holmes without being Holmes. Bell himself passed the credit back to his former student. If Conan Doyle failed to claim the honor for himself in his autobiography, he sprinkled clues throughout the Holmes stories to his apparent sense of self-identification, and Richard Lancelyn Green's attractive suggestion that Conan Doyle's Southsea years with his younger brother Innes were the origin of the Sherlock Holmes life-style and the Holmes/Watson relationship cries out for study.[5]

And yet it is not so simple. Conan Doyle may well have been Sher-

---

5. Those are vital years in which Conan Doyle laid the foundations of his future as an author, a sportsman, a family man, a propagandist, a public figure, and a psychic investigator; the origins of Sir Arthur Conan Doyle the world-famous celebrity, the Knight-Errant against the forces of injustice, the Spiritualist missionary, are all to be found in his Southsea years in the 1880s. Helping to overcome our relative ignorance of the details of that important period of his life will be the publication sometime this year of *A Study in Southsea, from Bush Villa to Baker Street: The Portsmouth Life and Times of Dr. Arthur Conan Doyle*, by Geoffrey Stavert (Horndean, Hants.: Milestone Publications, 1987).

lock Holmes in certain ways, and the creation of Holmes an act of conscious, calculated artistry on his part, but he was also a great many things that Sherlock Holmes definitely was not. A difficult, even tragic, early life might lie behind Sherlock Holmes' personality, but Holmes never remained all his life under the strong and sometimes smarting influence of his mother. Holmes never permitted himself a single romantic relationship, let alone one like Conan Doyle's with his dying wife and Jean Leckie. Holmes never felt, much less succumbed to, a yen for military adventure or agreed to lead social reform movements. Despite his, and Conan Doyle's ardor for justice, Holmes never undertook quixotic public campaigns on behalf of men possibly innocent of crimes of which they had been convicted. Most emphatically Sherlock Holmes never experimented with the occult, became a Spiritualist, defended the claims of spirit and fairy photographers, and traveled around the world as a missionary of a new faith. Arthur Conan Doyle did all these things, products of a more complicated psychology than most commentators have been willing to grant to the man who created in Sherlock Holmes English literature's paragon of austere, cold-blooded, misogynistic rationalism.

Conan Doyle was uninterested in elaborating a personal psychology for the delectation of his readers. The closest he came was an introversive poem of unknown date published in a rather extroversive 1898 collection of poetry, *Songs of Action*:

"The Inner Room"

It is mine—the little chamber,
  Mine alone.
I had it from my forebears
  Years agone.
Yet within its walls I see
A most motley company,
And they one and all claim me
  As their own.

There's one who is a soldier
  Bluff and keen;
Single-minded, heavy fisted,
  Rude of mien.
He would gain a purse or stake it,
He would win a heart or break it,
He would give a life or take it,
  Conscience-clean.

And near him is a priest
  Still schism-whole;

He loves the censer-reek
    And organ-roll.
He has leanings to the mystic,
Sacramental, eucharistic;
And dim yearnings altruistic
    Thrill his soul.

There's another who with doubts
    Is overcast;
I think him younger brother
    To the last.
Walking wary stride by stride,
Peering forwards anxious-eyed,
Since he learned to doubt his guide
    In the past.

And 'mid them all, alert,
    But somewhat cowed,
There sits a stark-faced fellow,
    Beetle-browed,
Whose black soul shrinks away
From a lawyer-ridden day,
And has thoughts he dare not say
    Half avowed.

There are others who are sitting,
    Grim as doom,
In the dim ill-boding shadow
    Of my room.
Darkling figures, stern or quaint,
Now a savage, now a saint,
Showing fitfully and faint
    Through the gloom.

And those shadows are so dense,
    There may be
Many—very many—more
    Than I can see.
They are sitting day and night,
Soldier, rogue, and anchorite;
And they wrangle and they fight
    Over me.

If the stark-faced fellow win,
    All is o'er!

If the priest should gain his will,
   I doubt no more!
But if each shall have his day,
I shall swing and I shall sway
In the same old weary way
     As before.

Some of the "many influences, not all consistent and not all positive" in Arthur Conan Doyle can be discerned in this unusually self-revealing poem. But while his psychology may well be reflected in this and other literary work, and in public and private actions, considerably more explication than his biographers have given us so far will be needed to resolve some of the enigmas of his life.

ii

The first breakthrough toward a truer understanding of Arthur Conan Doyle as a person occurred in 1978 with Michael Baker's publication of *The Doyle Diary*,[6] a discovery that demonstrated that at least one of the most important episodes of Conan Doyle's life had gone unnoticed and unappreciated. Charles Higham two years before had briefly mentioned the sad fate of his subject's father, Charles Altamont Doyle, but Michael Baker's examination of a sketchbook that Charles Doyle had done in 1889, while an inmate of the Montrose Royal Lunatic Asylum, provided insight lacking in all previous accounts.

Baker's praiseworthy investigation revealed that Montrose was only one of at least four asylums to which Charles Doyle had been committed, from approximately 1879 (when he was forty-seven years old, and Arthur was twenty) until his death in 1893, at the age of sixty-one. Initially Charles Doyle had been committed as a result of his alcoholism, Baker learned, and later epilepsy was diagnosed as well. A century ago, disorders such as these were sufficient to result in commitment to a lunatic asylum and to the corresponding imputation of insanity. Was Charles Doyle insane? "Keep steadily in view," he had written at the beginning of the sketchbook, on March 8, 1889, "that this Book is ascribed wholly to the produce of a MADMAN. Whereabouts would you say was the deficiency of intellect? or depraved taste?"

The sketchbook is a fascinating relic, displaying a good deal of the artistic talent of the Doyles and revealing Arthur's father (as summed up by Michael Baker) as Irish and a staunch patriot, a devout Catholic, possessing considerable wit and learning, with a distinct penchant for puns

6. Baker, *The Doyle Diary*, xxix + 91 pp.

and whimsy, and of an unworldly and careless disposition. Despite feeling abandoned by his family, he obviously still adored his wife Mary and harbored affection for his children. Although Arthur himself may have committed his father to these institutions, still Charles Doyle took pride in his son's burgeoning literary achievements, recording in his sketchbook the publication of two of Arthur's early novels and quoting from their reviews.

Michael Baker concluded that Charles Doyle was not mad, though "subject to headaches and prolonged periods of depression." The unhappy inmate himself recorded wryly in his sketchbook that

> I believe I am branded as mad solely from the narrow Scotch misconception of jokes. . . . Many cases are definitely settled only by the force of the doubt expressed, as many things are best expressed by stating what they are not—as for instance my claim for sanity is not best made by enlarging on my commonsense. . . . I would have thought, however, that it would be the duty no less than the pleasure of refined Professional Gentlemen to protect men like myself—than otherwise—and not endorse utterly false conceptions of sanity or insanity to the detriment of the life and liberty of a harmless gentleman—

"But if Doyle was not mad," Baker continued, "the pages of his book did reveal a man of melancholic disposition (perhaps understandable in the circumstances), given to bouts of depression, neurosis and morbidity. His devout Catholicism . . . combined with this condition to produce an almost obsessive preoccupation with death, especially death as a deliverance from his fate."[7]

The description of Charles Doyle as "of an unworldly and careless disposition" would seem to understate considerably the problem he had posed at home. Certainly he had never been a close, attentive father for his large family (ten children, seven of them surviving childhood) nor anything like the provider that they needed. "He was unworldly and impractical and his family suffered for it," Arthur Conan Doyle wrote in *Memories and Adventures*, at a time when his memories of his father were much mellower than they had once been. Charles Doyle's alcoholism, carefully concealed from the world for many decades, actually made him a shameful burden on his family, one that fell largely on Arthur as the oldest boy—a heavy responsibility for a young man not yet ready to make his own way in the world. Years later he hinted at his feelings about this in *The Stark Munro Letters*, bestowing a similar fate on the protagonist of his autobiographical novel:

7. Ibid, p. vii.

Of course I could only answer that I was willing to turn my hand to anything. But that interview has left a mark upon me—a heavy ever-present gloom away at the back of my soul, which I am conscious of even when the cause of it has for a moment gone out of my thoughts. I had enough to make a man serious before, when I had to face the world without money or interest. But now to think of my mother and my sisters and little Paul all leaning upon me when I cannot stand myself—it is a nightmare.

Unfortunately, attention to Conan Doyle's psychology in recent years has been more psychosexually speculative than well grounded in biographical research. Samuel Rosenberg's previously discussed 1974 study *Naked Is the Best Disguise*, a free-association romp through Conan Doyle's fiction, the Sherlock Holmes stories especially, produces a highly speculative description—*sans* explanation—of the author's psychology. While Ronald Pearsall's own psychosexual approach to Conan Doyle was very different from Rosenberg's—the latter saw him as a brilliant and quite conscious allegorist, the former as unconsciously reflecting the sexually repressive neuroses of fellow cultural plebians—Pearsall was equally speculative and probably even shakier. Higham (psychosexual in his own way) has gone furthest of the biographers to propose a complicated psychology behind Conan Doyle's literary work; Nordon the furthest in describing (a rather different) one; and Edwards the furthest in explaining what might account for Conan Doyle's psychology, at least in his early, pre-Jean Leckie years. But no one yet has done all this definitively in an integrated manner, correlating the more recent evidence of a less than transparent Arthur Conan Doyle with findings from a careful analysis of his literary output.

iii

If Michael Baker's *Doyle Diary* first proved that the definitive biography of Arthur Conan Doyle had not yet been written, other notable work since then has helped fill in other parts of the portrait. Valuable biographical research into Conan Doyle's career as an writer has been done by Richard Lancelyn Green and John Michael Gibson: their detailed notes for *A Bibliography of A. Conan Doyle*;[8] the introductions to their three "Unknown Conan Doyle" volumes, *Uncollected Stories*, *Essays on Photography*, and *Letters to the Press*;[9] and Green's extended sketch of

8. Oxford: Clarendon Press, 1983.
9. London: Secker and Warburg, 1982, 1982, and 1986 respectively.

Conan Doyle as the creator of Sherlock Holmes in *The Uncollected Sherlock Holmes*.[10] Samuel Rosenberg's intriguing but often exasperating literary psychoanalysis can now be measured against Christopher Redmond's infelicitously titled, but much less exasperating, *In Bed with Sherlock Holmes: Sexual Elements in Arthur Conan Doyle's Stories of The Great Detective*.[11] And in *Medical Casebook of Doctor Arthur Conan Doyle*,[12] Alvin E. Rodin, M.D., and Jack D. Key have exhaustively examined Conan Doyle's medical education, writings, and experiences, and their impact on his outlook and fiction—the value of which groundwork is all the more important if we recall Conan Doyle's view, quoted earlier by Richard Lancelyn Green, that medicine "tinges the whole philosophy of life and furnishes the whole basis of thought."

Recently there has also been, for the first time since Pierre Nordon's biography, an extended assessment of Conan Doyle's status as a literary figure. Regrettably, Don Richard Cox's *Arthur Conan Doyle* is a book whose useful linking of Conan Doyle's life to his fiction is only occasional. An example of the biographical interest of such linkage is Cox's acute observation of the parallels between the miseries of Conan Doyle's relationships with his dying wife and Jean Leckie, during the early years of this century, and the secret love affair theme in the *Return of Sherlock Holmes* stories written at that time.[13] Unfortunately, this example is fairly isolated in Cox's treatment, which is also flawed by an unsurprising but ill-considered concentration on Sherlock Holmes. He devotes 150 pages to Sherlock Holmes, but only 65 to all of Conan Doyle's other work. Omitted are numerous works of psychological interest like *The Parasite* and the *Round the Fire* horror stories. There is little discussion of *The Land of Mist* and none at all of *The Stark Munro Letters* and *A Duet*. Cox presents for the most part a very simplified and unrealistically ordered picture of Conan Doyle's life and work, with scant room for any complexities of personality or literary creativity, leading to a diminished vision of the writer and his achievement.

Though Cox did trouble to write a book about Conan Doyle's fiction, published in a "Literature and Life" series surveying writers as diverse as Henry James and Norman Mailer, Cox stands for the traditional academic dismissal of Conan Doyle when he concludes that

> Doyle is not "studied" today because there is no sub-text there to study. One does not usually finish a Holmes story and ask what it

10. London: Penguin Books, 1983.
11. Toronto: Simon and Pierre, 1984.
12. Malabar, Florida: Robert Krieger Publishing Co., 1984.
13. Don Richard Cox, *Arthur Conan Doyle* (New York: Frederick Ungar, 1985), p. 125.

"means," for the story that is presented overtly is the meaning: there is essentially no covert theme to be teased out of the characters and the action. *Moby Dick* is a novel about a whale that is really not simply a whale; *The Hound of the Baskervilles*, which is in many ways Doyle's most "literary" novel, is about a dog that in the end is really just a dog after all. And although we can see in *The Hound of the Basker-villes* a touch of naturalism, a hint of symbolism, the suggestion of a philosophical message, most critics today would relegate the novel to the category of "subliterature," because it merely entertains and does not broaden our understanding of the human condition.[14]

But while Cox offers this conclusion as if it were perfectly self-evident, no one listing Samuel Rosenberg's *Naked Is the Best Disguise* in his bibliography, as Cox does, is justified in asserting without any discussion of it that "there is essentially no covert theme to be teased out of the characters and the action" of the Sherlock Holmes stories.

For to the contrary, whatever one may think of Rosenberg's findings, he compiled a long and detailed case for Arthur Conan Doyle as a conscious and cunning allegorist—one who treated the characters and actions of his Sherlock Holmes stories, and of some of his other works, as expressions of a personal obsession with the theme of evil and punishment, disguising them in remarkably erudite sexual and religious symbol and metaphor. Rosenberg's case for this is hardly beyond criticism: his handling of psychoanalytic technique is naive, he offers only a few minimal facts about Conan Doyle to support his literary analysis, and he falls short of providing an interpretation of Conan Doyle's life. But despite all that, Rosenberg's various identifications of the sources of Conan Doyle's plots, characters, and images are frequently quite plausible; and while any given "discovery" of Rosenberg's may or may not be valid, overall he does appear to have found a richer bed of meaning and significance than most people had suspected might exist in the Sherlock Holmes stories.[15] To ignore this in a study that purports to reach conclusions about Conan Doyle's importance as a writer will simply not do. Alas, Sherlockians and academics alike are guilty (for very different rea-

14. Ibid, pp. 233–34.
15. It is impossible to do justice to Rosenberg's views of Conan Doyle and his fiction in a brief summary. See, in addition to *Naked Is the Best Disguise*, his introductions to new editions of Arthur Conan Doyle's *Hound of the Baskervilles* and *The Return of Sherlock Holmes* (both New York: Schocken Books, 1975), and his essay "Some Notes on the Conan Doyle Syndrome and Allegory in 'The Adventure of the Red Circle,'" in Harrison, ed., *Beyond Baker Street*, pp. 245–68.

sons) of preferring to ignore what Rosenberg suggests about the creative processes of Arthur Conan Doyle.[16]

Professor Moriarty, Sherlock Holmes told Watson, had authored a treatise on "The Dynamics of an Asteroid" so rarefied in its abstract mathematical thinking that there was no one capable of criticizing it. How strange it seems that there could be an allegorist so subtle that only one critic, however perceptive, was capable of detecting and analyzing it. Surely Rosenberg's arguments should be examined and, if ill founded, put to rest rather than ignored? Perhaps the charge of "subliterature" long held against detective stories has had something to do with this sort of academic neglect. But even if Rosenberg is dead wrong, "subliterature" is a somewhat threadbare term not entirely untinged by the snobbery of literary fashion. Raymond Chandler, the master of the American "hard-boiled" detective story, cynically observed forty years ago that "the mystery writer is looked down upon as a sub-literary being merely because he is a mystery writer rather than a writer of social significance twaddle."[17] He spoke as a somewhat embittered producer of fiction. But his comment reminds us of the intellectual problem faced by the academic and critical communities, even today, of how to think about certain kinds of "popular" or "recreational" literature. Anthony Burgess recently commented about this, in a tribute to the centenary of Sherlock Holmes:

> The truth is probably that our standards of esthetic judgment are insufficient to deal with Conan Doyle . . . our literary standards have more to do with Augustinian puritanism than with the guiltless gust of a rattling good yarn. If a book is hard going, it ought to be good. If it posits a complex moral situation, it ought to be even better. If it has a multitude of *sous-textes* and a battery of symbols it is supreme, fodder for doctoral theses and the stuff of tenure. To be a mere

16. I am indebted to Dr. Donald K. Pollock, Jr., of the Department of Social Medicine, Harvard Medical School, and the Department of Anthropology, Boston University, and my *Baker Street Miscellanea* co-editor, for these insights. The only meaningful attempt of which I am aware to examine Rosenberg's argument against the standard claims of a lack of deeper meaning in the Sherlock Holmes stories is Cameron Hollyer's brief essay, "Arthur Conan Doyle: A Case of Identity," *Pacific Quarterly* 3, no. 1 (January 1978): 50–61.

17. Quoted in Frank MacShane, *The Life of Raymond Chandler* (New York: Dutton, 1976), p. 10. (Not that Chandler was any great fan of Conan Doyle's work: "Found a two bit edition of Hound of the Baskervilles," he once wrote to a friend. "God, what tripe. It looks to me as if Lincoln was wrong. You can fool all of the people all of the time." Quoted in *Selected Letters of Raymond Chandler*, ed. Frank MacShane [New York: Columbia University Press, 1981], p. 159.)

entertainer is not enough. And yet to entertain is far more difficult than to enlighten.[18]

Edmund Wilson, that curmudgeonly old foe of detective stories, long ago examined in several famous *New Yorker* essays the pretentious claim of that genre, as he saw it, to be more than just genre pap. And he found almost all detective stories wanting. Yet he concluded even then that Sherlock Holmes is "literature of a humble but not ignoble sort," explaining that

> The old stories are literature, not because of the conjuring tricks and the puzzles, not because of the lively melodrama, which they have in common with many other detective stories, but by virtue of imagination and style. These are fairy-tales, as Conan Doyle intimated in his preface to his last collection, and they are among the most amusing of fairy-tales and not among the least distinguished. The Sherlock Holmes stories . . . were the casual products of a life the main purpose of which was something else, but creations that in some sense got detached from their author and flew away and had a life of their own. . . . For perhaps the only time in his life, he had hit upon a genuine spell.[19]

iv

But the question here is Arthur Conan Doyle and his standing, and whether he need be taken seriously. Sherlock Holmes is his main claim to serious consideration, but does Sherlock Holmes really matter in the final analysis? Does any writer deserve serious consideration as a literary figure of importance, one worthy of study, on the basis of such a creation? Is this work such to justify further biographical attention, whatever the defects of past attempts?

That depends in part on what one believes literature to be, of course. Chandler argued that "when a book, any sort of book, reaches a certain intensity of artistic performance, it becomes literature. That intensity may be a matter of style, situation, character, emotional tone,

18. Anthony Burgess, "The Sainted Sleuth, Still on the Case," *New York Times Book Review*, January 4, 1987, pp. l, 26–27; published in England in the *Independent*, January 10, 1987.

19. Edmund Wilson, "'Mr Holmes, They Were the Footprints of a Gigantic Hound,'" *New Yorker*, February 17, 1945, reprinted in *Classics and Commercials* (New York: Farrar, Straus, 1950), pp. 267–68.

idea, or half a dozen other things. It may also be a perfection of control over the movement of a story."[20] Here Chandler and Wilson, who did not possess a high regard for each other's views, appeared to agree about what constitutes literature. And if they are wrong—if Sherlock Holmes is not—those who say so must still contend with the truth of what T. S. Eliot wrote nearly sixty years ago, with much less justification then than if he were writing today: "Every writer owes something to Holmes. And every critic of The Novel who has a theory about the reality of characters in fiction would do well to consider Holmes."[21]

Even if Sherlock Holmes fell short of "literature" and were merely artistry of some popularly successful sort, the fact would still remain that Sherlock Holmes has much to say about the Victorian era and its ethos. "There are no better records of the profoundly normal oddity of Victorian England," the decidedly un-Victorian Kenneth Rexroth wrote two decades ago, "nor more humane ones, than the detective tales of Conan Doyle."[22] More imperative is the point that Sherlock Holmes has sung Conan Doyle's siren song of good versus evil, order triumphing over disorder, of justice attained however irregularly, to generation after generation of readers despite vast sea changes in the times and tastes. Pierre Nordon showed that Sherlock Holmes was a "product of a society which believed almost unanimously in its own values, resources and future." But that does not explain why Sherlock Holmes tenaciously retains a high place in the favorite reading matter of a society that appears, a century later, to have lost much of that self-confidence—not to mention having secured for himself a conspicuous place in other, often very different societies as well. Edmund Wilson said that for perhaps the only time in his life Conan Doyle had hit upon a genuine spell. But how many writers, of whatever kind, ever manage to hit upon even one spell that works as well and as long and as universally as Sherlock Holmes? There is some compelling archetypal quality about Sherlock Holmes that touches a responsive chord deep within the psyches of vast numbers of human beings. This is what Wilson meant by calling the Sherlock Holmes stories fairy tales.

The truth is, time and an undeniable cultural penetration have been on Sherlock Holmes's side and won Conan Doyle a higher repute as a writer than he ever expected or sought from that particular creation of his. His disdain for Sherlock Holmes has not been shared by his contem-

20. *Selected Letters of Raymond Chandler*, p. 69.
21. T. S. Eliot, reviewing *The Complete Sherlock Holmes Short Stories* by Sir Arthur Conan Doyle in the *Criterion*, April 1929, 555–56.
22. Kenneth Rexroth, "Sherlock Holmes," *Saturday Review*, April 27, 1968, 53, 58.

poraries or posterity, and today a critic like Hugh Greene may dare to aver that "more than half a century after his death one can say without much fear of contradiction that Conan Doyle was a great writer. His best creations, Sherlock Holmes and Dr. Watson, Brigadier Gerard, Professor Challenger, Sir Nigel Loring and Micah Clarke, show no signs of fading into oblivion."[23] Previously, the English-speaking academic and critical communities *were* prepared, more or less unanimously, to contradict such a statement: until very recently, Sherlock Holmes has had almost no part in the formal literary histories of England, nor has Conan Doyle's work ranked as literature in either England or America.

But now critics have broken ranks to suggest otherwise, and diehards (like Cox) may have failed to consider, for example, the excellent textual explications and thought-provoking reevaluations of Ian Ousby's chapter on Conan Doyle in his *Bloodhounds of Heaven: The Detective in English Fiction from Godwin to Doyle*,[24] Colin Wilson's essay "The Flawed Superman,"[25] Christopher Clausen's "Sherlock Holmes, Order, and the Late-Victorian Mind,"[26] and Kim Herzinger's "Inside and Outside Sherlock Holmes: A Rhapsody."[27] Their efforts and those of others make it clear that Conan Doyle did not merely add one more memorable but insignificant character to English fiction's repertoire. He created a moral hero vividly real in his given time and place, but able to transcend that time and place as well, in whose reality countless numbers of people have actually believed, many others have *wanted* to believe, and still others consciously *will* themselves to believe—an unequaled triumph of literary art over the normal limitations of its power to attract and sway and persuade.

"Great novelists do not merely tell stories, they create worlds," one of this volume's contributors has written elsewhere, "not only a particular location but also a particular set of values—a natural and moral order." Few have done that as well and with such enormous success as Arthur Conan Doyle did with Sherlock Holmes. In the gaslit 221B Baker Street of the author's imagination or in some lonely and sinister country house or on the windswept, haunted expanse of Dartmoor in *The Hound of the Baskervilles,*

23. Sir Hugh Greene, "Conan Doyle's Common Sense," *Listener*, February 27, 1986, 20.

24. Ian Ousby, *Bloodhounds of Heaven* (Cambridge, Mass.: Harvard University Press, 1976), pp. 139–75.

25. Colin Wilson, "The Flawed Superman," in Harrison, ed., *Beyond Baker Street*, pp. 311–33.

26. Christopher Clausen, "Sherlock Holmes, Order, and the Late-Victorian Mind," *Georgia Review* 38 (Spring 1984): 104–23.

27. Kim Herzinger, "Inside and Outside Sherlock Holmes: A Rhapsody," *Shenandoah* 36 (1986): 91–109.

Conan Doyle keeps his story alive on three levels—the literal, the ironic, and the mythic. . . . By attending to the sense of place in those and other Holmes stories we come to understand on a literal level the characters who act upon these stages. On another, rather more ironic level, we learn about character and plot from the actors' feelings about and behavior in their settings. And, most significantly, on a mythic level we feel the continual tension between the forces of disorder and the forces of order, between the forces of light and the forces of dark, between the forces of civilization and the forces of anarchy as they struggle for supremacy.[28]

The Hound of the Baskervilles does all that as surely, if arguably less profoundly in expression, as an acknowledged classic of English Literature like *Nostromo*—and for far more people than Joseph Conrad's admirable but less accessible work has ever been able to reach. Nor should the metaphysical shortcomings of the detective-story form be legitimate excuse to underrate the important purpose served by *The Hound*: in worrying about the mundane nature of the dog, Don Richard Cox overlooked the fact that Sherlock Holmes' concern was properly with the unknown evildoer who held the leash, and Conan Doyle's with the moral and philosophical predicament of antique evil lingering in a modern society supposedly advancing towards perfection.

If Arthur Conan Doyle has become great, it is through his greatness as a moral storyteller for his own time and ours, and very likely for our children's and grandchildren's as well. A man entranced by quests, he made his own life necessarily the subject of one if we are to know him and understand his significance. Marveling at the power of his greatest creation to imbed itself deeply in the consciousness of his culture, its unread members as well as the lettered, Anthony Burgess has posed a question that more than fifty years of biographical effort have not yet succeeded in answering: "No other character in our literature has so taken over a complete location and convinced the unliterary that he had a historical existence. If Conan Doyle was not great what was he?"[29]

The quest for Sir Arthur Conan Doyle is still incomplete. The true nature of the man and his life still eludes us. His works continue to be read avidly, some of them studied worshipfully as if they were revealed truth, but critically we are still unsure what to make of them—even the greatest and most exceptional of them. And yet, much valuable work has already been done, and many signposts along promising new roads of

---

28. David R. Anderson, "Grim Suggestiveness: Sense of Place in *The Hound of the Baskervilles*," *Baker Street Miscellanea*, no. 24 (Winter 1980): 11, 17.

29. Burgess, "The Sainted Sleuth," p. 27.

biographical interest now point the way. Perhaps Donald Redmond is correct that Sir Arthur's spirit is roaring with mighty laughter at the whole thing. But the joke would surely be on us, his readers in a world imbued with his creations, if no one traveled the rest of the distance and completed the quest.

CONTRIBUTORS

DAVID R. ANDERSON is assistant professor of English at Texas A&M University and the author of *Rex Stout*, a study of the author of the Nero Wolfe stories and novels.

JAMES BLISS AUSTIN, a retired industrialist, has compiled the best private collection of Sherlockiana and Doyleana in America and has contributed articles to many journals on those subjects.

PETER E. BLAU is a journalist, a Conan Doyle collector and bibliographer, and a former associate editor of the *Baker Street Journal* published by the Baker Street Irregulars.

DAME JEAN CONAN DOYLE is the daughter of the late Sir Arthur Conan Doyle and a retired Air Commandant of the Royal Air Force.

RICHARD LANCELYN GREEN is the co-compiler of *A Bibliography of A. Conan Doyle* and the editor or author of several other books on the subject as well, most recently *The Sherlock Holmes Letters*.

HOWARD LACHTMAN is a book and film reviewer for several newspapers in California and the author of *Sherlock Slept Here*, a history of Conan Doyle's North American speaking tours.

EDWARD S. LAUTERBACH is professor of English at Purdue University and a former board member of *English Studies in Transition*.

JON L. LELLENBERG is contributing editor for the independent quarterly *Baker Street Miscellanea* and the American literary agent for Dame Jean Conan Doyle.

ELY M. LIEBOW is professor of English at Northeastern Illinois University and the author of *Dr. Joe Bell: Model for Sherlock Holmes*.

ANDREW S. MALEC is the former Conan Doyle bibliographer for the University of Minnesota Library's Philip S. Hench Collection of Sherlockiana and the author of a number of related monographs.

CHRISTOPHER REDMOND is director of publications at the University of Waterloo, Ontario, and the author of several books about Arthur Conan Doyle, most recently *Welcome to America, Mr. Sherlock Holmes*.

DONALD A. REDMOND is principal librarian at Queen's University, Kingston, Ontario, and the author of several books about Conan Doyle, including *Sherlock Holmes, A Study in Sources*.

PHILIP A. SHREFFLER is assistant professor of English at St. Louis Community College and the editor in chief of the *Baker Street Journal.*

NICHOLAS UTECHIN is a BBC Radio current affairs producer and the editor of the *Sherlock Holmes Journal,* published by the Sherlock Holmes Society of London.

INDEX

Page numbers for illustrations are in italics